MARXISM AND
DECONSTRUCTION

MARXISM AND DECONSTRUCTION

A Critical Articulation

Michael Ryan

The Johns Hopkins University Press
Baltimore and London

Originally published, 1982
Johns Hopkins Paperbacks edition, 1984
Second printing, 1986
Third printing, 1989

The Johns Hopkins University Press
701 West 40th Street
Baltimore, Maryland 21211
The Johns Hopkins Press Ltd., London

Library of Congress Cataloging in Publication Data

Ryan, Michael, 1951–
Marxism and deconstruction.

Includes bibliographical references and index.
1. Communism—Addresses, essays, lectures.
2. Criticism—Addresses, essays, lectures.
3. Derrida, Jacques—Addresses, essays, lectures.
I. Title.
HX73.R9   335.43   81-48185
ISBN 0-8018-3248-9 (pbk.)

For Gayatri

In memory of
Walter Rodney
(1942-1980)

Philosophy has become secularized, and the striking proof thereof is that the philosophical consciousness itself has been pulled into the torrent of struggle. . . . If the construction and preparation of the future is not our business, then it is the more certain what we do have to consummate—I mean the ruthless criticism of all that exists. . . . I am therefore, not in favor of planting a dogmatic flag; quite the contrary. We should try to help the dogmatists to clarify their ideas.

—Karl Marx

Articulation is difference. . . . The relationship . . . is one of seriality without paradigm.

—Jacques Derrida

Contents

Abbreviations

NGC Rainer Nagele, "The Provocation of Lacan," *New German Critique*, no. 16 (Winter 1979), pp. 7-29.

OLI Paul Hirst, *On Law and Ideology* (Atlantic Highlands, 1979).

PA *Priorities for Action* (New York, 1973).

Pos Jacques Derrida, *Positions* (Paris, 1972).

PSE *Planning a Socialist Economy*, ed. L. Y. Berri (Moscow, 1977).

PT Andreas Faludi, *Planning Theory* (London, 1973).

Rev Karl Marx, *The Revolutions of 1848* (London, 1973).

SP Jacques Derrida, *Speech and Phenomena*, trans. David Allison (Evanston, 1973).

TSV Karl Marx, *Theories of Surplus Value* (Moscow, 1971).

VH Stanley Hoffmann, "A View from Home: The Perils of Incoherence," *Foreign Policy* (Elmsford, 1979), pp. 463-91.

WD Jacques Derrida, *Writing and Difference*, trans. Alan Bass (Chicago, 1977).

Preface

A "critical articulation" neither makes similarities into identities nor rigorously maintains distinctions. It is more akin to the weaving together of heterogeneous threads into a new product than to the scholarly and disinterested comparison of homogeneous masses whose distinction is respected. This book might be called an alloy, rather than a comparative study. The alloying of the two distinct entities into a new compound requires an account of the materials used, but merely to enable the location of common properties that facilitate the making of the alloy.

Not all deconstruction can be used for this endeavor. Except for the work of such radical critics as Gayatri Spivak[1] and others who use it to analyze institutions, political discourse, and ideology, American deconstruction is too far removed from the concerns of marxism to be of any value in an articulation of the sort undertaken here. The work of Jacques Derrida, the initiator of the deconstructive critique of metaphysics, is more accessible to this process.

Marxisms abound, and Alvin Gouldner argues that there are at least two major schools, the "scientific" and the "critical."[2] Scientific marxism is grounded in the axioms of the Soviet Union's celebrated metaphysics, "dialectical materialism." It interprets the world in one way at all times, and, therefore, it remains closed to new advances in philosophy and critical analysis, such as deconstruction. Because critical marxism is less the designation for a school or a system, and more the provisional tag for a plurality of movements, it can more easily be articulated with deconstruction.

In economic theory, critical marxist movements tend to be characterized by a rejection of the model of authoritarian central state communism. They favor models of socialism which are dehierarchized, egalitarian, and democratic. Whereas the Soviet model privileges productive forces (technology, heavy industry, and the like) over productive relations, thus permitting the preservation of capitalist work relations, critical marxists demand a complete transformation of the form of work and of all social power relations, in the "private" as much as in the "public" sphere. They see capital and patriarchy as equally important adversaries. Historically, patriarchy precedes free enterprise capitalism as a mode of oppression, and in the so-called socialist countries it postdates capitalism as a mode of oppression. Capitalism and patriarchy are inseparable in practice, though distinct in theory. Therefore, a socialism that removes capital while preserving patriarchy remains a form of oppression from the point of view of critical marxism.

Critical marxists depart from the leninist tradition in that they call for political organizational forms that are not exclusive, elitist, hierarchical, or disciplinarian. The postrevolutionary "arrangement of things," to use Marx's phrase, should include the political advances made by the bourgeoisie (such as democracy and civil rights), just as a socialist economy must necessarily presuppose the technological and economic advances that capitalism produces. Socialism should not destroy all "bourgeois rights" (hypocritical as some of them may be) and return to seventeenth-century absolutism. Democratic socialism would further the displacement and defusion of power relations, the institution of radical democracy, and the development of forms of self-management and of self-government.

Deconstruction consists of a critique of metaphysics in all its classic and current forms — idealism, transcendental phenomenology, crude materialism, logical positivism, and so forth. The closest approximation of deconstruction on the left is the work of Theodor Adorno and Walter Benjamin. More recently, the work of Tony Bennett, Ernesto Laclau, Paul Hirst, and others in England has reflected aspects of Derrida's work. Derrida published his major works between 1967 and 1975. Although he continues to publish significant documents, his work has become increasingly difficult, self-referential, and esoteric. If one has not read the early works, it is difficult to understand the later. The marxist vocabulary is present in Derrida's work only analogically, and his interests often seem alien to the political project of marxism. This difference in part explains the necessity of this book. I have attempted to explain certain aspects of Derrida's work which can be used within critical marxism. This is by no means an exhaustive introduction, and, at times, it is not even an accurate account, because my purpose has been to interpret Derrida in a way that is politically useful to nonfrancophile activists. My concern has been more pragmatic than scholarly.

This is not to say that deconstruction has nothing in itself to do with marxism. Derrida has declared publicly that he is a communist;[3] he remarks on the affinities between his work and the work of Marx;[4] and, in organizing a "defense of philosophy" against the French government's plans to curtail the number of hours philosophy is taught in the schools, he points out that the real target of the reform measures is marxism.[5] All of this does not make him a marxist, of course, although it does cast suspicion on those conservative deconstructionists who use Derrida for antimarxist ends. In a recent interview, Derrida spoke of himself as a marxist, although he was careful to distinguish the "open marxism" which he identifies with the work of Marx and with which he thinks deconstruction can be articulated from those marxisms (what I call "scientific" marxism here) which set themselves up as formal dogmas or as totalizing closures, whether philosophically or institutionally: "I would reaffirm that there is some possible articulation between an open marxism and what I am interested in. . . . Marxism presents itself, has presented itself from the beginning with Marx, as an open theory which was continually to transform itself. . . . It is one which does not refuse *a priori* developments of problematics which it does not believe to have itself engendered, which appear to have come from outside."[6]

This book, then, is devoted to elaborating that "possible articulation." It consists not only of a comparison of contents, but also of an attempt to develop a new form of analysis which would be both marxist and deconstructionist and would also encompass modes of political and social organization. One of the major arguments of the book is that how we read or analyze and how we organize political and social institutions are related forms of practice.

This book was written over a period of four years. I was working in its double subject matter about ten years ago, when I was a beginning graduate student in comparative literature, and my first published piece was a review of two Latin American novels in the *North American Review*. One of the novels was by a leftist and had to do with revolution. The other was by a modernist and related to the movement in French thinking in which I was just then becoming interested. Those two strands of thought never quite meshed, in the review or in my subsequent years' work. It was only after having finished my dissertation that I began to try to work them together more systematically and concretely. I felt there was some radical potential in French philosophy which had interested me in it in the first place, but my own radicalism was limited to an uninformed conversion to maoism in high school; participation in the student movements of the late 1960s and early 1970s; sympathy and identification with Latin American socialism, especially in Cuba and Chile; pursuit of marxist literary theory, especially that of George Lukacs, Lucien Goldman, and Benjamin, during graduate school; a cursory reading of Marx and Engels; an interest in the French radical philosophy of Foucault and Deleuze; a culture- and urban-starved seeking out of the near-marxists (historians, mostly) at Iowa; and a kind of fashionable *mechancété* within the profession of comparative literature.

It was not until I went to France that I began to read the marxist tradition in politics and economics with any care or seriousness. It helped that Derrida was doing Gramsci in his study group. Meeting Colin Gordon and Jonathan Ree of the English Radical Philosophy Group helped put me in contact with what was going on in Britain. For a time, I rejected deconstruction entirely in favor of marxism. As I pursued my work, I began to perceive similarities between marxism in its philosophic critical mode and deconstruction. It was not an accident, I concluded, that Derrida should be interested in Gramsci. I began to see that deconstruction could be used as a mode of marxist political criticism, although Derrida himself did not seem to be interested in pursuing this angle of work. For a time, I was worried that deconstruction's critical impact on marxism would be politically disabling, just as, at a certain point, I had thought that marxism's broader concerns made the deconstructive undertaking seem trivial. Long arguments with Gayatri Spivak and close readings of Sheila Rowbotham and Antonio Negri helped me to work out that problem; perhaps the kind of marxism that deconstruction disabled deserved to be disabled, and perhaps the opposition between the macro-public-political and the micro-private everyday world itself needed to be deconstructed?

It was not until 1978 that all of the thinking and worrying and fighting that I had been doing on the subject began to come together as a book. I wrote Chapter 3 that year in Los Angeles. Chapter 4 was completed in draft form the following summer in Austin, Texas. Chapters 5, 7, and 8 were completed during the following year in Ithaca, New York. I wrote the rest, except Chapter 9, the summer following in Austin and revised the entire manuscript that fall (1980) in Charlottesville, and again in the summer of 1981, when Chapter 9 was also written, incorporating work I had done in the meantime on Negri. I never expected to bring ten years' work to a punctual conclusion and I have not done so. Perhaps the subject is one that cannot be concluded. But if the articulation I have attempted here has taught me anything, it is not hopelessness, as some, familiar with American versions of deconstruction, might expect, but rather the necessity of the virtue of perseverance.

I thank the Alliance Française for permitting me to work in Paris. I am grateful to Jacques Derrida for making it possible for me to study with him at the Ecole Normale Superieure and to work with GREPH, the Research Group on Philosophic Teaching. Colin Gordon provoked me to begin writing about the politics of deconstruction by inviting me to present a paper at the Radical Philosophy conference in 1977. The University of Virginia provided a summer research grant that enabled me to continue working in France. My chairs in the Department of English at Virginia, Robert Kellogg and Del Kolve, very kindly allowed me to take leaves of absence without which the book would not have been written.

The Mellon Foundation made it possible for me to spend one of those leaves as a teaching fellow in comparative literature at the University of Southern California. I thank the Society for the Humanities at Cornell University for inviting me to be a teaching fellow for the year 1979-80.

Many of the ideas for this book were produced through interaction with my students and with colleagues, all of whom I could not hope to name. My friend and teacher, Gayatri Chakravorty Spivak, did more in this regard than even she is aware. Mark Kann, Doug Kellner, Fay Hanson, John Forrester, Peter Hohendahl, Fred Jameson, and Harry Cleaver gave extremely helpful criticism of individual chapters. Doug Kellner also helped refashion the outline for the final draft. The readers of the final draft, Terry Eagleton, Michele Richman, Gayatri Spivak, Susan Buck-Morss, and Jonathan Ree, cannot be thanked enough for their time and labor. I am grateful to Richard Barney for his painstaking and expert reading of the final proofs.

MARXISM AND
DECONSTRUCTION

Introduction

Marxism and deconstruction can be articulated, but in one fundamental way they cannot be related. Deconstruction is a philosophical interrogation of some of the major concepts and practices of philosophy. Marxism, in contrast, is not a philosophy. It names revolutionary movements, based among other things on Marx's critical analysis of capitalism, the theory and practice of which aim at the replacement of a society founded on the accumulation of social wealth in private hands with one in which freely cooperating producers hold social wealth in common. Millions have been killed because they were marxists; no one will be obliged to die because s/he is a deconstructionist.

Nevertheless, I will argue that deconstructive philosophy has positive implications for marxism and that these implications are not only philosophical, but political. One common conclusion promoted by both movements is that philosophy cannot be apolitical and that politics often rests upon philosophic or conceptual presuppositions. To articulate deconstructive analysis with marxism, therefore, does not imply comparing philosophemes or ideas. Rather, it consists of two activities: first, the winnowing out of metaphysical elements in the conceptual infrastructure of marxism, especially regarding its adherence to classical dialectics; and second, the use of deconstructive analysis as a weapon of marxist political criticism and as a means of providing a theoretical underpinning for the antimetaphysical and postleninist practical advances that are already under way within marxism. Crucial in this latter regard will be the relationship between what deconstruction accomplishes as a critique of institutions and the new developments that are occurring in socialist feminism and in the theory of autonomy.

For the most part, I have avoided doing what most obviously might be expected from a book with this title. I have not compared deconstruction with recent marxist philosophy, although I have tried to show the philosophical relationship between Derrida and Marx, as well as between

1

deconstruction and dialectics. I have taken this approach in part because I wished to perform a more political and less scholarly service by showing how what I consider to be an important critical philosophy might be of political use to marxists and in part because the term "marxist philosophy" has always struck me as being peculiarly oxymoronic, particularly when the term designates theoretical battles over the nature of knowledge without any concern for their immediate relation to the various social struggles. Consider the example of volume 1 of *Dialectics and Method, Issues in Marxist Philosophy,* in which the editors lament the inability of marxist philosophy to date to confront "the really fundamental philosophical issues," and they argue that "Marxist philosophy can only advance if it reaches down to the most general and abstract of philosophical categories." One could also argue that marxist philosophy cannot "advance"—that is, further the advent of socialism—unless it addresses concrete issues instead of abstract categories. The editors of *Issues* do not confront the question of what it means for marxist philosophy to "advance" in and of itself, separate from race, class, and sex struggles. They do express "hope" of a possible "link up" between philosophy and the workers' movement, which "might draw" upon marxist philosophy "in its struggle against capital."[1] It would seem, then, that marxist philosophy, from the point of view of the editors at least, is not directly bound up with the struggle against capital, the patriarchy, and racial chauvinism.

One of my purposes in this book is to argue that philosophy need not be separated from politics. Even such a nonmarxist philosophy as deconstruction can be put to political use, simply because philosophy, as the conceptual apparatus we inherit from our culture, is in the world, as well as in the academy. To a certain extent, philosophy does not need to be politicized because, as it exists in the conceptual infrastructure of everyday life practices, it is already political. But a marxist philosophy that confines itself to academic questions without attacking the "worldly" operations of philosophy can nevertheless manage to remain politically removed.

How can deconstructive philosophy that is a critique of idealist theories of meaning and of consciousness in language philosophy be of relevance to marxist political criticism? To understand how this articulation might be worked out, it will help to turn to a political theorist who makes clear the relationship between a conception of language and of meaning and a conception of political institutions—Thomas Hobbes.

In Hobbes's *Leviathan,* it is possible to see the sort of metaphysical operations which deconstruction attacks at work as political ideology. Deconstructive analysis can be used to reveal the metaphysical underpinnings of the political theory of conservative liberalism, that amalgam of possessive individualism, philosophic and scientific rationalism, authoritarian statism, and natural law market economics which has served so well as the philosophy of the capitalist class, as well as to reveal the ideological nature of intellectual enterprises that give themselves out to be rational, scientific, axiomatic, and self-evident. Deconstruction teaches one to attend to gestures of exclusion. What is the operation of exclusion in a philosophy that permits one group, or value, or idea to be kept out so that another can be safeguarded internally and turned into a norm? How is that norm impossible without an excluded other that is inferior, derivative, and secondary in relation to the primary value? How might one find what is excluded—something that usually is a variety of difference or repetition in metaphysics—at work determining that from which it supposedly derives? Can the metaphysical norm of conservative liberal theory be shown to be merely an abnormality in relation to a "normality" and a law it is the business of metaphysics not to recognize? And is this why metaphysics serves so well as ideology?

Hobbes not only cloaks class interests in the assumptions of universal reason and natural law; he goes one step further: he lays claim to absolute knowledge, and he identifies the deductive reasoning procedure with the presumption of axiomatic authority in the absolutist state. This is fertile ground indeed for articulating a critique of philosophical procedures with a critique of political institutions. For Hobbes demonstrates the relationship between the metaphysical concept of the logos as a point of absolute cognitive authority, from which laws issue in an unequivocal language that excludes all possibility of ambiguity of intention or interpretation, and the absolutist political concept of a sovereign who represents the whole state and who is the unique source of laws whose authority is incontestable. In Hobbes, metaphysical rationalism and political absolutism are mutually supporting, and this is made clear in the way an absolutist theory of meaning in language hinges with an authoritarian theory of law. The authority of the sovereign's law depends on the establishing of unambiguous proper meanings for words. Perhaps this is why Hobbes associates ambiguity, equivocation, and improper metaphor with sedition. Such absolute meaning requires the possibility of absolute knowledge, of a logos in which meaning and word coalesce as law. The absolute political state is necessarily logocentric because it depends on law, which in turn depends on the univocal meaning of words, which can be guaranteed only by the metaphysical concept of the logos, a point at which knowledge and language attain an identity that can serve as an absolute source of authority. This is why Hobbes began by defining terms, the first of which is the *mind*, when he wrote the *Leviathan*.

Philosophical deconstruction usually focuses on assumptions like those above which privilege the absoluteness of proper meaning and of the knowledge proper meanings afford metaphysical philosophy. In this case, it would ask what is excluded by this norm, and the answer would be metaphor, the "illegitimate" and unsanctioned transfer of meaning, improper analogy. A metaphor says one thing is something quite different; it implies the possibility of transformation and change, a questioning of the absoluteness of proper meaning and, consequently, of law. Metaphors lead astray; in metaphor, a thing becomes other than itself. The law of identity, which is the law of all sovereignty, be it of meaning or of the state, is broken. Such transformations of supposedly self-identical things into different things are irrational; hence, they trouble the rationalism of fixed, legitimate, proper meaning. And, according to Hobbes, metaphors arouse passion by inciting feelings that may not be compatible with a political institution whose laws require a rational acceptance of unequivocal definitions of words. Hence, he says, they should be avoided.

Derrida would argue that metaphor might in fact name an actual state of things, characterized by transformation, alteration, relationality, displacement, substitution, errancy, equivocation, plurality, impropriety, or nonownership, against which Hobbes's doctrine of proper meaning and his institution of propriety or ownership, to which meaning is linked, serve as antidotes. Might it not be that impropriety is fundamental, that metaphor founds language instead of being a derivative accident in relation to an absolutely univocal language? Given the dependence of Hobbes's political theory on the doctrine of absolute meaning, the consequences of such a conclusion would indeed be grave. If metaphor and sedition are interrelated, then sedition and civil disobedience rather than absolute sovereignty would be the foundation upon which political theory should be built. In other words, we would be on our way toward a theory of popular sovereignty and a functional theory of the state—not a goal Hobbes would cherish. And yet (the deconstructive argument would run) Hobbes's own text permits such a conclusion. For what is the "Leviathan," the analogy between the state and a natural being, but a metaphor? "For by art is created that great Leviathan called a Commonwealth, or State, in Latin Civitas, which is but an artificial man."[2] Hobbes's entire theory, then, rests on a linguistic form—metaphorical displacement, transposition, and analogy—that he will later exclude and banish as seditious. Does this seemingly unavoidable metaphoricity indicate a necessity that has implications for the political theory itself? Is the unavoidability of metaphor also the unavoidability of sedition? And is the naturalness of absolute meaning thus transformed into the mere forceful repression of a force and a necessity that works against the absoluteness of meaning, conceived as absolute propriety purged of all metaphorical displacement? Does this suggest that natural sovereignty is also the forced repression of sedition? And if the possibility of sedition indicates the permanently open possibility of an alternate form of popular sovereignty, does this imply that Hobbes's sovereign is himself seditious of that popular sovereignty? Metaphor against metaphor, force against force, sedition against sedition—these differences do indeed trouble the supposedly seamless universality which absolutism, in language and in the state, assumes. If Hobbes's incapacity to avoid what he condemns indicates the work of a norm of metaphoricity and, by Hobbes's own logic, of sedition and civil disobedience, then Hobbes's theory consists not of an absolute truth shining through exact, proper names which preexists the workings of metaphor, but instead of concepts produced by the impropriety of metaphoric displacement; not of a doctrine of universal sovereignty supported by "scientific" and "rational" principles, but of a particularistic class interest that seditiously displaces all other possible types of sovereignty by placing itself at the center; not of a norm, but of a deviation from a norm of displacement, of permanent revolution.

I say "permanent revolution" because that is precisely what Hobbes fears, and this open possibility (which in many ways is the deconstructive possibility expressed politically) is precisely what the institution of absolute sovereignty is designed to counteract and to manage. A similar (and also necessarily related) form of management is executed by the doctrine of absolutely proper meaning, which masters the open possibility that words might have different meanings in different contexts, or that their "proper" meaning might be "improperly" displaced in a metaphor seditious of sovereign meaning. Derrida says that such displacement, which is a force of difference that resists the desire in metaphysical thinking for identity (the identity of a proper meaning or of an absolute sovereignty), is usually excluded by metaphysics in the name of some norm or value such as, in Hobbes's case, proper meaning or absolute sovereignty. The open possibility of displacement which metaphor represents (once done once, the law that would prevent it from happening again endlessly has already been broken) makes the absolute propriety of meaning and of sovereignty impossible. This is why it must be banished. Like sedition, it indicates a fissure in the supposed plenitude and universality of sovereign meaning. Where the possibility of sedition manifests itself, there sovereignty is shown its limit. Where metaphoric displacement begins, there also the power of sovereign law as the absolutely proper name of a universal meaning is shown its limit. Both of these limits are necessarily "internal"; their very possibility retroactively conditions what they limit. There is no sovereign meaning outside of the possibility of displacement, which is therefore a condition of possibility of sovereign meaning. And there is no political sovereignty outside of the possibility of sedition. Without sedition, there would be no necessity for sovereignty. The name for that state beyond sovereignty would be revolutionary democracy, purely participatory self-government, without delegational or representational mediation.

Both absolute meaning and absolute sovereignty (and the two are mutually conditioning) thus lose their generality and their power. Hobbes's absolute sovereignty itself is simply one displacement among others in a potentially infinite series. This is what he fears, and this is why Derrida speaks of the deconstructive affirmation of the ever-open possibility of displacement as hope or trust. The assertion of absolute sovereignty in meaning as in the state is always an economy of distrust, desire, and fear. Like the presence of white blood cells, it is the best indicator of disease, in this case a force of displacement that undermines sovereignty and makes antidotes necessary. Hobbes's own theory is a negative affirmation of the open possibility of displacement, both in meaning and in politics, a possibility of irreducible, repetitive difference.

Standard philosophic deconstruction consists of showing how what a norm of sovereignty or identity (of meaning, say) excludes is in fact an "internal" necessity for that norm. Usually, what is excluded is some sort of crisis that could befall the norm. Metaphysical thought would say that this eventuality is absolutely external to the norm; the deconstructive argument consists of saying that if it could happen (sedition or metaphor, say), then it must necessarily be part of the internal structure of the norm it eventually disrupts, as a latent possibility. Furthermore, the crisis is usually something that would make the norm impossible. The displacement of metaphor and the impropriety of sedition make absolute meaning and absolute sovereignty impossible; their very existence indicates nonabsoluteness; hence, Hobbes rightly declares, they must be banished. The final point of a deconstructive analysis would be to say that sovereignty is itself merely a form of displacement, that it cannot define itself other than as the displacement of the ever-open possibility of displacement. Absolute meaning is the displacement of metaphor, is, in other words, the metaphor of metaphor. As the displacement of displacement, absolutely proper meaning becomes a name for metaphor. The part turns out to exceed the whole, and the whole becomes a point in a seriality it was supposed to transcend. Absolute political sovereignty, in turn, is the displacement of sedition, is, in other words, the sedition of sedition. What Hobbes's political sovereignty excludes is civil war; the sovereign demands obedience in return for security against the civil war in nature of all against all others. The deconstructive argument asserts that rather than be the purgation of civil war, absolute sovereignty is itself a form of civil war in that it must be defined as the suppression of sedition. The exclusion of civil war must take the form of a civil war against civil war; the attempt to exclude division absolutely is the absolute internalization of division. Intended to transcend difference, sovereignty instead is situated within difference, as a form of difference. The limit to its absoluteness is internal. Absolute transcendence, in meaning or in the state, is impossible as what it claims to be; universal transcendence is itself merely a situated point in the seriality it is supposed to encompass. What Hobbes excludes as that which makes sovereignty impossible is in fact the condition of possibility of sovereignty.

Derrida's work focuses in part on the side of this argument that shows the way supposedly sovereign or proper meaning is situated within an open seriality of metaphoric displacement. The norm is displacement; hence, all attempts to establish a normative identity of meaning which transcends and regulates that seriality as a sort of all-encompassing paradigm that excludes further metaphoric displacement can be shown to be a *construct*, a fiction. This is the meaning of the word *deconstruction*—to show the fictive nature of such constructs. Derrida occasionally suggests that this argument has implications for political, sexual, and economic institutions, and Hobbes certainly allows one to see how this might very well be the case. Rather than to anarchism as some might contend, this critique leads, I shall argue, to a radical socialism that is more akin to the participatory and egalitarian models of self-government and self-management proposed by democratic socialists, socialist feminists, and autonomists than to the hierarchical and party-elitist, central state, leninist variety that exists in the East. Concretely, the critique of political sovereignty (and the argument can also be made for the projection of particularistic interests into normative universals in sexual, racial, and economic sovereignty) implies that all representational (or party delegational) government that necessarily must present itself as the whole state is a fictive construct. The people who rule are merely people with common particularistic interests that attain uncommon propriety and universality only as a socially sanctioned fiction. They are inscribed in a cultural and historical seriality that prevents them from attaining the transcendence that is the claim of sovereignty. This critique points toward a necessary displacement of all such fictions toward a political institutional form that would be predicated upon the ever-open possibility of a displacement along a serial chain that could not be transcended by any kind of sovereignty that is not itself inscribed in the chain, that, in other words, is not sovereign: permanent revolution, continuous discontinuity, radical difference, but also, more concretely, a governmental form that does not pretend to be sovereign, perhaps something like the sort of alternating representation, subject to immediate recall, in which the representer and the represented are interchangeable because equal, which Marx describes in the Paris Commune.

Hobbes, then, permits us to see how language and politics, metaphor and sedition, an absolutist theory of meaning and an authoritarian theory of the state, a deconstructive critique of meaning and a political critique of absolute sovereignty, might be articulated. In such a slightly more liberal thinker as John Locke one encounters a sense of the antiabsolutist historicity and contextuality of meaning and of words. To pursue the equation, one could say that Derrida's sense of the open dissemination of meaning and the infinite extendability of reference, which is resistant to the sublative paternalism of politically conservative, idealist theories of meaning, is the philosophical accompaniment of a radically democratic and egalitarian socialism, in the same way that Hobbes's nominal absolutism balances his theory of absolute political sovereignty.

Deconstruction designates a state of things in materiality (it would be a mistake simply to call it material, because deconstruction, like contemporary speculative physics, advocates a critique of substantialism) which resists the desire for conscious categorical mastery of the sort at work in Hobbes. There is no such thing as an absolutely proper meaning of a word, which is not made possible by the very impropriety of metaphorical displacement it seeks to exclude. That impropriety of displaceability of meaning and of the infinite openness of syntactic reference beyond that circumscribed by proper meaning is a material force. The imposition of a conclusive, self-identical meaning that transcends the seriality of displacement is therefore metaphysical or idealist. Its political equivalent is the absolute state (be it dictatorial or liberal) that imposes order on the displaceability of power through sedition. The political equivalent of displacement—that force deconstruction foregrounds against absolutist philosophies of identity—is continuous and plural revolutions, the openness of material forces which exceeds the imposition of power.[3]

One of my primary assumptions, then, is that there is a necessary relationship between conceptual apparatuses and political institutions. The domain of philosophy articulates with the various ways power is exercised; concepts are also forces. But equally, the deconstructive critique of absolutist concepts in the theory of meaning can be said to have a political-institutional corollary, which is the continuous revolutionary displacement of power toward radical egalitarianism and the plural defusion of all forms of macro- and microdomination. In many ways deconstruction is the development in philosophy which most closely parallels such events in recent critical marxism as solidarity, autonomy, and socialist feminism. It marks a critical opening, a reexamination of the conceptual infrastructure which informs institutions and practices, a reexamination which is necessary if the other openings are to be given a theoretical basis and a justification against the mobilization of reactive, hierarcho-absolutist concepts of "socialism" against them. To affirm the abyss deconstruction opens in the domain of knowledge is politically to affirm the permanent possibility of social change. Deconstruction both opens the possibility of an infinite analytical regress in the determination of final, absolute truths and implicitly promotes an infinite progress in socially reconstructive action. It opens the possibility of further social, political-economic, sexual-political, and cultural revolutions, as opposed to closing them off in the aprioristic monumentality of a formal scheme, or in the generality of a universally inclusive institution, or through the coercive power of a norm of transcendental "science" conceived as absolute knowledge.

❧ 1 ❧

Deconstruction:
A Primer, A Critique,
The Politics Of

Derrida is not a marxist philosopher, nor is deconstruction a marxist philosophy. This does not mean, however, that deconstruction does not have radical political implications and uses. Before elaborating on those uses and implications, I will provide an introductory account of deconstruction, including a critique of some of its principles and an appreciation of its politics.

In very broad terms, deconstruction consists of a critique of metaphysics, that branch of philosophy, from Plato to Edmund Husserl to Paul Ricoeur, which posits first and final causes or grounds, such as transcendental ideality, material substance, subjective identity, conscious intuition, prehistorical nature, and being conceived as presence, from which the multiplicity of existence can be deduced and through which it can be accounted for and given meaning. Standard practice in metaphysics, according to Derrida, is to understand the world using binary oppositions, one of which is assumed to be prior and superior to the other.[1] The living presence afforded by the "expressive" voice of consciousness is a more authoritative oracle of truth for Husserl than the dead absence that characterizes "indicative" signification.[2] The second term in each case is inevitably made out to be external, derivative, and accidental in relation to the first, which is either an ideal limit or the central term of the metaphysical system. The reason why this is so, according to Derrida, is that the second term in each case usually connotes something that endangers the values the first term assures, values that connote presence, proximity, ownership, property, identity, truth conceived as conscious mastery, living experience, and a plenitude of meaning. The second terms usually suggest the breakup of all of these reassuring and empowering values, such terms as difference, absence, alteration, history, repetition, substitution, undecidability, and so on.

9

Derrida characterizes metaphysics in this way:

1. The hierarchical axiology, the ethical-ontological distinctions which do not merely set up value-oppositions clustered around an ideal and unfindable limit, but moreover subordinate these values to each other (normal/abnormal, standard/parasite, fulfilled/void, serious/non-serious, literal/non-literal, briefly: positive/negative and ideal/non-ideal); . . . 2. The enterprise of returning strategically, ideally, to an origin held to be simple, intact, normal, pure, standard, self-identical, in order then to think in terms of derivation, complication, deterioration, accident, etc. All metaphysicians, from Plato to Rousseau, Descartes to Husserl, have proceeded in this way, conceiving good to be before evil, the positive before the negative, the pure before the impure, the simple before the complex, the essential before the accidental, the imitated before the imitation, etc. . . . The purity of the within can henceforth only be restored by accusing exteriority of being a supplement, something inessential and yet detrimental to that essence, an excess that *should not have been* added to the unadulterated plenitude of the within. . . . This is the gesture inaugurating "logic" itself, that good "sense" in accord with the self-identity of *that which is*: the entity is what it is, the outside is out and inside in.[3]

Through the strategy of opposition and prioritization, metaphysics represses everything that troubles its founding values. Indeed, Derrida argues, its founding concepts—presence, ideality, and the others—come into being as the effacement and repression of such secondary terms as absence and difference. Deconstruction consists of upending the metaphysical system of oppositions and priorities by showing how what metaphysics excludes as secondary and derivative in relation to an originary concept of foundation—difference, say, in relation to identity—is in fact more primordial and more general than the metaphysical original. Difference is not derived from identity; rather, difference makes identity possible and, in so doing, makes impossible a rigorously pure self-identity in the metaphysical sense, one absolutely exempt from differential relations. Once this initial reversal of a metaphysical opposition is accomplished, Derrida usually sets about proving that all concepts of foundation, ground, or origin must be similarly displaced. They are in fact points situated in relation to larger systems, chains, and movements, which Derrida often characterizes by using terms that in metaphysics name secondary and derivative elements, difference and writing being the most infamous. For instance, Derrida points out that in order to be at all, self-identity must presuppose difference from something else. Difference and identity relate to each other within each other, mutually supplementing each other in a way that precludes a rigorous hierarchical and oppositional division between the two. Derrida claims that this movement of supplemental differentiation is more primordial than any metaphysical opposition or grounding concept of substance or presence. Indeed, it is what makes such things possible. But equally, it is itself not a ground or foundation in the metaphysical sense, because differential supplementation implies an indefiniteness of movement and an open-endedness of operation which could never be closed off in the form of a final stopping point, which would also be an absolute origin. Hence, Derrida will say that deconstruction reveals beneath the foundation of metaphysics an indefinite root system that nowhere touches ground in a transcendental instance that would itself be without roots or ancestors. Worded differently, there is no outside to the text, if by "text" we mean the nontranscendable, unfounded radicality of differentiation and supplementation.[4]

Supplementarity and iteration are two names for such ungrounding movements. I will give an account of them as found in three texts by Derrida: *Speech and Phenomena,* a reading of Husserl, *Of Grammatology,* on Rousseau, and "Limited Inc," a response to John Searle on the occasion of Derrida's critique of J. L. Austin's theory of speech acts. First, I will define some crucial problematic terms Derrida uses—differance, undecidability, and textuality. The French word *"différance"* is a neologism that combines two verbs—to differ, as in spatial distinction or relation to an other, and to defer, as in temporalizing or delay. In coining it, Derrida wanted to catch a more "primordial" spatio-temporal movement than any of the "founding" concepts or axioms of metaphysical phenomenological philosophy—the logos, being defined as presence, the priority of consciousness, intuition, the clear correspondence of logical concepts to concrete objects. For these grounding principles to serve as foundations upon which philosophical systems can be constructed, they should be absolutely self-sufficient or self-identical. They cease to be primordial grounds once they can be derived from something else. Derrida's point is that there are no primordial axioms, no instances of absolute truth or self-identity, and no founding principles that are not produced by (and therefore derived from) differance. Everything is only as it differs from or defers something else. And differance is not a ground, nor can it serve as a first principle or an origin upon which a philosophical system can be based, because it is what undoes all "indifferent" self-identity, the necessary premise of a ground.

To picture how differance can undo self-identity, one needs to think of the nature of elements in a series or in a structure. Each element has substance, or "is," only as it relates to other elements. Each element possesses being or presence only as it differs from, defers, or delays other absent elements. And that other presence is caught in a similar web of delay and difference. The "presence" of those other elements is also hollowed out and extended by other-relations; even a finite structure is thus infinite with regard to the possibility of a final closure or determination of its "being." No presence as such is ever arrived at which annuls and transcends the movement of spatio-temporal differentiation, absorbing seriality into a paradigm, be it ontological (being) or theological (meaning). The differential constitution of elements in a series or in a structure can be understood in linguistic terms. The letter "n" has existence only in relation to the rest of the alphabet. The word "for" takes on a meaning and function only in a language chain that relates it differentially to other words, from which it differs in use, function, and place in the chain, and which it defers, in the sense that such other words as "of" are implied by "for," but their onset is delayed or put in reserve if "for" occupies the focus. In language, there are only relations. Derrida cites Ferdinand de Saussure's linguistic principle of the differential character of signs, wherein "the system of signs is constituted by the differences between the terms, and not by their fullness" (*SP*, 139). The elements of signification have no substance of their own apart from the relations of similarity and difference which bind them to other elements. Throughout his work, Derrida generalizes this principle: there is no self-identity of words, thoughts, things, or events that is not produced by differance. By differance, misspelled with an "a," he means a combined movement of deferment in time and differentiation or distinction in space or in kind. In saussurian linguistics, the flat phoneme "t" has sensible fullness only as it defers and is distinct from—differentiates—a class of other "t"s which are constituted in a similar systemic, relational way.

Differance is thus more "primordial" than the substance or presence of each element in the series or structure. The apparent self-identity of each element is an effect of its difference from and deferral of other elements, none of which has an identity of its own outside the "play" of differential relations. Each element is "other" at the same time as it is selfsame. Its identity is made possible by that otherness or alterity, which makes its uniqueness impossible at the same time, because to be other is to be non-self-identical. To be at all, each thing must be constituted so it escapes the traditional metaphysical category of being, if being is, as it always is, according to Derrida, defined as a form of presence. Differance can never be present, even though it constitutes presence.

Derrida also argues that such philosophical oppositions as nature/culture, theory/practice, mental/manual, and life/death are differentially constituted. Of concepts, he writes: "The signified concept is never present in itself, in an adequate presence that would refer only to itself. Every concept is necessarily and essentially inscribed in a chain or a system, within which it refers to another and to other concepts, by the systematic play of differences" (*SP*, 140). Such chains are both systemic and historical. Husserl pretends to operate without presuppositions, but the presuppositionless ground he resorts to, the punctual present moment or point of presence, is, Derrida points out, a concept and a word (*stigmè*) inherited from a long metaphysical tradition. Pursuing this historical argument into the domain of linguistic and conceptual systemic determination, Derrida, following Heidegger and Nietzsche, argues that certain concepts in philosophy may be only the effects of dominant linguistic forms—being, for example. In another vein, he points out that J. L. Austin, in describing so-called "standard" speech acts, attempts to pass off an ethical and ontological determination, whose roots extend back to the metaphysical distinction between nature and culture, as a "neutral" methodological decision. Such neutral theoretical technicity is sanctioned, tautologically, by the very opposition of culture to nature which it advances. When we consider that this opposition also underwrites the hierarchical division between mental and manual labor, we can begin to perceive a certain ideology-critical potential in deconstruction:

> We could thus take up all the coupled oppositions on which philosophy is constructed, and from which our language lives, not in order to see opposition vanish, but to see the emergence of a necessity such that one of the terms appears as the differance of the other, the other as "differed" within the economy of the same (e.g., the intelligible as differing from the sensible, as sensible differed; the concept as differed-differing intuition, life as differing-differed matter; death as differed-differing life; culture as differed-differing nature). [*SP*, 148]

All of the conceptual oppositions of metaphysics which deconstruction undoes can be said to hang on the frame of the interiority/exteriority binary. What is inside, according to metaphysics, is "own," proper, good, primary, original, unadulterated; what is outside is other, improper, bad, secondary, derivative, degraded. Metaphysics tends to arrange the world conceptually into oppositions that adhere to this general pattern. Presence (of the mind to itself in the interior speech of consciousness, for example) precedes and is better than absence (of the living being, in writing). The same can be said for the other oppositions metaphysics employs in its desire to master the world through formally complete conceptual schemes—the positive and the negative, good and evil, nature and culture, truth and fiction, the real and the artificial, the physical and the technical, life and death, presence and representation, theory and practice, and so on. Derrida argues that by examining the bases used to determine the opposition between the logically or ethically prior term and the secondary, derivative term, one concludes that the possibility always exists that the axioms used to determine this system may not apply in all cases. It is possible to locate "marginal" cases that are undecidable in reference to the axioms and therefore put the completeness and consistency of the system in question.

This logic of incompleteness or inconsistency imposes itself because the "inside," which is the criterion for determining an "outside" (absence is outside presence, fiction outside truth, death outside life, and so on), can be shown to be in economic or differential relation to the outside, if it is to be at all. The exclusion of an outside in order to determine an inside already installs a differential relation between the inside and the outside, so that neither one exists apart from the other; it is itself only inasmuch as it is *different* from something other, as well as the other's *deferment.* The logic of priority and derivation can thus be reversed and displaced, as can the general axiomatic structure of inside and outside.

Every case of a binary opposition is marginal because the self-identity of each case is defined as a margin between the two poles of the binary. Each case is differential, both poles of a binary at once and neither one exclusively. In the binary opposition of theory and practice, the margin is the limit where theory and practice both meet and divide, where theory establishes what it is, its self-identity, in relation to what is other than or different from it—practice. The selfsameness of theory is its difference from practice. The margin that differentiates the two is always made up of both—this but not that, that and not this. The margin, in other words, is differential—both at once, but neither one exclusively. The margin is "between." Derrida's point is that each case of either theory or practice is marginal in that it is differentially constituted as both but neither one exclusively. All theory is either a theory of a past practice which it describes, or of a future practice toward which it aims, in addition to being itself a practice. Pure practice (antitheoretical, voluntarist activism) is always itself a certain theory of practice—part of a series, in other words, rather than something that transcends seriality as an unalloyed paradigm. Metaphysics sunders the differential margin that problematizes the absoluteness of the binary opposition by isolating, hypostatizing, and privileging one or the other of the terms. As idealism, it privileges theory; as vulgar (nondialectical) materialism, empiricism, or positivism, it privileges practice.

Derrida uses the term "radical alterity" (the inscription of other-relations in the selfsame) to name the irreducibility of differance. He takes philosophy back to the *diapheron* of Heraclitus, the one differing from itself, the selfsame that is other. The implication of this "diaphoristics" for knowledge is that there can never be an isolated, unique, proper, selfsame thing that would be the object of an absolutely adequate proper name. Otherness or alterity is to that extent radical. One cannot locate a proper ground of substance or subjectivity, ontology or theology, being or truth, that is not caught up in a web of other-relations or a chain of differentiation. All determinations of identity are broken apart by the necessity of alterity, reference beyond to an other. Derrida's words for that differential relation of alterity which breaks apart all "presence" of being or of conscious thought is "trace."

The trace is not a presence but is rather the simulacrum of a presence that dislocates, displaces, and refers beyond itself. The trace has, properly speaking, no place [*avoir lieu*—also does not take place], for effacement belongs to the very structure of the trace. . . . Differentiation is what makes the movement of signification possible only if each element that is said to be "present," appearing on the stage of presence, is related to something other than itself but retains the mark of a past element and already lets itself be hollowed out by the mark of its relation to a future element. This trace relates no less to what is called the future than to what is called the past, and it constitutes what is called the present by this very relation to what it is not, to what it absolutely is not; that is, not even to a past or future considered as a modified present. [*SP,* 142-43]

Presence—defined either as thought, the self-presence of the mind to itself in consciousness, or as being, the truth of the thing itself revealed in its presence—cannot be primordial in philosophy because it is an *effect* of differentiation. Differentiation or trace is effaced by the presence it constitutes.

Think of the image on a television screen. It is a plenitude of presence, but on closer, micrological inspection, it turns out to be a series of points. The substance of the image is made up as much of intervals as of points, of a spatialization that is also a temporalization, because the points and intervals must repeat and maintain the image; otherwise it would be too fleeting to constitute a presence. That presence, then, is double, both continuous presence and discontinuous differentiation. Derrida criticizes philosophies of presence, from idealism to positivism, for taking an effect to be a cause when they implicitly assume presence to be primordial. Yet Derrida also refuses to accord a constitutive, original, or primordial status to differentiation. Clearly, Derrida here is moving toward a philosophy that defines thought and being in radically historical terms:

If the word "history" did not carry with it the theme of a final repression of differentiation, we could say that differences alone could be "historical" through and through and from the start. . . . Differences . . . are the effects produced . . . that do not have as their cause a subject or substance, a thing in general, or a being that is somewhere present and itself escapes the play of difference. . . . We shall designate by the term differentiation the movement by which language, or any code, any system of reference in general, becomes "historically" constituted as a fabric of differences. [*SP,* 141]

In the essay "Différance," Derrida points to Hegel, Nietzsche, Freud, Saussure, and Heidegger as predecessors. He might also have named Spinoza, Marx, or the Benjamin of the *Trauerspiel* study, who offered a prototype of differentiation in his image of the constellation, which exists only as the interstitial relations between star points. Differentiation acts through space and time, yet it is neither intelligible (in the sense of being ideal) nor sensible (in the sense that it is like a physical force that is imperceptible, yet whose effects register on other media).

Another prototypical kind of "diaphoristics" or economy of forces is decipherable in Marx's description of exchange value. Exchange value is a concrete social relation, but it has no sensible existence outside of the play of differences between commodities or the difference of forces between capital and labor. One cannot study the "truth" of exchange value as the thing itself revealed in its presence without recourse to a differential system that breaks up presence into an economy of forces and deploys the "thing itself" along a chain of referential serial relations. In a foreshadowing of Derrida's more philosophic critique of substantialism, Marx says repeatedly that capital and exchange value are not substantial things, but instead "relations." As in physics, "insubstantial" force permits matter to congeal, and that substance of matter does not lend itself to being a primordial ground in the philosophic sense, because it is an effect of a differential of force.

Perhaps the most important of Derrida's terms requiring definition is "undecidability." Derrida borrowed it, while working on the problem of the origin of geometry in Husserl, from Gödel's work on metamathematics. He then used the principle to criticize the assumption in philosophy that a set of formal logical axioms can be constructed which provides a complete account of the truth or meaning of the world, as well as of the related assumption that a single foundation—"Being," for example, in Heidegger—could be posited which saturates every aspect and moment of life and into which everything in the world ultimately resolves itself. In each case, the system of knowledge, as formal logic or as the founding category, is assumed to be complete and absolute. It has no outside, hence no limit or margin demarcating an inside from an outside. Such a system necessarily presupposes the possibility of transcendence, either in the form of a transcendental consciousness (Husserl) that produces the logical forms that describe the world without itself being a part of the world (having been removed from it by phenomenological reduction), or in the form of a general category that encompasses all of existence while not being part of specific historical or worldly existence and to which all worldly existents refer for their truth or meaning ("Being"). Each, therefore, presupposes the possibility of a metalevel that allows the closure or sealing off of seriality in a complete paradigmatic system that has no limit and, therefore, no outside.

For the formal system to be complete, to have no outside, it must assume the possibility of a transcendental position that is not simply one item of the formal logic; it must assume an outside to the series that acts as a paradigm. Otherwise, the axiomatic system or the master principle will simply be part of the world being described formally. To be a complete system, formal schematism requires a metalevel that must be outside the field of seriality formalized by the system. But how is the metalevel position from which the system is constructed to be accounted for? An account of it simply generates another metalevel, which requires accounting for, in an infinite regress. What allows any complex system to be complete also seems to render it incomplete in one move.

To use Gödel's terminology, the system is necessarily "undecidable," because it generates elements that can be proved both to belong to the system and not to belong to it at the same time. The axiomatic system is necessarily incomplete. Gödel allowed translators to render *entscheidungs-definitif* (decidable) as "complete."[5] A formal system of axioms is undecidable if it is incomplete, and, according to Gödel, all such systems are undecidable. Derrida's persistent posing of the question of a limit, a point at which an outside, and hence, also, incompleteness, might be defined for a formal system, can thus be crucial for criticizing the pretensions to absolutely complete knowledge or truth in philosophy. Gödel's theory suggests that for any axiomatic system, cases will be derivable from the axioms in which it will be impossible to decide whether or not the element in question belongs to the system. The system is incomplete because the element can either satisfy or not satisfy the requirements established by the axioms for belonging to the system. Undecidability "is only a sign that the system could be extended. For example, within absolute geometry, Euclid's fifth postulate is undecidable. It has to be added as an extra postulate of geometry, to yield Euclidean geometry; or conversely, its negation can be added, to yield non-Euclidean geometry."[6] The addition of an axiom scheme to account for the undecidable elements necessarily gives rise to the same problem. New undecidable elements arise. The process of completion can never be completed. Schematization is possible, but it is also embedded in a seriality (the necessity of extension) that makes any one final paradigmatic scheme that resolves the series into a complete synoptic form inevitably incomplete and potentially self-contradictory. The implications for science and for logic are radical.

Jacob Bronowski summarizes Gödel's theorems and their consequences:

> The first theorem says that any logical system which is not excessively simple . . . can express true assertions which nevertheless cannot be deduced from its axioms. And the second theorem says that the axioms in such a system, with or without additional truths, cannot be shown in advance to be free from hidden contradictions. In short, a logical system which has any richness can never be complete, yet cannot be guaranteed to be consistent. . . . An axiomatic system cannot be made to generate a description of the world which matches it fully, point for point; either at some points there will be holes which cannot be filled in by deduction, or at other points two opposite deductions will turn up. And when a contradiction does turn up,

the system becomes capable of proving *anything,* and no longer distinguishes true from false. That is, only an axiom which introduces a contradiction can make a system complete, and in doing so makes it completely useless. . . . Turing's and Church's theorem [states] that it is impossible to decide for every instance whether it is a consequence of the axioms. And finally, Tarski's theorem demonstrates . . . that there cannot be a universal description of nature in a single, closed, consistent language. . . . The laws of nature cannot be formulated as an axiomatic, deductive, formal and unambiguous system which is also complete. . . . Any finite system of axioms can only be an approximation of the totality of natural laws.[7]

Much of Derrida's work consists of showing how attempts within philosophy to construct a complete, axiomatic system for describing the totality of the world encounter the same problem that arises in the search for an absolute ground of truth in science. The set of philosophic axioms inevitably proves to be incomplete. Undecidable elements arise that are necessary for the completion of the system, but also contradict its axioms. For example, Husserl wishes to prove that formal logical propositions can be deduced simply from mental intuition, purified of all experiential detritus. The language of intuition should necessarily be expressive, rather than indicative, because indication would imply a referential difference that contradicts the axioms of a lived plenitude of presence in intuition. Indication implies a dead moment, a sign that is not a pure emanation from the living mind. Derrida proves that Husserl's argument and his axioms necessarily require such an indicative sign in order to be complete, but the addition of an element that contradicts the axioms of the theory also proves the theory to be inconsistent. The indicative sign is a moment of undecidability in Husserl's system.

Husserl's system, then, both theoretically or axiomatically excludes, yet practically requires, an element that is undecidable—both internal yet external to the system. It is, therefore, incomplete; it cannot pretend to be a single, consistent system for describing the truth of the world. Essentially, deconstruction consists of showing the incompleteness of systems such as that of Husserl which pretend to be absolute. Incompleteness, or undecidability, implies that every axiomatic system has a limit defined by elements that are both inside and outside the system. Deconstruction consists of locating such limits, for example, word-concepts like *pharmakon* (meaning both poison and cure in Plato), whose intractable ambiguity allows the completion of an axiomatic system, such as Plato's, while simultaneously introducing a contradictory element that puts the completeness of the system in question. Another example is the graphic mark on a page in relation to the literary critical school of thematics, whose axioms suggest that all the material signifiers in a text can be reduced to ideal meanings that assemble, unify, and transcend the fragmented, graphic aspect of the text. Derrida argues that such graphic marks (and the white spaces that lend them contour) are necessary for essential meaning to be produced. Yet, such marks are "meaningless"; they remain behind, a fallen aspect of language which denies sublation into ideal meaning. The graphic of a text, therefore, is undecidable in relation to the axiomatic system of thematic meaning. It allows ideal meaning to be produced, and in that sense it is necessary for the completion of the system of thematic meaning. But it also contradicts the axiomatic premises of thematics, because it is a nonideal graphic remainder that cannot be raised to the level of meaning, defined as the gathering together of graphic fragments into a homogeneous ideal plenitude. Thematics is incomplete (and inconsistent) as an axiomatic system for understanding texts and the world, and the graphic is the undecidable element that indicates that the system can be extended.

The problem with extension, of course, is that any new set of axioms will give rise to the same inconsistency or undecidability. The generation of limits where the completeness of a system becomes problematic cannot be closed off. Limits, points where the possibility of absolute saturation is troubled by the emergence of an outside that is not decisively enclosed by the system, become potentially limitless. Systems such as Hegel's that attempt to delimit most absolutely are also most open to this sort of deconstructive critique.

In a recent text, "The Law of Genre," Derrida speaks of incompleteness or undecidability in the literary taxonomy of genre classification in a way directly related to its mathematical origin:

> The law of the law of genre . . . is a principle of contamination. . . . In the code of set theories, if I may use it at least figuratively, I would speak of a sort of participation without belonging — taking part in without being part of, without having membership in a set. The trait that marks membership inevitably divides; the boundary of the set comes to form . . . an internal pocket larger than the whole; and the outcome of this division and of this overflowing remains as singular as it is limitless. . . . The principle of genre is unclassifiable, it tolls the knell of the . . . classicum, of what permits one to call out orders and to order, the manifold without a nomenclature. . . . There should be a trait upon which one could rely in order to decide that a given textual event, a given "work," corresponds to a given class (genre, type, mode, form, etc.). And there should be a code enabling one to decide questions of class-membership on the basis of this trait. For example . . . if a genre exists (let us say the novel . . .), then a code should provide an identifiable trait which is identical to itself, authorizing us to determine, to adjudicate whether a given text belongs to this genre or perhaps to that genre. . . . This supplementary and distinctive trait, a mark of belonging or inclusion, does not properly pertain to any genre or class. The re-mark of belonging does not belong. It belongs without belonging. . . . If re-marks of belonging belong without belonging . . . then genre-designations cannot be simply part of the corpus. . . . The designation "novel" . . . does not, in

whole or in part, take part in the corpus whose denomination it nonetheless imparts. Nor is it simply extraneous to the corpus. . . . It gathers together the corpus and, at the same time . . . keeps it from closing, from identifying itself with itself. This axiom of non-closure or non-fulfillment enfolds within itself the condition for the possibility and the impossibility of taxonomy.[8]

Here, Derrida describes the problem of generic belonging and of deciding what belongs and what does not in a way that recalls the mathematical theory of undecidables. A set of generic axioms upon which decisions of belonging or nonbelonging can be based can be completed by an element that belongs to the set while yet not belonging, thus indicating incompleteness and the necessity of extension. An absolutely decidable generic taxonomy is made impossible by the condition of possibility of generic inclusion—the mark of generic belonging, the principle of generic classification. That mark is both included and excluded from any specific generic class, like the set of all possible sets in mathematics. For example, it permits one to mark off novels, but is not itself novelistic. It is also the mark of a potentially limitless extension or overflow, because classifying it would require a further mark of generic belonging that would be inside, yet outside, the class. The metalevel becomes infinitely extendable precisely because it cannot attain a formal language of classification which would escape the problem of undecidability. It can never transcend the problem of incompleteness which haunts the level of which it supposedly provides a decisively taxonomic account.

Perhaps Derrida's most famous text on this problem is "The White Mythology," in which he argues that, because all language is metaphoric (a sign substituted for a thing), no metametaphoric description of language is possible that escapes infinite regress. He is criticizing the transcendental impulse in general, the desire to construct truths through a language supposedly so formal that it renders the truth of the thing itself in its presence without any representational mediation. Any absolute knowledge, conveyed in necessarily metaphoric language, would, therefore, also have to provide an account of all metaphors, but such a metametaphorics is impossible without recourse to yet one more metaphor, the language of the formal description itself, a metaphor that would be undecidable because it both participates in and remains outside of the system it helps enunciate. To account for the language of the account would require another account—and a potentially interminable repetition of the problem. Derrida emphasizes representation, inscription, and graphics so heavily because any system of absolute knowledge or truth would require representation and would have to be inscribed somewhere (even in the cortical matter of the brain), and that material practice can never be fully absorbed, without remainder, into the ideal system of truth being enunciated. The very means of communication is always undecidable in relation to the ideas communicated.

The implication of undecidability for marxism is that the formal axioms of scientific marxism—that revolutionary change is necessarily a result of developing productive forces, that dialectical materialism is *the* way of understanding the world, and so on—are necessarily, like any such system, incomplete. To cling to them in the name of transcendental science, which is absolute in its truths, is to contradict the findings of modern science concerning the incompleteness of all such formal systematizing. Within the system of scientific marxism, the revolutions in Russia and China are examples of undecidables in that, as socialist revolutions, they derive from the axioms of the system, but they do not satisfy the axioms because they occurred in countries where the productive forces had not sufficiently developed. This development required some adjusting of the original axioms. Cases were possible in the world which satisfy their criteria of truth or provability, yet which also did not. The possibility of such undecidability remains open. A more recent case is the emergence of socialist feminism in the West in the 1970s. As a demand for the emancipation of female reproductive labor (among many other things), it is recursive (that is, derivative) in relation to the axioms of the system of scientific marxism, yet as a movement that refuses to consider patriarchy as subordinate to capital, it disqualifies itself as a term consistent with scientific marxism. Without socialist feminism, however, scientific marxism is incomplete, because the emergence of the new term reveals an area not covered by, but nevertheless derived from, those axioms. A materialist and historicist analysis necessarily leads to the socialist-feminist conclusion. Scientific marxism, therefore, is incomplete and requires extension. One can generate the same conclusion using the solidarity and autonomy movements.

Marxism, as a historical mode of theory and practice, is from the outset undecidable, that is, open to extension according to what history proffers. To constitute marxism as an axiomatic system immune to the historical opening of undecidability (the revelation of incompleteness) and the necessity of extension is both antimarxist and antiscientific. To refuse an undecidable element such as socialist feminism, because it questions the presently existing axioms of historical materialism, is to deny both history and science. History is another name for undecidability as the ever-open possibility of extending an axiomatic system, and marxism, if it is a science, is a science of history. From the moment at which its axioms are established, it opens itself to extension according to the movement of history. Its axioms are always provisional, because history is a domain of change, modification, and extension—open-ended. The word "science," in the hands of scientific marxists, has acquired a meaning inimical to scientific inquiry, which, if anything, celebrates undecidability as the constant possibility of modifying the axioms of any given system. Rather than an unmodifiable set of formal axioms which once and for all explain the absolute, decisive truth of the world, "science" should mean the attempt to discover undecidability, the limit at which present axioms cease to be complete and begin to require supplementation. Science does not mean the absoluteness of truth (in the vulgar sense of Althusser), but rather the persistently maintained possibility that any presently existing truth may prove not to be absolute.

Another important term is "text" or the "general textuality" of the world. By this, Derrida does not mean that the world is nothing but a linguistic object, or that things would not exist if we did not name them. He does mean that, by analogy, just as in a text, the differential relation of discontinuous linguistic elements produces an *effect* of homogeneous ideal meaning, where reference seems to stop and which seems to exist apart from the materiality of the text in a realm of pure intelligibility, so also, the world is a texture of traces which exist autonomously as "things" only as they refer or relate to each other. They are therefore "signs" in that, like signs, their "being" always lies elsewhere (because a sign is always the sign of something else; it cannot not refer to something other). Its "being" is predicated upon reference. The semblance of "being as presence"—a perceptible plenitude in the present moment—is thus simply an effect of complex chains of relations whose texture is never "present" as such. As Marx would have put it, had he lived to be a critic of phenomenology, to privilege perception is to limit oneself to "things," at the expense of the imperceptible social relations that produce them. As each word of a text cannot exist in isolated uniqueness, but must relate diacritically or differentially to the web of words which makes up the rest of the text if it is to make "sense," so also, no entity—no subject or substance—has a unique being (the object of a singular appellation or proper name) apart from the web of relations and forces in which it is situated. "The thing itself always escapes" (*SP*, 104), because reference along that web is irreducible. "The system of the sign has no outside,"[9] because the intelligible meaning, which (according to phenomenology) transcends, precedes, and determines a text and stands outside the play of sensible linguistic representation, is itself possible only on the occasion of the text and is itself caught up in a web of references that constitutes another text. The intelligible, which phenomenology would want to privilege as a realm apart, is itself inscribed in the sensible and in the indefinite texture of reference. Meaning is not ideal in the sense of a spiritual plenitude possessed by consciousness. Consciousness is itself, according to Derrida's reading of Freud, inscribed; it refers to a prior inscription in the material space of the mind.[10]

Similarly, in analytic philosophy, the outside of the text—the real or the material—cannot be exempted from reference or the structure of the sign. No entity or event that one might pretend to describe or to name adequately is not an effect of forces, histories, and structures, which are not themselves isolatable or determinable as self-identical entities or events. The real or the material cannot, therefore, be said to be "outside" the dissemination of reference which Derrida calls the "text." No entity or event can be named "properly" or adequately, because to do so would require tracing out the web of referential roots which produces it from an "outside" that is internal to the makeup of the things. "Text" names that interweaving of inside and outside through the process of reference which puts in question the philosophical desire to posit a pure outside to space, history, and materiality — as a transcendental realm of ideality (meaning) — or a pure outside to differentiation and referential relations as a positivist materiality that would be of a completely different order than the differential or relational structure of a language which refers to it (idealism turned inside out), or a pure nature prior to all culture, institution, technology, production, or artifice, by virtue of which such things can be termed derivative degradations rather than "natural" necessities. In other words, the "nature" (pure presence, self-identity) of an idea, a concept, an ideal truth, or a meaning consciously conceived is impossible without the "cultural" institution of representation. Not only are all ideas re-presentations (not the natural presence itself), but also all ideas are "inscribed" in the matter of the mind (in the sense that Freud describes). The realm of conscious ideality, which is the point of departure for all idealisms, is inseparable from "unnatural" representation and "material" inscription. There is no ideality, then, that is not from the outset already "outside" itself, other, as spatialization or re-presentation. Put another way, mental labor is always manual. It cannot dispense with that passage through history and the world. The strategy of idealism is to declare that spatial passage in all its forms (for example, writing, as we shall see) to be an accident, a purely external and contingent supplement that represents a fall from the self-presence of consciousness as ideality. Idealism, especially in its hegelian and husserlian forms, recuperates that exteriority as a moment in the coming to self-present being of mind and consciousness. History is simply an allegory of mental development, just as language is simply an expression of ideal meaning, which retains its ideality despite its passage through spatial representation.

Derrida's concern for the autonomous history and being of language is designed to counter that idealist conception of it as nothing but a vehicle for ideal truth, a temporary detour, by which conscious meaning departs from itself only to return to itself intact, as ideality devoid of all spatial, historical, or material impurities. Breaking that circle of departure and return to an already intact origin of consciously intended meaning is one point of deconstruction. Hence, Derrida emphasizes Freud's concept of the unconscious as a psychic inscription that produces the self-presence of consciousness as an effect, thus questioning the originality of consciousness in idealism. He points to the insurmountable possibility of "lateral reference" in language, which permits a text, against the conscious will of the author, to "disseminate" meanings that are not consciously intended. He even points to the space upon which inscription takes place, as well as to the etymological history of language, as necessary presuppositions, components of the prephilosophic "already there" that dislocates the originarity of consciously conceived meaning. Logocentric philosophy privileges consciousness as an origin of ideal meaning and truth. Derrida deconstructs the self-evident nature of that model of self-presence by showing that it is *constructed,* a product of numerous histories, institutions, and processes of inscription which cannot be transcended by consciousness conceived as a domain of pure ideality. By demonstrating that consciousness, rather than being a pure origin of meaning and truth, is a "text," a weave of many strands which are not of the nature of "presence" or "meaning," Derrida gets at one of the roots of idealism.

The point of the deconstructive metaphorics of textuality and "writing" is not, as some American deconstructors argue, to privilege language, rhetoric, or "literary texts," but rather, to situate what idealism privileges—conscious ideality as self-presence or self-constituted meaning—in two ways: first, as a regional function produced by a more extensive, asemantic (nonidealizable as conscious meaning) weave of differential relations, institutions, conventions, histories, practices; and second, as something whose natural priority is produced retroactively as an effect by the institutionality and spatiality of language, which, according to the idealist scenario, ought to be secondary and derivative in relation to ideality, consciousness, and ideal truth.

Derrida's generalization of the concept or metaphor of the "text" onto history and the material world can be understood in the two ways I used above. First, historical events are produced by concatenated chains that feed into the supposedly homogeneous event and determine it as a multifaceted, multirooted "matter" whose truth (in the sense of the revealed presence of the thing itself) could never be fully plotted out or resolved into a presence to which a decisively absolute and all-inclusive meaning could be assigned, because of the micrological strands of differential relations in and around the event. In this sense, the historical event is a "text" which can be deciphered endlessly without ever rendering an ultimate meaning-determination or a full truth or even making present all the microscopic webs of relations that determine the event. To focus or center on an event is necessarily to blur edges or margins, just as to locate the meaning or truth of a text in conscious intention is to blur the margins where the outside of the text, in the form of history, personal life, social relations, institutions, conventions, and so forth, bleeds into the inside, corrupting the purity of that conscious intention and supplying a dimension to the text that is unconscious, but also indispensable and decisively determining. To isolate a single event in history, then, is to a certain extent to overlook history.

Second, if an event or a thing is determined, if a decision is made to short-circuit the play of differential relations that mixes inside and outside at the margin and makes analysis potentially interminable, that determination is not a natural revelation of truth conceived as the presence of the thing itself, but instead an institution. It blurs the marginal differential where inside and outside become confused and resolves it into a clean-cut identity. If one accepts that the historical world is produced as a process of differentiation in which specific events are subsumed by larger chains, series, structures, and sequences, then one must also acknowledge that all knowledge of it which isolates self-identical entities or events from that differential seriality is necessarily institutional, that is, conventional and constructed. It cannot pretend to consist of the natural, spontaneous, or intuitive revelation of a full truth, the presence of the thing itself, based solely on self-evident axiomatic assumptions and devoid of all strategic exclusions. This, to use a marxist word, would be an example of ideology.

Derrida's readings of Husserl and Rousseau are similar in many ways, and in each he elaborates upon the crucial deconstructive concepts of supplementarity, difference, and repetition. Derrida finds Husserl in some ways paradigmatic of metaphysics. For Husserl, the decisive instance of absolutely certain truth is conscious intuition of the presence of an object to the transcendental ego, outside empirical history and the world. Such truth requires a logical language, and in the *Logical Investigations*, Husserl attempts to develop a purely formal grammar free of all empirical contamination. To do so, Husserl must distinguish between expressive signs, which are welded to the immediate presence of the internal voice of consciousness, and indicative signs, which pertain to worldly communication and imply empiricity and mediation. For Husserl, clearly, expressive signs are privileged, and indicative signification is to be avoided, because it would contaminate the immediacy and the purity of expressive presence, along with the absolute truth it affords. Expressive language is operated by voluntary consciousness and meaning-giving intention, but the certitude of internal consciousness does not itself require signs; immediate self-presence can dispense with the mediation of signification altogether — almost.

Derrida's deconstructive critique chips away at Husserl's idealist metaphysics on several fronts. First, he suggests that signification, with two of its characteristics, repetition and difference, may not be derived in relation to a primordial presence located in transcendental conscious intuition that is the locus of absolute truth, and that this insight is indicated in Husserl's text, against Husserl's better intentions. Husserl describes presence as breaking up into two different sorts of signs — expressive and indicative — but, Derrida asks, if such a differentiation is possible, can it be merely accidental, or does it not hint at difference — the difference between the signs—as a necessary possibility already at work within the supposedly seamless presence of conscious intuition? In fact, Derrida argues, the "present moment" upon which Husserl's argument rests is produced by its differential relation to nonpresence; the ground of truth, in other words, is structured by what within the system is considered to be excluded as the domain of nontruth. Husserl is an idealist, and, to pertain to ideality, intuitive presence and conscious intuition must be infinitely repeatable, that is, they must transcend empirical instantiations and historical alteration, thus remaining the same over time. But repetition implies a relation to a nonpresent future other as well as a re-presentation of a nonpresent past other. Within presence, then, repetition and difference, which are supposedly derivative in relation to presence, are at work constituting presence. This is a deconstructive reversal of a hierarchy and its displacement into a differential movement. The foundation and center of Husserl's phenomenology is the "present moment," a unique and original point of plenitude from which repetition as re-presentation and difference, the displacement of presence, supposedly derive. But those "secondary" operations can in fact be shown to be conditions of possibility of a unique "present moment," the supposedly primary instance. The differential movement into which the center is displaced is at this point called "trace" by Derrida.

Produced like a phoneme in linguistics by a differential chain, presence can never be what Husserl desires it to be, self-identical and self-sufficient, a ground of absolute truth. Presence is in itself only as it hinges with alterity, the other in the selfsame. Therefore, there can be no presence "as such." It is always deficient. The name for the filling of that deficiency originally by what supposedly comes second is "supplementarity." A supplement, by virtue of the principle of differential constitution, "produces that to which it is said to be added on" (*SP*, 89). What is said to be added on in this case is signification, that with which pure conscious intuition can supposedly dispense. But to attain that ground of truth which is intuitive presence in transcendental consciousness, the world must be completely left behind. And the more transcendentality retracts from the empirical world, the more it becomes dependent on signs, because outside of the world, it is without signs of its own. To a certain extent, then, there can be no purely intuitive truth that is not contaminated by the mediacy of signification.

In addition, Derrida points out that no sign can provide the undivided unicity and immediacy that Husserl's present moment of intuition requires in order to be expressed. A sign can function only by repeating something prior to it—the code that allows one to recognize it as a sign—and by being repeatable beyond the point of its utterance, most relevantly in the eyes and ears of the beholder. The sign cannot occur without being internally split by the structure of repetition which makes it possible and simultaneously renders its self-identity impossible. Husserl wishes mediacy to be derivative and secondary in relation to the immediacy of the expressive sign which is the direct oracle of conscious intuition. But, in fact, no sign could occur without mediacy as repetition.

The final opposition that Derrida deconstructs in Husserl is between sense and nonsense. Husserl's pure logical grammar determines sensible meaning and absolute truth as the conscious intuition of an object in its presence to the mind. This is the norm of truth against which the abnormality of statements conveying no intuitable object—"the green is where"—is defined. Derrida argues that what Husserl thinks abnormal or nonsensical—the absence of an intuited object in its presence—is in fact the condition of possibility of all speech communication. Signs can function only in the absence of the intuition of the speaker and of the presence of the object of the statement; once again, "writing" is the prototypical name for this general condition because it is defined as functioning in the absence of both its subject and its object. The presence of a speaker or of an object is not necessary for a statement to have meaning, that is, truth; indeed, the very existence of the statement presupposes their absence from the statement. Indication, therefore, that form of signification which entails mediacy and absence, may not be derived or secondary in relation to expressive speech, which is supposedly more primary and more directly linked to presence; without indication or indicative mediacy, according to Derrida, there could be no expression. Signification is not added on to expression; rather, it dictates expression. The ground to which Husserl wants to return in order to found an opposition that relegates indicative mediated signification to a secondary and auxilary status is in fact an effect of mediacy.

In *Of Grammatology*, Derrida focuses on the metaphysical opposition of speech to writing in Rousseau's account of the origin of languages. The conceptual chain determining this opposition goes back to the distinction between nature and its others—culture, technology, artifice, institutions, production, history, and so on. Speech is natural, good, and original because it is the medium of the voice of consciousness in its self-presence. Writing in the history of languages comes later; it is an evil, artificial, external accident that befalls more natural speech from without. Rousseau arranges this process as a continuous history of degradation from origin to fall. Derrida's deconstructive reading consists of showing how in Rousseau's text, one thing is declared by Rousseau—the exteriority of writing to speech—and another thing is described—the priority of writing, as the name here of supplementarity and of differance, to speech. As befits a good logocentric metaphysician, Rousseau would like to assure the value of living natural presence and the centrality of consciousness and of its medium, speech. But he cannot help but reveal a more primordial, decentering movement of differance and supplementary substitution which, according to Derrida, is in fact the condition of possibility of presence and of conscious speech. Whereas Rousseau declares a degradation through history from natural speech to technical writing, Derrida insists that he describes the differential and supplemental interrelation and mutual constitution of all the polar opposites that sustain the initial opposition—nature/culture, need/passion, gesture/voice, and so on. Writing "in the general sense" is the word Derrida uses to name this movement of mediacy, which makes possible the supposedly underived immediacy of speech and of presence. He chooses it because writing "in the narrow sense" is detached from any natural link to living presence; it is worldly, historical, and graphic, and these characteristics make it resistant to the spiritualizing idealization with which speech in metaphysics is identified as the possibility of unmediated self-presence in consciousness. For Derrida, writing names the system of differences which situates Rousseau's origins—speech, nature, and presence—as determinate effects of larger movements of differential relations which undermine simple notions of originality and opposition.

One important characteristic of writing is that it is always the signifier of a signifier, a signifier of conscious speech, for example, which is itself another signifier of an object or an idea. Writing can never present an unmediated signified that would transcend the mediacy of signification; it is the name for mediacy and the nonimmediacy of presence. The origin of languages in Rousseau's text is subject to a similar mediacy. If all the poles of opposition used to isolate and prioritize that origin supplement each other, so that one cannot be isolated apart from a differential relation to the other, then that systematic differential relationality and intersubstitutability precedes and makes possible the natural, original presence which Rousseau privileges as a predifferential, prehistorical origin. One basis for this argument is something Derrida later calls "parasitism." Parasitism suggests that something that supposedly comes second in fact is necessary for what comes first to be first, and this troubles the logic of priority and derivation. Nothing occupies the "first" place. Rousseau declares writing to be secondary to natural speech, but he describes speech in such a way that it suggests that writing —as a name for differential relationality and supplementary substitution—is in fact what produces speech as one of its effects. For writing in the narrow sense to take the place of speech, a process of substitution must already be possible and at work, a process that, Derrida argues, has the characteristics of writing in the general sense—differentiation, supplementarity, reference from signifier to signifier without reaching a signified that transcends the chain, and so on. As he puts it, postoriginary degradation, that is, the substitution of writing for speech, implies preoriginary repetition, that is, a process of supplementary substitution which is prior to speech and within which speech is situated as an effect.

And such substitution necessarily implies an open-ended chain of substitutions which would never arrive at a transcendental presence exempt from differential relations. Like writing, it will always lead to yet another signifier. When Derrida looks at Rousseau's account of the origin of languages, he finds that speech is a substitute for gesture, which is a substitute for a cry. And even the original melody of sound is shaped and constituted by differences of quantity. The origin is itself constituted by differential supplemental relations in a larger system or texture. Like writing, it refers beyond itself without providing access to a natural, living presence that would be indifferent. According to Derrida, because difference and supplemental intersubstitution are primordial, one can never hope to arrive at a self-present or self-identical point, in discourse or in the world, at which differential relations would be transcended. The point of transcendence would simply be one more point in the chain.

Derrida therefore finds in Rousseau's opposition between speech and writing a paradigm of metaphysics. The priority of speech is determined by the centrality accorded the logos and by the value of presence, conscious life, proximity, and property—what is own, internal, selfsame, not other. Writing is deprivileged because it represents a departure from presence and property. The living subject or logos is absent in writing, which is a sign of distance, displacement, and detachability. Writing can belong to anyone; it puts an end to the ownership or self-identical property that speech signaled. In writing, meaning can be gleaned only through the differential interrelations of the parts with each other; speech dispenses with mediation (alterity, the constitutive relation to an other) and provides access to meaning as an immediate punctual plenitude of consciousness. Writing implies differentiation in space, between the parts of a sentence, for example, as well as temporal deferment, because a sentence cannot be read at once, nor does its meaning reveal itself at one go in a flash of immediate presence.

In metaphysics, then, speech is the mode of spirituality, and writing implies the temporal and spatial extension of history and materiality. Derrida describes the subordination of writing to speech as a replay of the traditional metaphysical lording of transcendent spirituality over fallen and degraded worldly spatialization. He might have added, of mental over manual labor. His deconstruction of that hierarchical opposition will be to say, as did Marx before him, that what passes for spirituality is merely a determined moment in (spatial) differentiation and (temporal) deferment, what might, in another, more macrostructural vocabulary, be called materiality and history.

Metaphysical idealism declares differentiation, as history and materiality, to be outside, absolutely external to the locus of property and presence—the logos, consciousness, and cogito—which, in all the metaphysical scenarios, from Plato to Hegel to Husserl, "falls" into history and materiality only to recuperate them as aspects of its ideal substance. Like Marx, who argues that what appears as a spiritual idea is an effect of a material process, Derrida deconstructs metaphysics by showing how the most pervasive model of idealism—presence and property as the selfsame being of what is—is also an effect of differentiation, that which it supposedly excludes in determining property as a substantial, self-identical plenitude extracted from spatiality and history.

Derrida's critique of J. L. Austin's theory of speech acts or performative utterances is an example of how deconstruction can be brought to bear on Anglo-American as well as Continental philosophy. A performative speech act is a promise, a request, a command, a speech event that does something. In his first essay on Austin, Derrida relies heavily on the notion of repetition discussed above. Austin calls certain speech acts standard or normal; others such as citations in a play he calls infelicities, and he excludes them from his analysis of ordinary language. According to Derrida's logic of "parasitism," anything that is excluded as an accident that occurs to a system must be considered at least a structural possibility of that system. The exclusion of infelicities thus leaves its mark on the norm of standard speech acts. A citation is a sort of repetition, and repetition, according to Derrida, is the condition of possibility of the functioning of all signifying forms in communication. The sign must be repeatable, one might say, citable, both in regard to a code and in the absence of its sender. For Derrida, then, the so-called standard speech act is itself constituted by a more general version of the abnormality Austin seeks to exclude, that is, citation. Indeed, Derrida argues that all speech acts presuppose a general citationality. To work at all, a speech act must be acknowledged as citing a previously established code, convention, or repeatable model, and it must be repeatable from the outset in other places, other contexts. Repetition or citationality makes possible and establishes the identity of the signifying form, but equally, it makes a pure or rigorous identity impossible, because it implies that the speech act can occur only as a citation and that it can be cited, or repeated, elsewhere, in other contexts. Repetition makes identical, but it also alters or makes different. Without a movement of self-differentiating repetition or citation, there could be no event, no presence of the speech act. This is why, here, Derrida replaces the word "repetition" with the word "iteration," which contains the double meaning of repetition and alteration or difference. Similarly, the centrality of conscious intention and of self-identical meaning is here displaced; it must operate within an already given system and structure that is unconscious, as well as an imminent possibility of displacement which exceeds its control. There can be no absolute anchor, then, of the sort Austin implicitly assumes for intentional consciousness; there are only multiple contexts into which speech acts can be grafted at will, that is, without reference to the legislative power of will. Citation, fiction, and convention might, Derrida suggests, be more important to so-called standard language than Austin realizes.

In his response to John Searle's response to this critique, Derrida advances ideas that are by now familiar: that philosophy always proceeds on the basis of an anonymous tradition of a code, chains of concepts, and a nonconceptual process of production; that absence marks present intention in advance; that identity is delimitable only through differential relations and is in consequence never fully self-present; that repetition gives signification its movement and that this dehiscence within the supposed identity of the speech act renders it possible while making its purity impossible; that the necessary structural possibility of removing speech acts from their context to cite them elsewhere cannot be controlled by any single code or context; that oppositions such as that between serious philosophy and literary play become problematic when considered in terms of the iterability or citationality that constitute them; that the standard is always capable of being affected by nonstandard speech acts; that iteration subverts the nature/convention opposition; and that both Austin's treatment and the speech events he treats are marked in advance by the possibility of fiction either as the possibility that they can be cited or as the system of conventions which gives them meaning. This is so because iteration, which comprises both repetition and alteration or becoming other, implies the structural possibility that, to occur, an act must already be citational, that it must contain the possibility of being repeated and thus potentially of "being mimed, feigned, cited," and so on. The standard language act cannot, therefore, be distinguished in rigorous opposition to fiction or convention. And the value of nature which would allow such an oppositional determination to be made cannot be justified by the usual claim to impartiality. Derrida insists that Austin's analysis, with its unquestioned assumption of a natural standard, is structurally condemned to unnatural partiality:

> Prior to the hypothesis of such neutrality, the opposition serious/non-serious . . . literal/metaphoric, etc., cannot become the object of an analysis in the classical sense of the term—strict, rigorous, serious—without one of the two terms, the serious or the literal, or even the strict, proceeding to determine the value of the theoretical discourse itself. This discourse thus finds itself an integral part—part and parcel, but also partial—of the object it claims to be analyzing. It can no longer be impartial or neutral having been determined by the hierarchy even before the latter could be determined by it. [LI, 211]

Derrida concludes that this problematic condition of possibility deprives the theory of the scientificity it claims for itself. He criticizes Searle along similar lines. He suggests that "the language of theory always leaves a residue that is neither formalizable nor idealizable in terms of that theory of language" (LI, 209). In this case, Searle overlooks the fact that his own theoretical utterances elaborating an abstract, ideal, and systematic theory of speech acts are themselves speech acts. Because Searle's justification of the theory rests on an analogy, that is, a metaphorical comparison of speech act theory with other sciences, Derrida points out that even "in Searle's terms, it is based *ultimately* on the metaphorical, the sarcastic, on the non-literal" (LI, 209). Finally, suggesting the possibility that fiction might not be derived, Derrida argues that both Austin's supposedly neutral methodological exclusion of infelicities and Searle's justification of that exclusion as a case of logical dependence are "pretended forms" of discourse. In other words, the most apparently natural assumption of scientific neutrality is a form of fiction. Austin and Searle assume logic to legitimate an alogical decision, the attribution of an "ethical-ontological" pathology of deterioration to a differential relation between standard and infelicitous speech acts. In so doing, they themselves cite a characteristic gesture of metaphysics.

The point of this analysis is not simply to write off conscious intentionality, that traditional privileged center in metaphysics, but to situate it within larger structures and movements that allow it to function but deprive it of any empowering centrality or originality. Conscious intention can never be fully actualized or made present to itself, because iterability, which makes it possible, introduces a constitutive dehiscence or doubling that renders such purity impossible. In consequence, the operation of the logos, that is, logic, must also be resituated. Derrida writes: "The matter we are discussing here concerns the value, possibility, and system of what is called logic in general. The law and the effects with which we have been dealing, those of iterability, for example, govern the possibility of every logical proposition, whether considered as a speech act or not. No constituted logic nor any rule of a logical order can, therefore, provide a decision or impose its norms upon these prelogical possibilities of logic" (LI, 235). Derrida also speaks of the presemantic possibilities of syntactic play in language which allow semantic content to come into being without itself assuming the form of meaning. Prior to logic, the law of iterability, that is, of repetition as alteration or differance, dictates that even serious logical discourse contains the structural possibility that it might be mimed, cited, parodied, and turned into literary play. Similarly, literary play—"the green is where," for example—can be cited in a different context and made into a serious purveyor of objectively valid content.

Derrida's point, then, is that it is illegitimate to exclude, even provisionally or methodologically, such elements as infelicity or citation from the rigorously determined system of speech acts, because these are merely examples of the general operation of citationality or iterability that is at the root of the system of the theory of speech acts. Derrida concludes by suggesting that this root opens up a "topology of the unfounded" that removes language from its philosophical jurisdiction. The operations that govern it are not themselves governable by the order of philosophic truth, and no metalanguage can give an account of them without being subject to their laws.

Brutally summarized, then, the deconstructive "revolution" consisted of questioning some of the most treasured mainstays of bourgeois philosophy, both in its idealist (Continental phenomenological) as well as its positivist (Anglo-American analytic) mode: the possibility of a complete system of formal axioms which would provide absolute knowledge; the primacy of consciousness; the secondariness of semiological reference to preconstituted ideal meaning; the value of truth as absolute adequation of reference from word to world; the self-evidence of the binary opposition (physis/techné, nature/culture, sensible/intelligible, and the like); the logical and ethico-political priority of identity, unity, and homogeneity over difference, alterity, and heterogeneity; the desire to reduce antagonism and differential force through models of selfsameness which privilege the repression of mediacy (of history, of temporal delay and spatial deferment, of rhetorical detour, and the like) in favor of a fictive immediacy of seamless presence or proper substance (ontological or ideal, being or meaning); the desire for security through cognitive mastery of dissonance and uncertainty; the construction of philosophical descriptions based on circularity (the return of language to a preexisting ideal meaning or to a stable material world exempt from the structure of reference, or not produced as effects of differential relations); the desire for fixed grounds where reference beyond to something other stops; the centralizing of the logos as a norm and an ultimate point of reference for determining the truth of the world; the belief in the property (*propriété*, selfsameness, ownness, self-identity) of entities, ideas, and events detached from alterity or other-relations; the concept and value of a prior nature conceived as an origin or cause that defines history and institutions as secondary; the establishing of norms based on such self-evident values as presence or property defining something else as degraded, deviant, accidental, or secondary; the overlooking of the differential interconstitution of such hierarchical oppositions; and so forth.

Derrida insists that there is no transcendental truth that theologically commands the deconstructive undertaking as a rational order of first principles, axioms, and postulates that determine its discursive line from the outset; deconstruction consists of "a strategy without finality." Derrida uses the word "series" to describe this strategy. Deconstruction consists of a series of polemics with philosophy rather than of the elaboration of a philosophical system, and its point is to show that all philosophical systematizing is a matter of strategy which pretends to be based on a complete system of self-evident or transcendental axioms.

Deconstruction criticizes definitions of idealized truth as absolute completeness, adequation, self-identity, or transcendence. Yet it also questions the position of critique, the assumption that one can decisively criticize from outside the field of differentiation that holds both the critic and the object of critique in its sway. According to Derrida, there is no transcendental, suprahistorical critical position, and most of his seemingly self-indulgent autobiographical ruminations can be accounted for as attempts to confront this inability to step out of differentiation as history or as the microstructural movement of everyday life.

Marx's more politicized version of this position is to renounce "interpretation" in favor of practice. Theory could no longer aspire to transcendental validity or truth; it is situated in and exceeded by history and materiality, which it no longer controls in the way that philosophy has traditionally mastered the world, by constructing absolutely adequate representations or formal logical systems that correspond to a proper presence, an eternal and universal substance or subject. If there is a notion of "radical alterity" in Marx of the sort that Derrida thinks exceeds the traditional philosophical definition of truth, it is the thematic of relationality. Exchange value is a relation that is never present as such. It is of the nature neither of a subject, because it belongs to the socioeconomic system, nor of a substance, because it is produced by differences and relations. The relational definition of the world destroyed the idealist pretensions of theory, the ability to construct a single, adequate logical concept whose generality would encompass everything and saturate it with meaning. Relationality imposes on theory the necessity of acknowledging that it is a practice in history, the tracking down and working out of relations, rather than the proper naming of the world from a critical or theoretical position supposedly extracted from the field in which the named object exists. Theory is labor and has value only as such. Marx, like Derrida, thus undoes two presuppositions of idealism: the distinction between mental and manual, and between theory and practice.

Whereas Marx's "strategy" (no longer a matter of a philosophic critique based on transcendental first principles) has a finality, composing a death warrant on capital, Derrida's, at least according to Derrida, has none. The "radicality" of this counterfinality can be defined historically and contextually in reference to the philosophic orthodoxy prevalent in France in the late 1950s and early 1960s when Derrida first wrote—the self-validating, circular finality of phenomenology and of idealist dialectics. Nevertheless, there is a finality to his strategy, and that is the undoing of finality in all its philosophic forms—the founding axiom, the all-inclusive system, truth defined as the revelation of the presence of the thing itself, self-identity, adequation, and the rest. Derrida is subject to his own principle of differentiation. To exclude finality "strategically" is to subject oneself to it: to counter finality is to engage in the finality of countering finality. To close the door too precipitously may mean that at least there is an opening within the closure, but, equally, to keep the door open with excessive care is to indicate that closure is always a real possibility and that the keeping open is the closing off of closure.

I will now outline some preliminary critiques of deconstruction, or at least of that nonexhaustive segment of it which I have just presented.

My first critique would be that deconstruction lacks a social theory and that this is not an extrinsic or accidental oversight but an intrinsic fault, because deconstruction points toward the possibility and necessity of such theory without ever providing one. Deconstruction describes the logical or structural necessity of turning such metaphysical principles as consciousness, ideal meaning, presence, and nature inside out and into a "social text." These principles are intrinsically exposed to exteriority. Repetition constitutes the propriety or ownness of what seems self-identical or unique, but by virtue of this property, repetition situates what it constitutes in a system of differential relations to what is other or not own. Derrida elaborates upon this insight on the level of philosophical argument and successfully wields it to demolish certain foundations and strategies of bourgeois philosophy and social science, but he fails to pursue its logical consequence: an analysis of the social constitution of consciousness through the unconscious, of the repression of sociohistorical etiology through recourse to models of nature, of the political function of rationalist paradigms in social policy, and, on the most general level, of the part played by logocentric operations and procedures in the everyday pursuit of race, sex, and class oppression. Similarly, Derrida's notion of the ungrounded rootedness of all metaphysical grounds leads theoretically to a radical sociology of knowledge, a historism that would resist metaphysical historical models of continuity, periodization, and personalization by opening a potentially infinite field of analysis within a finite space. Here, Derrida confines his work to analyses of chains of philosophical concepts.

One point of deconstruction would be that such analysis is itself social, that is, anchored in history. Consciousness and concepts are material. Philosophical concepts are dependent for their transmission on such nonphilosophical forces as publishing and education, and this dependence tends to break down the rigorous metaphysical opposition between the philosophical or conceptual and the social or cultural-political-economic institutional. Nevertheless, Derrida's own analysis remains confined to concepts and to language rather than to social institutions. This can be accounted for in a sociohistorical way that is appropriate for the point I am making. It is possible that the rigorous and isolated disciplinary training French philosophers receive simply works against extending philosophy into social theory, even when that philosophy arrives at a philosophical justification for such a move. Even French marxist philosophy (especially that of Althusser), which should be social in content, manifests an idealist tendency. The force of repetition may make possible and limit conscious intention, but equally, the force of a sociohistorically produced disciplinary institution can make possible and limit the conscious intention of a philosophy of repetition. And that should waylay any urge to give priority to repetition over social institutional causality. Derrida is not guilty of this, and he suggests that repetition operates in institutions as a force of reproduction. The one convincing and rare example he gives is his own position as a *repetiteur* or tutor in the French school system.[11] His activity of repeating is made possible and limited by the general repetition that operates the teaching institution, which in France is closely linked to the state. His teaching is not only a voluntary activity, but also an instantiation and guarantee of a broader repetitive movement that assures the reproduction of the school and of the state. This argument seems to find reinforcement in the marxist theory of reproduction, both economic and ideological, and certainly has a bearing on Marx's analysis of the way history repeats itself in the eighteenth Brumaire.

But the example also makes clear the operation of a force that is not one of repetition, but upon which repetition, as a sociohistorical movement, depends. For the general repetition at work in an institutional system to operate, it must instantiate itself in empirical practice and through social agents. Even if the conscious intent of those agents needs to be deflated in terms of the already-there of language, history, and the unconscious, their intent and action are nonetheless required for the force of repetition to be effective. Derrida, like other French structuralists, tends to write off the subjective factor excessively, and this is understandable considering the excessively subjectivistic humanism of the various phenomenologies and existentialisms against which they sharpened their critical claws. I do not want to seem to capitulate to those Anglo-American empiricist or positivist critics of deconstruction who cannot accept that the material world might be made to work in part by counterintuitive and nonempirical forces such as a drive to repetition. But I take their side, especially the side of sociohistorically oriented marxists, to the extent that I think Derrida's emphasis on repetition and difference is lopsided. As Anglo-American literary critics prove, it can itself become a metaphysics. A general force of repetition may make an institution such as the capitalist system seek self-reproduction, and a difference between need and surplus, use and exchange value, may even be said to force the so-called natural and self-identical force of labor, but repetition and difference could not operate without being instantiated, and that instantiation is in each case social and historical and noniterated or nonrepeated in character. In other words, repetition is a force that works, but it is not the only force at work. The concept of repetition allows empirical presence to be turned inside out, but repetition itself by that very token can be accorded no self-identity of its own. It necessarily turns outside in, because it can subsist only in differential relation to its other, that is, insubstantiation in empirical history. Repetition as ideological and economic reproduction may make capitalism work systematically, but so do workers. And the force that makes workers work is not only repetition. The need for sustenance which is the basis of the reproduction of labor power may function as a difference of quantity, but that level of use value remains an unencroachable minimal limit without which life would cease and cease to repeat. Derrida would argue that this means that life parasitically contains within it the necessary possibility of an external opening onto death, but that neoexistential philosophical conclusion remains irrelevant unless it is translated into concrete political-economic terms: necessary labor, the minimum wage required to reproduce the labor power of workers, is not a self-identical or natural thing, but instead a variable limit between contending forces, that capitalist force which attempts to decrease it as much as possible toward the limit of death, and the force of workers' struggles which attempts to expand needs as much as possible against capitalist domination. Used in this way, the philosophical insight becomes political: work for survival is not a natural or self-identical part of life; rather, it is an agonistic limit, a difference of forces, in which life is defined as a limit by the threat of absence, privation, and death.

The law of parasitism—that external accidents or secondary eventualities betoken internal or prior possibilities—clearly does not easily translate into a social principle. Stalin's misappropriation of Marx may indicate the necessary possibility of misreading inscribed in Marx's text, but it does not indicate the necessity of Stalin in Marx. The Yale School's politically conservative use of deconstruction also testifies to the possibility of bizarre effects, in this case, the translation of a complex philosophy into an old-model new criticism from which the muffler has been removed, creating more noise without noticeably improving the speed. That does not change Derrida's avowedly leftist politics, although it is easy to see how his emphasis on the passivity of the subject under the weight of heritage could underwrite a conservative traditionalism, as well as how his placing of logic and truth within larger movements that do not reduce to those instances could generate an epistemological nihilism that anoints the status quo while appearing to rage against it.

When I said at the beginning of this chapter that Derrida is not a marxist philosopher and that deconstruction is not a marxist philosophy, I meant that his overt intent and its explicit operation are not politically radical in character. The goal is not institutionally political, but institutionally philosophical, although within the institution of academic philosophy, the method puts in question the ideological bases of philosophical conservatism, as humanism, idealist transcendentalism, logical positivism, intuitionism, logocentrism, meaning theory, and so on. Thus it is potentially very useful for a marxist critique of ideology, and by "ideology" here, I mean the set of ideas and practices which reproduce class rule. Ideology as the dominant paradigm of the bourgeois social and hard sciences often depends on precisely the sorts of things deconstruction questions. The critique of Searle's scientism shows how this can be the case. It should be evident also that a deconstructive critique would severely circumscribe any notion of individual freedom which does not take into account those movements of general repetition which are played out through apparently intentional action and which guarantee institutional reproduction. Executed in and through the most unconscious everyday practices are concepts, word histories, and institutional forces whose work may not be manifest, but whose power of repetition operates to secure class hegemony.[12]

A few years ago, in an interview, Derrida criticized revolutionary voluntarism and suggested that radical practice needed to adopt plural strategies that were angled or indirect. This view is in keeping with his critique of the privilege of consciousness in logocentric metaphysics. The historical arena is too deeply sedimented and one is too unconsciously embedded in it to assume that what one wants or intends is what one effectuates or gets, or even is what is really going on. Marx calls this being able to make history only in terms of what history proffers. Derrida's vision is more cautious and skeptical, but it is not, as some leftist critics insinuate, reactionary. The one aspect of deconstruction that raises political objections most often is the situating of truth within broader processes that constitute it without being subject to its jurisdiction. I interpret this as implying that an absolute or whole truth is indeterminable, but that truths are possible and that such truth is often plural. Marx's labor theory of value accounts for an object that, as has recently been shown, can also be accounted for solely using the price of commodities.[13] Two true descriptions (with admittedly differing political implications), the same object. There are limits, of course; a possible plurality of truth descriptions does not imply a liberal pluralist vision of the equal validity of all political positions.

I will now turn to some possible political implications of deconstruction.

The concepts of difference and repetition have implications for the possible development of socialist and democratic political institutions in three ways. First, they undermine the legitimacy of typological or categorical thinking. Such thinking creates self-sufficient and exclusive categories or types that order the world conceptually as well as normatively.

When institutionalized, such categories or types can become the guiding principles of social policy, themselves helping to mold a world in their own image. For example, a certain typological thinking would arrange all the different forms or "topics" of English language usage according to a normal type—white bourgeois English—and abnormal deviations from this norm—all the various nonwhite or "sub"-white dialects. Here, plural differences are reduced to a binary opposition that is also a normative hierarchy of good and bad and can serve as the ideological basis for the rationalization of speech usage. One also thinks of categorical types that distinguish domains of knowledge—politics, economics, law, sociology, and so on—which, when institutionalized as the disciplines in which we acquire technical expertise and as the different domains of social policy, can actually make the world seem to be constituted by such purely exclusive, isolated domains. Categorical typing can permit economics to become a matter of technical adjustments to laws that supposedly function independent of sociology, law, or politics, all of which are given out to be autonomous conceptual and real domains. A deconstructive approach would insist that any topical or empirical instance of such a typology undermines its efficacy as anything but a theoretical or ideal fiction. Politics is necessarily, constitutively bound up with economics; sociology and law are only formally separable. Any concrete example of the category would immediately break the formal rule of the category or type by revealing the interrelationality (one might say the differentiality) of the categories.

The second way that difference and repetition act is to question the distinction between sensible and intelligible, mental and manual, which, according to Marx, is the basis of the division of labor. The critique of this distinction usually takes the form in Derrida's work of a critique of meaning, conceived as an ideal self-identical plenitude that transcends the process of signification that communicates it between consciousness and serves as a cause and stopping point for signification. For idealism, meaning stands outside the text, if by "text" we mean the tissue or web of differential relations and references that, for Derrida, envelops both linguistic processes and the historical world. The doctrine of ideal meaning, whose universalist validity supposedly transcends topical historical specification and difference, is thus a modern version of the idealism Marx called "German ideology," a philosophy that was equally anxious to oppose and to prioritize the ideal to the empirical or historical material (whether in the form of social institutions, economic production, or language). By suggesting that ideal meaning is not a cause or ground, but instead an effect of forces usually condemned by idealism to the realm of historical materiality as merely instrumental and meaningless, forces such as difference and repetition, Derrida, like Marx, puts in question the bases of the division of labor. Difference and repetition, he claims, are neither sensible nor intelligible, ideal nor material, and they constitute, while deconstructing, all idealist oppositions that support or derive from such distinctions. They cannot serve as the legitimating basis for a social and political economic institution that would presuppose the validity of such oppositions and put them to work legitimizing the division between mental or managerial and manual labor.

Finally, deconstructive philosophy as Derrida practices it implies that authority should be conceived (and practiced) as a function, rather than as an instance. One could say that as a philosophical critique of metaphysics, deconstruction consists of transforming what are taken to be instances (that is, seemingly self-identical ideas or entities that are supposedly extracted from differential relations and repetitive alteration, such as consciousness, meaning, absolute truth, nature, presence, and so on) into functions (that is, provisional points situated within larger chains, historical root structures, differential and relational systems). This transformation of instances into functions undermines the authority, as final cause or ultimate determinant, which is usually attached to such instances. To situate the metaphysical instance of conscious intuition as a function within larger networks that are unconscious in nature—the presemantic, preconceptual, hence, preconscious historical tissue and autonomous referential productivity of language, for example—is to attenuate the authoritative finality that is assigned to consciousness both in philosophical theory and political practice. The instance of methodological impartiality and neutrality in the social sciences can also be situated as a function of the unavoidable premethodological decisions (that of serious/nonserious or standard/nonstandard in Austin, for example) that necessarily predetermine the so-called scientific and objective nature of the "merely technical" analysis. And here, of course, from a deconstructive point of view, true science would consist of taking into account the ultimate impossibility of such a thing as a true science that would attain a metalevel of theory that would transcend even the practice of that theory. The set of all sets always lacks at least one set and in consequence is infinitely extendable. The undecidability or structural incompleteness that opens the possibility of infinite extension can lead to epistemological nihilism and a nonpolitics of abdication. The absolute reduction of authority, from instance to power vacuum rather than to function, simply leads to an implicit affirmation of whatever authority is operative or most agile. This accounts for the political conservatism of the Yale Schoolmen. But the displacement of instantial authority into functional authority also has implications that are radically democratic and socialist in character. As I have already noted, the closest example in the marxist tradition is Marx's description of the Paris Commune, in which authority became rational, revocable, distributional, and functional.

The move from instance to function in analysis also entails a move from absolutes to differential, situational relations. A reading of the historical text of World War II which bases itself "metaphysically" on empirical presence, for example, would say that the causal instance in an absolute sense of the Pacific war was the Japanese attack on Pearl Harbor. Political interests are served by this limitation of causality to the presence of an observable event. To deconstruct that privilege of presence and to find the nonpresentable, nonobservable root system of the event would necessitate tracing the history of trade relations between Japan and the United States during the 1930s. One could even reach the conclusion that Japan was at least in part provoked into launching its attack by protectionist trade sanctions and the cutting off of access to raw materials and markets. The deconstruction of the presence of the observable event and of the authority of the single cause transforms that causal instance into a function within a larger differential text or tissue, a multiply determinate root system that constitutes the presence of the event without being reducible to the simple form of presence. The political-economic interest served by the instantial model of monocausality would be interested in going to war against an apparently external enemy. A deconstruction of the presence of the event and of the authority of the cause permits us at least to suspect that the enemy is in part internal and that a certain internal political-economic interest solicited the external enemy for its own ultimate profit. Predictably, perhaps, it is an interest that tends to transform the function of authority into an instance of power.

Such a deconstructive analysis of historical causality could lead to an infinite extension that would conclude that the historical text is "unreadable." But this conclusion is as absolute in its own way as the conclusion of monocausality. Instead of laying down a law of one cause, it lays down a law of no determinable cause. The practical equivalent of the theoretical transformation of instance into function is provisionality, that is, the recognition that one operates in a historical scene with determinate interests and that one must choose sides. There is a difference between the angelic disinterestedness accompanying the hypothesis that no truth is determinable, no text readable, and the provisional limitation of a potentially unlimited and indeterminate textuality in the name of the political interest of countering the structures of power whose interests are served implicitly by the angelic disinterestedness of liberal detachment.

The displacement of instance into function would operate politically and economically as the replacement of privilege, bureaucratic control, autocracy, and hierarchically invested power by radical democracy and as the replacement of the instance of economic power by a social function of distribution, autonomous self-control, and dissemination, that is, production and circulation without exchange. It is for this reason that I would argue that deconstruction is a philosophical pretext for a socialism that would be radically democratic and egalitarian in nature. The instances of conceptual or methodological power which Derrida attacks in metaphysical philosophy have always served political-economic interests. It is no accident that a normative concept of propriety developed in seventeenth-century England, at the same time that property right became the basis of civil government, replacing the traditional hereditary privilege of the aristocracy with the mark of power of the ascendant mercantile middle class. Perhaps it is also no accident that in the late twentieth century a philosophy appeared that advocates the antinormative, non-concept of impropriety, non-self-identity, and nonownership. Not that ideas produce history, but, if the rise of the bourgeoisie is an act worth following or an example worth heeding, then the philosophical justification of a new political economic form appears early in its formation, often before it actually attains ascendancy. It could be, then, that one cannot yet speak of the politics, or even the economics, of deconstruction. Perhaps they must remain for the moment at least a subject of speculation rather than description, a topic for future construction.

I will now turn to the question of the relationship between deconstruction and marxist philosophy, political economy, and social theory. The question I will address is: does deconstruction have direct applicability to such questions, or does it, like dialectics, need to be stood on its head? Is it possible to locate a political or an economic kernel within the philosophic shell? In laying the groundwork for an answer to that question, it will help to pursue further the relationships between deconstruction and the marxist tradition, first in regard to Marx and then to dialectics.

❧ 2 ❧

Marx
and Derrida

Derrida admits his work occupies a marginal cultural sphere. Collections of love letters and autobiographical reviews of Parisian art displays[1] have little perceivable immediate pertinence to such questions as the proletarianization of peasants or the poisoning of the world by transnationals. Nevertheless, capitalism is not merely political and economic, but also cultural and social, not merely economically exploitative, but also patriarchal and racist. Indeed, to succeed as political-economic domination, capital requires power in these other spheres. Writing critiques of bourgeois models of communication and representation, philosophizing, and so on may not be the best way to seize state power, but unless they pretend to be a substitute for other forms of struggle (i.e., the Frankfurt School), they can have an important place. In fact, I would argue that a narrow focus on questions of political-economic power, at the exclusion of other plural, multisectoral critiques and reconstructions, can be as self-defeating as a narrow focus on cultural concerns. It is not accidental, after all, that Lenin's crude philosophic objectivism accompanied an equally crude vision of socialism. Without further apologies, then, I will try to show that the critical methods of Marx and Derrida can be compared and that deconstruction can be articulated with critical marxism. There are four reasons why this comparison is possible: first, because Derrida follows Marx as a critic of metaphysics; second, because the deconstructive rewriting of the classical dialectic removes the justification for the conservative marxist model of a linearly evolutionary and finalistically resolutive progress to socialism, while implicitly furthering a politics predicated upon a more realistic assessment of the antagonistic forces and irreducible differences that characterize capitalist social and productive relations; third, because deconstruction can provide the principles necessary for a radical critique of capitalist-patriarchal institutions that is not merely oppositional but undermines from within the legitimating grounds for those institutions;

43

and fourth, because deconstruction can supply conceptual models for the economic and political institutions required in egalitarian and nonhierarchic socialist construction.

Here, I will deal with the first point, the critique of metaphysics in Marx and Derrida, and I will be concerned primarily with questions of method of analysis and of the critique of knowledge. I will begin with a comparison of the concepts of relation, difference, and antagonism in Marx and Derrida. Then, I will work out the similarities and differences between their critiques of positivism, idealism, naturalism, and objectivism.

Derrida has not always been willing to consider himself a marxist. In early texts, he suggests that marxism itself is subject to deconstruction, that it belongs to the metaphysics of presence. He pitches together the materialist dialectic with the speculative idealist dialectic and accuses both of being metaphysical, that is, of adhering to the horizon of presence and of self-identity, of positing a resolutive telos of noncontradiction and indifference, and of reducing the infinite displacement of the trace (the inscription of alterity in what seems selfsame) to stable, homogeneous structures of meaning and of being: "I don't believe there is a 'fact' which permits us to say: in *the* marxist corpus, *the* notion of contradiction and *the* notion of dialectics escapes *the* domination of metaphysics. . . . I don't believe one can speak, even from a marxist perspective, of a homogeneous marxist text which would instantaneously liberate the concept of contradiction from its speculative, teleological, and eschatological horizon."[2] The interview quoted here occurred in 1971. In a later text (1972), he reverses himself and suggests that Marx's postscript to Hegel escapes the metaphysical urge for logocentric closure and sublative resolution through the speculative dialectic. In "Hors Livre" he describes Marx's difference from Hegel by considering the status of the "preface" in their texts. In attempting, like Hegel, to avoid "formal anticipation," Marx, unlike Hegel, did not seek a result that would be a "pure determination of the concept, even less a 'foundation.'" Derrida then cites one of Marx's prefaces, saying that it exhibits a "quantitative and qualitative heterogeneity of developments, and the whole historical scene in which it is inscribed." He concludes: "Thus, the asymmetrical space of a post-script to the greater Logic is sketched out. An infinitely differentiated general space . . . a force of historical non-return, resisting every circular re-comprehension in the reflexive domesticity (*Erinnerung*) of the Logos, re-covering and proclaiming truth in its full speech" (*Diss*, 41). Perhaps Derrida gave the question more thought between 1971 and 1972. Certainly, in earlier texts, his condemnation of all forms of the dialectic is unremitting. I quote from *Of Grammatology*, published in French in 1968: "All dualisms, all theories of the immortality of the soul or of the spirit, as well as all monisms, spiritualist or materialist, dialectical or vulgar, are the unique theme of a metaphysics whose entire history was compelled to strive toward the reduction of the trace. The subordination of the trace to the full presence summed up in the logos [is] an onto-theology determining the archeological and eschatological meaning of being as presence, as parousia, as life without differance" (*Gram*, 71). By 1972, Derrida markedly changed his tune. In between 1968 and 1972 stands the 1971 interview with Jean Louis Houdebine and Guy Scarpetta during which he was first publicly (in writing) taken to task on the question of marxism.

After 1972, such pieces of Marx's vocabulary appear in Derrida's work as capitalization and surplus value. In 1976, during an interview, Derrida redefined the relationship of deconstruction to "marxism." The deconstructive question, he said, concerns "the philosophical project inasmuch as it calls for a foundation and an architechtonics, systematics, and therefore as well the onto-encyclopedic *universitas*. . . . Does marxism (inasmuch as it contains a system named dialectical materialism) present itself as a philosophy, elaborated or to be elaborated, as a *founded* philosophical practice, as a 'construction'. . .? I don't know a marxist discourse—considering or calling itself such—which would respond negatively to that question. Nor, I would add, which poses it or even recognizes it."[3] Derrida wisely limits his reservation to marxist philosophy and to dialectical materialism, but he mistakenly equates marxism with a philosophical system. Once that is done, marxism can be reduced to althusserianism or Communist party diamat, both of which are indeed subject to the deconstructive question, because both apply founded systematic constructions to the world. Each in its own way is more concerned with the scientific or philosophic purity of the conceptual edifice or construct than with practice carried out in a problematic historical arena whose heterogeneity makes complete systematic formality questionable. It is not surprising that both philosophies have been accused of effacing class struggle, that practical war of forces which makes the construction of "marxist" philosophical *systems* seem irrelevant.

In the same interview Derrida spoke of the necessity of the marxist problematic of ideology, and he suggested ways deconstruction might engage the question by considering such oppositions as science/ideology and ideology/philosophy. He said marxists would do well to address the texts of Nietzsche and Heidegger in terms of ideology. And, while criticizing "dogmatic" marxism, he nonetheless expressed distaste for the "derisory and reactive" French "post-marxists." He did the same in the 1979 interview from which I have already quoted and in which, for the first time in print, he speaks of himself as a marxist. There also he provides a sympathetic description of marxism: "Marxism presents itself, has presented itself from the very beginning with Marx, as an open theory which was continually to transform itself and not become fixed in dogma, in stereotypes."[4]

Derrida, then, is a critical philosopher who undertook a deconstruction of bourgeois philosophy in its most powerful incarnations, from Rousseau to Hegel to Husserl to Heidegger to Searle, who made the uninformed mistake early on of lumping Marx's materialist with Hegel's speculative dialectics, who, after reading Marx, corrected the misattribution and acknowledged the parallel nature of Marx's undertaking to his own (inasmuch as Marx's was methodological or philosophical), and who still maintains a critical distance in regard to Soviet diamat and to dogmatic, precritical marxist "philosophy."

I am convinced that if marxists were to cease pretending to be "philosophers" and to stop mistaking the construction of "marxist" philosophical systems for a political practice that calls itself marxist and also to cease mulling over such conceptual abstractions as "mode of production" or "determination in the last instance" or "relative autonomy," and instead to carry the critique of capitalism and of bourgeois culture into the home turf of bourgeois philosophy and thought, the result would be something *like* a politicized version of deconstruction. Not exactly the same, because an analysis of the circuit that leads from John Searle's reactionary philosophic study to David Rockefeller's bank office, to the torture chambers of Santiago de Chile, requires supplementing Derrida's fine micrological critique of the structural principles and operations of the institutions of power and domination in philosophy with a more macrological and social mode of analysis.

I will begin to plot the similarities between Marx and Derrida as critics of epistemology by discussing the concepts of relation, difference, and antagonism as they appear in Marx's Introduction to the *Grundrisse*. My purpose throughout will be to argue that the conceptual breakthrough one sees at work in both Marx and Derrida has necessary political implications and that the methodological or conceptual radicalization in each instance is irrelevant, even in the development of a "science," unless those political implications are immediately called forth.

Marx's Introduction to the *Grundrisse* allows one to bring him together with Derrida in regard to the concepts of relation, difference, and antagonism. Marx admits that a category like "production in general," which seems to reduce difference to identity, is a "rational abstraction" that fixes a "common element" that nonetheless is "itself segmented many times over and splits into [*Auseinanderfahrendes*] different determinations."[5] The category of knowledge is therefore an institution, a conventional construct, rather than a naturally corresponding proper name or representation of the presence of a self-sufficient thing in itself, an institution whose abstract generality prevents it from ever being fully adequate to the historical specificity of each segmented form of production. Marx's term to name that segmentation is "essential difference": "The elements which are not general or common must be separated out from the determinations valid for production as such, so that in their unity . . . their *essential difference* [*wesentliche Verschiedenheit*] is not forgotten. . . . The categories of bourgeois economics possess a truth for all other forms of society . . . but always with an essential difference [*Unterschied*]" (*Grun*, 85, 106; 7, 26). The emphasis is on essential difference because what Marx criticizes in bourgeois political economy is the tendency to "smudge over all historical differences and to see bourgeois relations in all forms of society" (*Grun*, 105; 26). The reduction of difference to identity serves a political function. Marx criticizes "those modern economists who demonstrate the eternity and harmoniousness of the existing social relations" (*Grun*, 85; 7) by "forgetting" this essential difference. Because of historical particularity and essential difference, general categories such as "production in general" exist only in the mind as cognitive institutions: "There are determinations [*Bestimmungen*] which all stages of production have in common, and which are established as general ones by the mind [*von Denken*]; but the so-called *general conditions* [*Bedingungen*] of all production are nothing more than these abstract moments with which no real historical stage of production can be grasped" (*Grun* 88; 10).

Essential difference makes it impossible that the general category, which collapses difference into identity, should be a proper name, to use the derridean term, an adequate representation of the world or of history. Recourse to such institutions or categories is always therefore a theoretical fiction, as well as a political instrument or strategy. Marx wrote: "This eighteenth century individual—the product . . . of the dissolution of the feudal forms of society . . . —appears as an ideal whose existence [the eighteenth-century prophets] project into the past. Not as a historic result but as history's point of departure" (*Grun*, 83; 5). Derrida later spoke with equal force against the conversion of differentially produced effects (consciousness, for example) into natural origins, although he did not pursue an analysis of the political function of this conversion. For Marx, the general category of the individual effaces the mediation of individuals by society. Social relations constitute an otherness that could never be reduced to an identity—the individual—that could then be idealized as a general category—itself an identification of differences—that transcends essential difference and specific historical "segmentation." The constitution of a general category of identity in the mind requires the location of a self-identical object in the world. For such a project to succeed, alterity—the antagonistic social relation for Marx—must be effaced. And as an ideological claim declaring capitalism to be homogeneous and natural, it does indeed succeed.

The question of the status of the category, then, is not merely methodological, but also political. On it hangs the question of ideology, the representation of the world through images and concepts that pretend to be natural, adequate, and proper, but in fact operate through a sifting of differences, antagonisms, social relations, and historical claims.

The political nature of categorization is particularly clear when Marx speaks of relations. A relation always involves more than one item. Something is in relation to an "other." Relation therefore implies otherness or alterity. A relation is never singular or composed of one unique element. The uniqueness of each element in a relation depends on an other. To say that what appears to be a simple "thing" is in fact a "relation" is to say that alterity precedes and produces identity. In discussing the relation between production and consumption, Marx writes: "Each of them, apart from being immediately [*unmittelbar*, unmediatedly] the other, and apart from mediating the other, in addition to this creates the other in completing itself; itself as the other [*sich als die andre*]" (*Grun*, 93; 14). This is a classic statement of the hegelian dialectic of interrelation. Marx is arguing against those political economists who would separate production and consumption as distinct categories, hence as distinct things. Marx's point is that the "thing" cannot exist except in relation to its "other." Production examined alone is an "empty abstraction": "This again shows the ineptitude of those economists who portray production as an eternal truth while banishing history to the realm of distribution. The question of the relation between this production-determining distribution and production belongs evidently within production itself" (*Grun*, 97; 18). Here, Marx's description of the double act of elevating production to an eternal truth and of debasing distribution by relegating it to history is in its form very similar to Derrida's description of the initiating metaphysical act of elevating consciousness, ideal meaning, self-presence in the mind, and therefore speech to an eternal truth, and of simultaneously debasing spatialization, history, social institutionality, and therefore writing through banishment to an outside.

For Marx, once alterity, the relation to the other which is "internal" to the thing (production), is taken into account, one arrives at a full concrete determination, as opposed to an empty abstraction. It should be noted that the word "determination" [*Bestimmung*] does not mean a self-identical "thing," but instead a locus of relations whereby something is constituted by or in relationship to other determinations. Marx, therefore, always speaks, for example, of money, labor, exchange, and value as "relations" [*Verhältnisse*], not as "things" [*Dinge*]. This is why for methodology, Marx decides that categories such as "production" in general, which efface differences, relations, and history, are inadequate analytic tools. They presuppose self-identical things, which are eternal rather than historically specific, and unique rather than relational. Marx's point is that such categories make what is historically produced seem natural, what is segmented into different interrelated parts bound to specific historical moments seem eternal: "At the beginning these may appear as spontaneous, natural. But by the process of production itself they are transformed from natural into historic determinants, and if they appear to one epoch as natural presuppositions of production, they were its historic product for another" (*Grun,* 97; 18).

Marx criticizes the general category through two modes, one spatial — "general-historical relations in production" — the other temporal — "the movement of history generally" (*Grun,* 97; 18). You will remember that Derrida's concept of differance also includes a spatial mode — differing, distinction, becoming other — and a temporal mode — deferring, delaying, putting in reserve — intertwined. Like relationality in Marx, Derrida's concepts of trace and alterity also imply the inscription of the other in the selfsame.

Derrida contends that the constitutive scission or antagonism which a marxist would also see at work in the world is precisely what the most metaphysical forms of positivist knowledge — those based on immediacy, consciousness, and presence — filter out and efface. Where an ideologist sees a self-identical economy operating according to self-sufficient objective laws, a marxist sees strife, struggle, and the scission of antagonistic social relations. Derrida's version of this insight is more philosophical than sociopolitical. Metaphysical forms of knowledge, by emphasizing the seamless immediacy of knowledge, make the world appear undifferentiated, whole, nonantagonistic. By pointing out the difference, especially the difference of force, at work in all conceptuality, Derrida points toward, but does not develop, the conclusion that all knowledge (of the social world in particular) is a terrain of political struggle. His neonietzschean belief that ruling interpretations of the truth of the world are more the result of superior force than of superior truth value points toward a description of the war of interpretations as a political war whose stakes are the terms in which reality is defined and indeed "contructed." The reason or truth of any epoch may be so only because it is more empowered than any other version. Like Nietzsche, Derrida stops short of fully analyzing the linkage between the superior force of an interpretation of the world and the superior power of the political-economic class whose interest it supports. At times, it seems as if ideas have a force of their own for Derrida, independent of the social forces that use them. At other times, he is careful to anchor the reason of state in the rationality promoted by state educational institutions.

Antonio Negri argues that all of Marx's economic categories in the *Grundrisse* reduce to political categories of social antagonism between classes.[6] There are no autonomous laws of economic value which are not at bottom laws of the exercise of political force as exploitation. This is the political significance of Marx's rewriting of the metaphysics of identity as a conceptuality based on difference and relation. A similar argument could be made for Derrida on the level of conceptual knowledge in general. The deconstructive emphasis on difference, scission, and alterity opens the possibility of a political economy of knowledge that would see the question of truth as one of political force. Like the capitalist workplace, the workshop of scientific and philosophic conceptuality might also be a contested terrain where such a simple thing as analytic method can become a tool of class power, as a way of deciding who can know and what can be known.

I will now consider four brands of knowledge against which both Derrida and Marx, either explicitly or implicitly, write: positivism, idealism, naturalism, and objectivism. The purpose of this exercise, once again, is to demonstrate similarities between the deconstructive and the marxist critiques of knowledge and to argue that in each case the critique is not only philosophic, but also political in character.

Positivism is based on immediate "factual" knowledge: truth consists of the perfect adequation between the instruments of knowledge—concepts and words—and the world, which is assumed to be stable and fixed as the immediate presence of objects or events. Derrida argues that what seems positive, immediate, and present is caught up in a web of mediacy (becoming other in time, other relations in space). Presence is never original or unique; it always refers beyond itself to something other, and it is always an effect, a re-presentation. What seems immediate is derived in relation to the movement of differing, deferring, and becoming other (always bearing the *trace* of something beyond or other) that precedes and makes possible immediacy. Immediate presence thus breaks down into a complicated, problematic structure/movement of mediacy. (Not mediation of negation, because that implies the resolution into conclusive identity in the classic dialectic.) Nothing, in other words, "is" without presuppositions and effects, without itself being a presupposition and an effect of other things, and conditions and effects circulate and interrelate in ways that deny the stability of presence required by positivist knowledge. Positive immediacy, presence as such, is produced by the detours and the referential relays of differentiation.

Derrida's method here can be called reversal, showing how what seems immediate and original—the positive fact in its presence—is mediate and derived. The next step is a displacement of the possibility of a positive fact, or an immediate presence, which would function as a norm (the "natural" or "real") over against which something derived—the detour of metaphor, fiction, artifice, language, signs, institutions, production, history, technology—could be defined as other. Derrida's point is to show that the so-called natural or real is itself already structured and made possible only by virtue of detour, technology, repetition, representation, and so on. One cannot rigorously distinguish between the two as being a more original norm and a secondary derivation. The possibility always exists, as Derrida puts it, that fiction might not be derived. What we call natural might be a product of institutions and technology. For example, the real facts of the positivist might themselves be constructs or fictions fabricated through strategic exclusions. The pretense to "science" conceals a politics. Certainly, the positivist notion of a "person" when compared with a marxist definition of the social being qualifies as such a fact/fiction, whose political function in bourgeois society is not insignificant.

Marx's critique of the positivist method of classical political economy is executed through a practice similar to Derrida's reversal and displacement; he calls it "inversion." The best known example is the inversion of the inversion which classical political economy operates by claiming that circulation, not production, is the origin or source of profit. Here what is merely a result—price—is taken to be a cause. Marx is equally critical of the positing of positive "things" (land rent, wages, profit, and so on) which are not seen as being produced by networks of social relations that displace their immediacy and inscribe their presence to consciousness in a complex systematic structure and a multistranded history. For example, the positive entity "property" is in fact multiple, differentiated, and an *effect* of relations that exceed the circumference of its immediacy and its presence: "In each historical epoch, property has developed differently and under a set of entirely different social relations. Thus to define bourgeois property is nothing else than to give an exposition of all the social relations of bourgeois production. To try to give a definition of property as of an independent relation, a category apart, an abstract and eternal idea, can be nothing but an illusion of metaphysics or jurisprudence."[7]

Marx describes the relationality that becomes congealed in "things" like property as social. Derrida confines to philosophical terms the differential relations that produce entities and things without themselves being reducible to an ontology of "being." But the general pattern of reversal and displacement is analogous. The linking word is *effect*; what positivism would like to limit to a self-evident fact is the effect of differential relations, either microstructural, in the deconstructive sense, or macrostructural, in the marxist social-historical sense. Paraphrasing Thomas Hodgskin, Marx writes: "The effects [*Wirkungen*] of a certain social form of labor are ascribed to objects, to the products of labor; the relationship is imagined to exist in *thing-ly* [*dinglicher*] form."[8] Derrida adds, "What we need is to determine in another way, according to a differential system, the *effects* of ideality, signification, meaning, and reference. . . . Reading should not proceed here as a simple sublation of concepts, or words, as a statistical or static punctuation. One must reconstitute the chain in movement, the effects of a network and of a play of syntax" (*Pos*, 90; *Diss*, 221). Meaning is an aftereffect of the differential movement of syntax, not a preexisting spontaneous intuition in the mind.

Marx and Derrida are speaking of different things here, but there is a general methodological congruity. Marx accuses political economy of abstracting things from differential social and historical relations of which they are an effect. Those "things" are then accorded an original or causative status. Property, rather than a historically produced social relation, is transformed into the simple origin of wealth. This metaphysical reduction hides the role of production and of productive labor in the generation of wealth, and it conceals the origin of wealth, which is exploitation founded on an antagonistic social relation, a difference between classes. Similarly, in idealist and positivist philosophies of language, meaning is posited as an ideal source to which language attaches itself and which language expresses. A differentially produced effect is made the origin of that whose "chain" or "play of syntax" produces it. A "thing," meaning, sense, or ideal truth, takes the place of the differential relations between links in the discontinuous chain of language. The two gestures—the reduction of differentiation in political economy as in philosophy—belong to the same metaphysical system. And each functions politically. The first annuls the claims of labor to a just "return" on its investment of labor power. The second permits the immediate to be privileged over the mediate, the intelligible (ideal) over the sensible (material). One can say that the two political functions form an alliance. Each form of positivism, as the focus on circulation at the expense of social relation and historical production or on presence at the expense of the background network that constitutes it, supports the other. Attending to perceived presence and meaning implies remaining at the level of circulation, rather than flushing out the mode of production of such presence or such meaning. And this attitude supports the ideology that overlooks economic production (and class difference and antagonism) in favor of the apparent indifference, equilibrium, and homogeneity of economic circulation.

Marx's critique of idealism consists of more than accusing Hegel of having turned the world on its head, of having made the idea the origin of the material of which it was itself a derivative effect. The critique also insists that thought and ideality are possible only on the basis of the material practice of language, of accusing Proudhon of reducing the complex circuitry of the world to a simple logical system, of deriding the assumption that an intellectual elite (Bruno Bauer and company) can, through ideas, change the world, and of describing how the process of abstract thought in political economy collapses differences into identities, reduces out distinctions, effaces history, abridges transformation and extended circuits into unities, and fuses conflict and antagonism into a semblance of equilibrium and harmony. If the classical speculative dialectic turns the negative into a positive and resolves contradiction into identity, then the classical political economists are guilty of idealist dialectics; they see a negative downturn as a positive moment before an upswing and declare crisis to be unity: "It is entirely wrong, therefore, to do as the economists do, namely, as soon as the contradictions in the momentary system emerge into view, to focus only on the end results without the process which mediates them; only on the unity without the distinction, the affirmation without the negation. . . . They take refuge in this abstraction because in the real development of money there are contradictions which are unpleasant for the apologists of bourgeois common sense, and must hence be covered up" (*Grun*, 197-98; 112).

Derrida accuses all of Western metaphysics of a similar "idealism" —covering over rupture, difference, antagonism, and undecidability— with "onto-theological" concepts of presence and property—transcendence, meaning, being, absolute knowledge, phenomenological intuition, models of ideal truth, and the like. (To a certain extent, Derrida acknowledges, some such idealism is unavoidable, if knowledge is to be practiced and meaning communicated.) If we are to believe Derrida, "being" is constituted not as "presence" but by differences of force to whose effects idealist philosophy attempts to apply proper names or unique categories based on the logic of self-identity, but those relations withstand unique, proper appellations. Metaphysics posits concepts of ontological self-identity (being, entity, event, act, idea) or a logic of causality, development, and conclusion. Philosophical common sense demands "the substitution of the accomplishment of a *dynamis* for the substitution of a trace, of pure history for pure play, and . . . of a welding together for a break" (*Gram*, 187). Under metaphysical eyes, the class struggle becomes the harmonious development of a self-identical, nonantagonistic social whole.

In *The German Ideology* Marx is working with terms that are of a different philosophic order than Derrida's, but his characterization of idealism is similar to Derrida's picture of the operations of metaphysics. Marx, too, distrusts the substitution of a pure history for a more heterogeneous development:

> The individuals who are no longer subject to the division of labor, have been conceived by the philosophers as an ideal, under the name "man", and the whole process which we have outlined has been regarded by them as the evolutionary process of "man", so that at every historical state "man" was substituted for the individuals existing hitherto and shown as the motive force of history. . . . Through this inversion which from the first disregards the actual conditions, it was possible to transform the whole of history into an evolutionary process of consciousness.[9]

Derrida's counter to the metaphysical desire is to posit an immaterial, yet real (in the sense that force is felt but not seen except through effects on other media) process that escapes the metaphysical closure of "being as presence." Marx occasionally criticizes metaphysics in terms that seem to foreshadow Derrida:

> We have seen that the whole problem of the transition from thought to reality, hence from language to life, exists only in philosophical illusion, i.e., it is justified only for philosophical consciousness, which cannot possibly be clear about the nature and origin of its apparent separation from life. This great problem, insofar as it at all entered the minds of our ideologists, was bound, of course, to result finally in one of these knights-errant setting out in search of a word which, as a *word,* formed the transition in question, which, as a word, ceases to be simply a word, and which, as a word, in a mysterious superlinguistic manner, points from within language to the actual object it denotes; which, in short, plays among words the same role as the Redeeming God-Man plays among people in Christian fantasy . . . thus the triumphant entry into "corporeal" life.[10]

Here, Marx criticizes two idealist illusions that Derrida also contends with. The first is the "apparent separation" between consciousness and the world, and the second is the illusion of reference, that a word points from "within language" to the actual object in the world.

Both Marx and Derrida call consciousness, the seat of idealism and of the apparent autonomy of the thought process, a symptom, but whereas Derrida derives it from differentiation such as that which appears in Freud's description of the emergence of consciousness from unconsciousness, Marx relates it to social and historical structures: "The apparent absurdity of merging all the manifold relationships of people in the *one* relation of usefulness, this apparently metaphysical abstraction arises from the fact that in modern bourgeois society all relations are subordinated in practice to the one abstract monetary-commercial relation."[11] Derrida never provides an equivalent explanation for metaphysics. Nevertheless, both he and Marx argue that the work of speculative thought itself creates the conditions for idealism. Marx: "In consciousness . . . relations become concepts."[12]

A third major area in which Marx and Derrida can be compared is the critique of naturalism and objectivism. Marx critiques David Ricardo for claiming that capitalist production relations are natural; the antagonism and the coercion operating between classes is thus neutralized. Derrida makes a similar critique of the French state-run school system. To naturalize the scene of teaching is to dissimulate "the forces and interests which, without the slightest neutrality, dominate, master, and impose themselves on the teaching process, from inside an agonistic and heterogeneous field which is divided and operated by incessant struggle."[13]

Marx's discussion of the opposition nature/history provides a hinge for comparing Marx's critique of naturalism with Derrida's. Derrida's critique of Rousseau's naturalism is akin to Marx's repudiation of Mill's and Ricardo's conversion of historical institutions into supposedly natural things. Those "natural" things conceal the relational or differential character of capital as well as its historical genealogy, and they are in fact congealed relations that can only be conceived theoretically and not perceived empirically in a "natural" or objective form.

Derrida's argument against naturalism is related to the argument for "general textuality." Rousseau's metaphysical naturalism makes speech out to be the origin of language because it is most natural, that is, most proximate to the "natural voice" of consciousness, which, because of the logocentric character of metaphysics, is accorded ethical and logical priority. The concept of nature is bound up with the concept of logocentric truth, of universal law pronounced by a consciousness that transcends the empirical world. The value of nature, then, is more than a point of origin in a historical genealogy; it also is a value that is linked to the metaphysical opposition between inside and outside, mental and manual, the physical and the technological. In discussing the concept of the arbitrariness of the linguistic sign, which defines the institution of arbitrariness in opposition to the supposedly more "natural link" between sound and meaning in phonology, Derrida names what is at stake in the critique of naturalism: "All this refers, beyond the nature/culture opposition, to a supervening opposition between *physis* and *nomos, physis* and *technè*, whose ultimate function is perhaps to *derive* historicity; and, paradoxically, not to recognize the rights of history, production, institutions, etc., except in the form of the arbitrary and in the substance of naturalism" (*Gram*, 33). Not to recognize history, production, institutions is to perform the ideological gesture of Mill and Ricardo. What Derrida seems to target in metaphysics is the conceptual infrastructure of the naturalizing ideology of classical political economy. The myth of the immediate "natural" presence of meaning and sound in the mind permits history, production (technological artifice), and institutionality to be declared external, fallen, and secondary. They all represent death for the logos, the centerpiece of metaphysics. By expelling them as its other, an other it controls and owns because they are derivative in regard to the logos (speech/mind/law), a retroactive sense of full life as a spiritual parousia without mediacy, history, technology, or institutions is gained. That is the meaning of the metaphysical concept of nature.

This gesture of exclusion establishes the opposition between speech and writing, nature and culture (history, technology, production, institutions), but it also inscribes the supposedly internal nature of speech in exteriority. The necessary exclusion of institutionality and of history in order to ground the priority of nature relates nature intrinsically to history and to institutionality. The establishment of a norm of nature is not possible without an other against which its normativity is defined, an evil like unnatural writing which is expelled by natural speech. In that act of expulsion, the "instituted trace" ("where the relationship with the other is marked") manifests itself. Pure nature cannot be posited without a simultaneous affirmation of that which supposedly excludes nature—the outside as history, production, institutions. One could say, of human language at least, nature is instituted. Immediacy is derived in relation to the mediacy from which it must differentiate itself in order to be "itself."

There is no strict homology between Derrida's deconstruction of metaphysical naturalism and Marx's attack on the objectivist and naturalist ideologies of political economy, but the two relate in that deconstruction seems to get at the root of the naturalizing ideology of political economy and to plot out its system in relation to all metaphysics. Nevertheless, there are points of direct contact. By naturalism, Marx means the effacement of history and of social genealogy; something is made to seem outside the movement of time and the productive process of society. Derrida's argument is more philosophical or logical than historical or societal, but at times his critical weapon against naturalism—differentiation—takes on qualities that relate it to history, at least in the sense of the transformative movement of time in space, and of an infinite genealogy for which there is no theological origin. In his meditation on the metaphysical opposition between speech and writing, Derrida describes writing as being "thoroughly historical" and sets out to show how "writing" (as a name for trace or differentiation) precedes and produces speech as an effect, the supposedly natural ground of language and signification. Derrida argues that speech as the revelation of internal living consciousness would not be possible without differentiation: "The opening of the first exteriority in general, the enigmatic relationship of the living to its other and of an inside to an outside: spacing. The outside, 'spatial' and 'objective' exteriority which we believe we know as the most familiar thing in the world, as familiarity itself, would not appear without . . . differance [differentiation] as temporalization, without the nonpresence of the other inscribed within the sense [or meaning] of the present" (*Gram*, 70-71). Derrida is arguing against the naturalist and objectivist prejudices that posit either a nonsignifying, natural ground of intuition from which language as a process of reference derives or a purely objective, material (in the vulgar sense) presence which language designates and in which the process of reference ends. Both prejudices are ideological in that they program an effacing of history, relationality, and "general textuality," the fact that "things" are caught up in webs of reference which, because of the spatio-temporal movement of differentiation as of history, never touch an absolute or transcendental ground, where reference would stop or a purely ahistorical presence (of meaning or being) would reveal itself absolutely, and the fact that "natural intuition" is never original, but instead always a derived effect of psychic inscription and, by implication, social inscription.

I would suggest, then, that, although the terms are not identical, the critical, anti-ideological charge carried by the words "history" and "relation" in Marx is matched by that implicit in the words "trace" and "differance" in Derrida. If "history" is Marx's word for the breaking up of nature and for the onset of institutions and production, it bears a relation to Derrida's term, the "becoming-unmotivated" of the trace, the breaking of signification with the "natural attachment within reality." There is no nature of language or of thought which is not already institutionalized or becoming-unmotivated. Assuming that motivation names the natural attachment in general, we might weave Marx and Derrida together in a slightly illegitimate way by substituting the word "history" for the word "immotivated" in the following passage from Derrida: "Without referring back to 'nature,' the historicality of the trace has always *become*. In fact, there is no historical trace: the trace is indefinitely its own becoming-historical" (*Gram*, 47). Were such a transposition legitimate, it might prove the case for a radical concept of history in Derrida. But given that his concepts of trace and differentiation accomplish a critique of naturalism similar to the one accomplished by Marx's concepts of history and social relations, such a proof would be merely academic. Derrida is not Marx, but he has provided refined tools for furthering a marxist critique of naturalist prejudices that deny history and social relationality.

Marx's version of this undoing or deconstruction of the metaphysical as well as ideological opposition between nature and culture, nature and technology, hinges on the concept of labor, human constructive activity. What Ludwig Feuerbach takes to be a purely natural and objective materiality is in fact a subjectively cultured artifact:

> And so it happens that in Manchester, for instance, Feuerbach sees only factories and machines, where a few hundred years ago only spinning-wheels and weaving-looms were to be seen. . . . Feuerbach speaks in particular of the perception of natural science . . . but where would natural science be without industry and commerce? Even this "pure" natural science is provided with an aim, as with its material, only through trade and industry, through the sensuous activity [*sinnliche Tätigkeit*] of men. So much is this activity, this unceasing sensuous labor and creation, this production, the foundation of the whole sensuous world as it now exists that, were it interrupted only for a year, Feuerbach would not only find an enormous change in the natural world, but would very soon find that the whole world of men and his own perceptive faculty, and his own existence, were missing. [*CW*, 5:40; *MEW*, 3:13, 44]

Throughout the *Grundrisse*, Marx argues that the historical process of capitalist development consists of the "pulling-away of the natural ground" (*Grun*, 528; 426) of industry, so that what was previously superfluous becomes necessary, and what was an artificial effect or product of production becomes a condition of production—credit, for example, or fertilizers. Similarly, the "natural form of existence of the product" of labor "is stripped away," so that use value becomes exchange value. "Things" come to embody social relations. And those social relations are themselves historically constructed, "posited by society": "All relations as posited by society, not as determined by nature. Only this way is the application of science possible for the first time" (*Grun*, 276; 188).

Much of what passes for "objective" materiality or "natural" law in the economy is in fact a concretization of relations whose provenance is social and historical and which include a subjective component. This is the significance of defining constant or fixed capital as past objectified labor. Similarly, prices are "ideal" expressions of value. And a commodity, one of the most important features of capitalism, is as much "imaginary" as "corporeal": "When we speak of the commodity as a materialization [*Materiatur*] of labor—in the sense of its exchange-value —this itself is only an imaginary, that is to say, a purely social mode of existence of the commodity which has nothing to do with its corporeal reality" (*TSV*, 1:171; *MEW*, 26.1:141). The exchange of commodities requires an ideal operation of abstraction and equation which becomes real in the concrete form of money:

> Value is their social relation [*gesellschaftliches Verhältnis*]. . . . As a value, the commodity is an equivalent; as an equivalent, all its natural properties are extinguished. . . . Every moment in calculating, etc., that we transform commodities into value symbols, we fix them as mere exchange values, making abstraction from the matter they are composed of and all their natural qualities. . . . This third, which differs from them both, exists initially only in the head, as a conception, since it expresses a relation [*ein Verhältnis ausdrucke*]; just as, in general, relations can be established as existing only by being *thought* [*nur gedacht werden können*], as distinct from the subjects which are in these relations with each other. . . . This abstraction will do for comparing commodities; but in actual exchange this abstraction in turn must be objectified, must be symbolized. . . . Such a symbol presupposes general recognition; it can only be a social symbol; it expresses, indeed, nothing more than a social relation [*gesellschaftliches Verhältnis*]. . . . Doubling in the idea [*ideelle*] proceeds (and must proceed) to the point where the commodity appears double in exchange. . . . In the form of money, all properties of the commodity as exchange value appear as an object distinct from it, as a form of social existence separated from the natural existence of the commodity. [*Grun*, 142-45; 61-63]

Marx is careful to point out that money "is a product of exchange itself, and not the execution of an idea conceived *a priori*" (*Grun*, 144; 63).

Nevertheless, it is clear from the account of exchange value that this process is neither purely objective nor material nor natural. It is a process of social and mental mediation which is concretized in the exchange of money. The subjective mental process of abstraction and comparison, which necessarily "strips away" the natural and material form of the product, is implied in exchange. The intertwining of subjective and objective operations is what Marx means when he speaks of the "material and mental [*materiellen und geistigen*] metabolism which is independent of the knowing and willing of individuals" (*Grun*, 161; 79). The significance of Marx's early description of human life as productive activity (objectifying the subjective, subjectifying the objective) for the later economic theory is clear. The so-called objective economic structure is an embodiment of subjective labor, and it would not operate without the mediation of the mental process of abstraction which permits comparative relation and thus exchange. The seemingly objective "thinghood" of the exchange economy is the expression of a social relation: "As values, commodities are *social* magnitudes, that is to say, something absolutely different from their 'properties' as 'things.' As values, they constitute only relations of men in their productive activity" (*TSV*, 3:129; *MEW*, 26.3:127).

Marx condemned as fetishistic those economic theories which posit the economy as something natural, entirely "material" (in the positivist sense), or purely objective:

Capital is conceived [by capitalist ideology] as a thing [*Sache*], not as a relation [*Verhältnis*]. . . . The general exchange of activities and products, which has become a vital condition for each individual—their mutual interconnection [*Zusammenhang*]—here appears as something alien to them, autonomous, as a thing [*als eine Sache*]. In exchange value, the social connection between persons is transformed into a relation between things [*Verhalten der Sachen*]; personal capacity into an objective [*sachliches*] capacity. . . . The crude materialism of the economists who regard as the *natural properties* of things what are social relations of production among people, and qualities which things obtain because they are subsumed under these relations [*Verhältnisse*], is at the same time just as crude an idealism, even fetishism, since it imputes social relations [*Beziehungen*] to things as inherent characteristics, and thus mystifies them. . . . It is characteristic of labor based on private exchange that the social character of labor "manifests" itself in a perverted form—as the "property" of things; that a social relation appears as a relation between things (between products, values in use, commodities). This *appearance* is accepted as something real [*etwas Wirkliches*] by our fetish-worshipper, and he actually believes that the exchange-value of things is determined by their properties as things, and is altogether a natural property of things. No scientist to date has yet discovered what natural qualities make definite proportions of snuff tobacco and paintings "equivalents" for one another. Thus he, the wiseacre, transforms value into something absolute, "a property of things," instead of seeing in it only something relative, the relation of things to social labor, social labor based on private exchange, in which things are determined [*bestimmt*] not as independent entities, but as mere expressions [*Ausdrücke*] of social production. . . . The whole objective world, the "world of commodities," vanishes here [in Hodgskin] as a mere aspect, as the merely passing activity, constantly performed anew, of socially producing men. Compare this "idealism" with the crude, material [*materiellen*] fetishism into which the Ricardian theory develops. . . . . Capital more and more acquires a material [*sachliche*] form, is transformed more and more from a relationship into a thing, but a thing which embodies, which has absorbed, the social relationship, a thing which has acquired a fictitious life and independent existence in relation to itself [*Selbstständigkeit sich zu sich*], a sensuous-supersensuous [*sinnlich-übersinnliches*] entity. [*Grun*, 258, 157, 687; 169, 75, 579; *TSV*, 3:130, 267, 483; *MEW*, 26.3:125, 263, 474]

I cite at such great length simply to show how Marx would have opposed such "productive force marxists" as Martin Shaw,[14] who would claim that marxism is a science of objective economic laws which promotes the development of what is primary in economics, that is, productive force. This mistaken hypothesis relegates the question of subjective activity (hence labor) and the political question of productive relations to a secondary, auxiliary status. This hypothesis can become an ideology that justifies the equating of high productivity under capitalist work relations with socialism. Such fetishizing of the so-called material or objective aspect of production overlooks everything Marx says on the subject of productive relations, labor, and the social relational, hence politically antagonistic, nature of seemingly objective things like value.

Objectivist or naturalist fetishism, according to Marx, then, consists of erasing all marks of human labor from the social world, of converting historically and socially determined productive relations, which are irreducibly antagonistic, into purely natural, homogeneous, and objective "things." Marx suggests that the history of economic development has consisted of the conversion of nature into history, that is, of replacing natural needs, instruments, materials, relations, and so on with social products. The movement toward socialism will be a distanciation from the objectivist materialism that characterizes conservative marxism today, which would overlook the constitutive role of politically antagonistic social relations and social labor. Only such a strategic omission could justify equating socialism with the exacerbation of wage labor under the domination of the law of value and the preservation of antagonistic and exploitative productive relations.

Nature recedes as the world is converted into a product of technology and becomes historical. Technology — form-giving labor — is, according to Marx, the "nature" of human activity, thereby putting into question the distinction between nature and culture, at least as it pertains to human life. There would seem to be no moment of pure nature prior to technology. Even at a stage of pristine use value, the simple gathering of food, labor modifies both the external world by removing its "natural" product (itself manufactured, in that humans are not the only entities in nature which produce things), and the internal human world, by allowing humans to grow and reproduce. Inside and outside—the oppositional basis for the nature-culture, mental-manual binaries—is here undermined as an absolute opposition, because the subject of production, technology, and reproduction implies that human technology and the technology of nature which produces everything from apples to genes are interchangeable. The implication of this implicit deconstruction in Marx is that he would have given short shrift to modern economic ideologies, be they capitalist or state socialist, which claim that the economy is governed by objective and *natural* economic laws, next to which the strata of social relations is secondary, derivative, and accidental. The deconstruction implies that what seems secondary is in fact essential, but its essence is itself not of the nature of essence, that is, self-identity. Rather, it is the social, differential, non-self-identical scission of the antagonistic class relation, a relation that is itself determinant of the so-called natural and objective laws of economics. If politics always entails a difference of force, then we can say that politics as difference produces that from which a metaphysical political economy would say it is derived, the "natural" or objective identity of economic law. The value of nature which allows objective economic laws, independent of social relations, to be elaborated becomes untenable in the face of this critique. And this constitutes an example of how a deconstructive critique of a metaphysical value concept—here, nature—can hinge with marxist political economic struggle.

As differentiation imposes on Derrida the necessity of tracing out the chains of relations as opposed to a method that would resume the chains in movement into a punctual meaning or referent supposedly exempt from the movement of reference—"a simple sublation of concepts"—so also Marx's adherence to relationality imposes on him a method of investigation and exposition that entails working out the relations and avoiding stopping short at "indefinite notions" of seemingly selfsame "things": "The way in which the various components of the total social capital . . . alternately replace one another . . . requires a different mode of investigation [*Untersuchungsweise*]. Up till now, mere phrases have been taken as sufficient in this respect, although, when these are analysed more closely, they contain nothing more than indefinite notions, simply borrowed from the intertwining of metamorphoses that is common to all commodity circulation."[15]

In both Marx and Derrida, the critique of the misconceptions of metaphysics makes necessary the working out of a new practice of differential analysis. By differential analysis is meant a mode of investigation (and exposition) which treats the stable and fixed facts and entities of positivist science as effects of interrelating forces and structures whose transformations required extended exposition and a continuous displacement of the categories. Marx: "How, indeed, could the single logical formula of movement, of series [*Aufeinanderfolge*], of time, explain the structure of society, in which all relations coexist simultaneously and support one another" (*CW*, 6:167; *MEW*, 4:131).

One result of the conceptual breakthrough to difference and relationality is that both Derrida and Marx radically situate their theoretical work in history. I quote once again from the Introduction to the *Grundrisse*. Marx has just argued that the abstract general category of labor is conceivable only when in practice real labor has developed to a point where individuals are indifferent toward the particular kind of labor they perform, so that they can transfer from one kind to another: "The most general abstractions arise only in the midst of the richest possible concrete development, where one thing appears as common to many. . . . Labor shows strikingly how even the most abstract categories, despite their validity—precisely because of their abstractness—for all epochs, are nevertheless, in the specific character of this abstraction, themselves likewise a product of historic relations, and possess their full validity only for and within those relations" (*Grun*, 104-5; 25-26). Here, Marx renounces once and for all an idealist practice of analysis, along with the possibility of a transcendental critical position outside history from the vantage point of which one could know history using purely ideal conceptual instruments. His own concepts are products of history, profoundly bound up with the objects they name. That object is not an "outside" to which formal, logical categories correspond or are adequate. The object norms the concept as much as the concept determines the object. Theory is practice. History constructs the logic with which history is understood. Marx thus sets his analysis loose in history, without a paradigmatic first principle that is not historical, logically prior to all engagement with the world. Theoretical knowledge is immediately practice, which takes its cue from the historical world. No theoretic first principle or paradigmatic axiom anchors the analysis to a metahistoric, transcendental instance or criterion of truth. The analysis, as much as the object of analysis, is in history.

Derrida sets his analytic practice loose by renouncing philosophic responsibility (adherence to axiomatic first principles and progress toward an ultimate determination of absolute truth). He uses the word "errancy" to describe the strategy without finality that results. Giving up first principles and last truths also implies entry into history, renouncing the possibility of transcendence, refusing to conceive of the historical passage as a midpoint between an initial axiom and a conclusive goal of ideal meaning or truth. Derrida's notion of "undecidability" can be interpreted as naming the impossibility of decisive or absolute truth determinations which are not differentially produced, which do not therefore bear the trace of an alterity that transforms the supposed totalizing truth determination into a theoretical fiction that is necessarily incomplete or undecidable. Radical alterity implies that the field being determined cannot be reduced to the form of a presence or a proper thing that can be named in the form of truth (as adequation or correspondence between concept and world). Because the historical movement of differentiation splits presence and property (self-identity) and gives rise to undecidability, one could say that undecidability implies history, in the sense that decisive truth determinations, which do not take differentiation into account, constitute a denial of history. Errancy becomes another name for entry into history, giving up the transcendental security and the decided mastery which the dogmatism of final truths and the imperialism of first principles afford.

Marx's "philosophical" critique of what he called the "metaphysics" of classical political economy was linked to a political practice that was broad in its implications; it operated through class antagonism, historical developments, and the struggle for social power. "Metaphysics" meant a specifiable method that served an ideological power function in bourgeois society. Derrida's struggle against metaphysics remains for the most part confined to philosophical and literary texts. His attempts to broaden the effectivity of deconstruction are limited to references to other disciplinary domains. And because the object of deconstruction is the desire for onto-encyclopedic mastery — Hegel's absolute knowledge, for example — the politics that derive immediately from the critique seem at best antistatist.

Nevertheless, none of the critiques I have summarized is simply philosophical; each also engages political questions. Deconstruction criticizes the attempt to establish the truth of reality as positive factual, ideal, or objectively natural identity by revealing scission and difference to be the constituents of identity. Marxism characterizes this scission as a class antagonism and this difference as a difference of social forces and conflicting political-economic interests. Marxism thus adds a missing dimension to deconstruction by extending it into social and political-economic theory. But deconstruction also is crucial for the marxist critique because bourgeois ideology, in social science and social policy, has been able to write off the marxist contention that the social world is politically conflictual through and through as a merely external, sociological point unrelated to the internal, essential, purely philosophical or scientific, technical pursuit of true knowledge detached from politically interested, sociologically motivated concerns. Deconstruction, operating from within the outlines of bourgeois philosophy, shows how what that philosophy excludes is in fact internal to its makeup. Difference, scission, and antagonism constitute the "internal" domain of bourgeois philosophy and bourgeois science, as supposedly neutral, disinterested, universally valid technicity, rather than being merely "external," sociological, accidental, hence, dispensable corollaries to its essential operations.

The political implications of this articulation of the deconstructive and the marxist critiques of knowledge are not limited to bourgeois philosophy. They also extend to the determination of the truth of reality of socialism — of what will or will not be called socialism. All of the critiques I have covered imply that political economic structures do not have a positive, ideal, objective, natural existence, independent of subjective, social differences of force which constitute them in a nonpositive, mediated, relational, and differential way. The implication for socialist construction is that no amount of modification of the supposedly objective political-economic machinery will produce socialism, if the more fundamental questions of that social difference of force are not addressed. Preceding economic production, as Marx points out, is distribution, the differential distribution of social agents into roles and classes, a distribution of difference without which no production could take place, at least in its capitalist form. That difference, that irreducibly potential antagonism, will not be effaced by a technical "economic" adjustment based on positivist or objectivist or naturalist philosophical premises of the sort that now prevail in scientific marxism. The critique of those premises, therefore, both from a deconstructive and a marxist perspective, is politically crucial to the construction of a socialism that would do more than simply preserve capitalist productive relations under the title of "socialized" productive forces.

The classical, resolutive, essentialist, and totalizing dialectic provides a philosophic support for conservative marxist conceptions of capitalist development and the transition to socialism. This is so in large part because the classical dialectic is predicated upon the reduction of difference to identity. A deconstructive critique of classical dialectics might aid the formulation of more radically socialist conceptions of political strategy and of the strategy of transition. In the next chapter, I will give an account of such a critique, and in the subsequent chapter, I will consider its implications for marxist political economy as seen through a rereading of *Capital Volume One*.

❧ 3 ❧

Deconstruction
and Dialectics

The relationship of Derrida's work to dialectics is not unambiguous. In his early work, he uses such dialectical concepts as mediation as critical weapons against husserlian phenomenology. In this approach, as I shall argue, he resembles Adorno. In his later work, after he had written on Hegel, Derrida qualified his use of the dialectical vocabulary, and the speculative dialectic becomes a model for metaphysics. I will first give a theoretical account of the relationship between deconstruction and dialectics, and then I will plot out the similarities and differences between Derrida and such modern dialecticians as Sartre, Marcuse, and Adorno.

In "Différance," Derrida says that when he characterizes presence as a determination and an effect of a more primordial differential process, he is actually relaunching "hegelianism" (*SP*, 151). True, it is a hegelianism "beyond hegelianism," in that the process of differential supplementarity (the irreducible necessity of an other to constitute something "proper" or selfsame) encompasses the dialectic as one determined moment of its chain. Nevertheless, in his essay on Antonin Artaud, Derrida uses the word "dialectic" to describe the "originary repetition" which is the other-relation or trace within the selfsame: "Because if one thinks the *horizon* of the dialectic correctly—outside a conventional hegelianism—, one understands perhaps that it is the indefinite movement of finitude, of the unity of life and death, of difference, of originary repetition, the origin of tragedy as the absence of a simple origin. In this sense, the dialectic is tragedy, the only possible affirmation against the philosophic or christian idea of a pure origin."[1] Perhaps it is this positive sense of the relation between deconstruction and dialectics which provokes him to say at another point that the classical dialectic is always a dialectic of the dialectic, a reductive sublation of a possibly recalcitrant heterogeneity. The mainspring of that heterogeneity, of that "indefinite movement of finitude," is the concept of mediation. Derrida uses the word positively in his early critique of husserlian phenomenology. Against the theology of immediate presence, Derrida proposes the mediation of the relation to the other as nonpresence. Against the ground of expressive meaning, he uses the irreducible mediation of expression by indication, of ideal semantics by the institutional, practical, and syntactic side of language. What permits the closure of phenomenological truth as the identity of consciousness and its objects in the interiority of the mind simultaneously opens it to an outside irreducible to its ideal form. History is the possibility of being intrinsically exposed to the extrinsic. Truth and the logos are possible only through history, which makes them impossible as absolutes. Absolute Knowledge is an effect of the *marche*, of the machinery of language through which it must pass. And ideality in general is possible only as the mediacy of language and history.

After beginning an intense study of Hegel which culminates in *Glas*, Derrida drops the words "mediation" and "negation" from his vocabulary. "Mediacy" [*mediatété*] or "expansive mediacy" appear instead.[2] And in one of the rare moments when he uses the word "negation" in the later work to name the alterity that inhabits the repetition necessary for self-identity, it is within quotes. More and more, the dialectic comes to be inseparable from the desire to repress the dissemination of reference, to reduce alterity, and to cut off the indefinite movement of finitude.

Let us now look at the classical speculative dialectic to determine what about it struck Derrida as being of critical relevance and also what about it provoked him to use it as a paradigm of metaphysics.

The metaphysical concepts of presence and of property (selfsameness) will serve as examples of the ambivalent relationship of deconstruction to dialectics. Both concepts are grounding principles, that is, each is supposedly primary, original, unconditioned, nonderived in relation to anything that might be logically or historically prior to it. Both, therefore, are instances of truth. On the basis of their juridical normativity, the truth or untruth of things can be decided. The truth of Being is presence, the revelation of the presence of Being in the present moment to consciousness. The truth of an entity is the "proper" essence that distinguishes it from other entities, marks off its "property" or self-identical ownness. The first step of even the traditional dialectical critique would be to complicate these simple determinations of presence and of property. To determine Being as presence requires a corollary determination of Non-Being as absence, that is, of the other of Being which is also its negation. A negative otherness, or alterity, arises when one attempts to determine what any entity is in itself. One must immediately say that it is not something else; it is only as it *differs* from an other. Alterity, the differential relation to an other which is necessary for the constitution of a proper thing or a present moment, complicates that property (self-identity) and that presence. Identity presupposes alterity; the selfsame exists only in relation to its other, which, in classical dialectics, is always its opposite or negative. The second step of the traditional speculative dialectic, however, annuls this insight and sublates difference and alterity or contradiction. The other-relation that troubles the simple self-identity of an entity or a concept is negated, preserved, and turned into a moment in what is now a process of attaining a more complex, concrete self-identity, as opposed to the simple abstract identity one began with. Because simple identity suffers a fall into an other-relation that expropriates it, when it returns to itself out of the other and comes to recognize or appropriate the other as itself (as, say, Cause comes to be mediated by Effect in a complex unity), this self-identical property is stronger than ever. It manages to incorporate, and therefore neutralize, its own worst enemy — difference and alterity — as part of its own coming-into-being.

This "cunning" is perhaps why a thinker such as Derrida finds the hegelian dialectic to be at once fascinating and pernicious. It recognizes the mediated nature of all supposedly proper entities, their constitutive expropriation (nothing is self-sufficient), but it orders this potentially heterogeneous differential into a system of simple binary oppositions or contradictory negations (Being-Non-Being, Cause-Effect) and suppresses the heterogeneity of alterity and difference in favor of a theology of truth as self-identity or "propriation," which arises from the process of mediation — that is, the return of the other-relation into the self-identity of the entity, concept, or subject. Hegel's concept of mediation thus represents an annulment of the mediacy or other-relation (not negation or opposition, but differentiation) Derrida would like to use as a lever for subverting metaphysical self-identity.

Derrida criticizes metaphysics in general on the grounds that it follows the pattern of Hegel's dialectic by sublating mediacy into mediation, the inherent nonidentity and constitutive alterity of all supposedly unique, selfsame things into mediated identity which represses alterity. Mediacy is incorporated into the metaphysical system as a subordinate, derivative, and accidental element. Some mode of presence or property (intuition in Husserl, Being in Heidegger, Absolute Knowledge in Hegel, proper meaning and conscious intention in Anglo-American philosophy) is simultaneously declared to be primary and good. The subordinate element is secondary, derivative, or degraded, and it generally takes the form of history, difference, "writing," materiality, representation, and practice.

Derrida uses mediacy against the speculative dialectical law of mediated self-identity. He does so by showing how such metaphysical concepts of property and presence as intuition, essence, being, meaning, truth, and consciousness, which are primary grounds, absolute origins, and norms of truth in the classical speculative schema, are themselves derivative in relation to what they supposedly subordinate and exclude within metaphysical idealism—representation, spacing, empiricity, exteriority, difference, scission, history, alterity. For example, one subordinate part of the system of identity—difference—proves to be larger than the whole of which it is a part. Spatial identity is possible only as difference from something excluded from that identity. Temporal identity—infinite responsibility—is possible only as a succession of points, each different from the other. The primary ground of self-identity thus proves to be an *effect* of one of its own subalterns. The traditional dialectical subsumption of parts under the whole is undone because one part has proven larger than the whole.

The consequence is not that something more primordial is declared to be the prior ground. What Derrida questions is the very desire, which he calls "onto-theological," for a totalizing foundation such as presence or identity. When he puts differentiation in the place of the ground, he does so to make something a ground that cannot be one, that in fact puts in question the possibility of such an absolute ground, because differentiation is merely a process of disaggregating scission and discontinuous extension. The traditional hegelian dialectic acknowledges the existence of this process, but it represses it and lifts it up (*aufheben*) into a moment of identity. Derrida insists that identity could not exist without that process and that identity is itself merely a determinate moment of its chain. By so doing, he displaces the classical dialectic. Any dialectical totality will encounter a moment of undecidability (difference, for example, as a constituent of identity), which completes the system while also exceeding it.

In classical dialectics, then, one finds the critical principle of the other-relation that accompanies any determination, constituting as well as splitting its self-identity. But equally, one finds the metaphysical principle of mediation whereby the other-relation is characterized merely as a negation (not an undecidable or extendable seriality of differentiation or of traces) that can be negated and thus sublated back into self-identity.

Derrida never discusses the dialectic in connection with Marx. Nevertheless, Derrida's critique of classical dialects may be related to Marx's understanding of the dialectical relations between capital and labor. Capitalism performs a classical ideological sublation by subordinating labor (capital's historical, practical, empirical "other") and making it a moment in the development of capital. Labor is incorporated or reflected into capital; it loses independent existence and has no meaning "outside" the capital relation. The political-economic equivalent of the deconstructive operation is to reverse the hierarchy that places capital over labor (the moment of revolution) and to displace it so that such an opposition no longer exists (the moment of socialization). The goal Marx posits is more deconstructive than hegelian, more an overcoming of opposition (hence, of hierarchy, because the division into opposites operates the division of labor), than a sublation of contradiction into a resolutive identity. The deconstruction of the capital/labor dialectic, which reflects labor into an identity with capital, requires a realization of the antagonistic scission implicit in repressive identity. This realization occurs as an assertion of autonomy from the relation on the part of labor, a denial of the dialectically reflected identity through a refusal of the identitarian logic of the equal exchange of work for wages in order to expand capital value. As in Derrida's deconstruction of Hegel, breaking that logic requires an assertion of the difference, discontinuity, and scission implicit in any identity, especially one based on the dialectical reflection of alterity or otherness into oneness, so that the dialectic of reflected identity which reduces the alterity of labor to the self-identity of capital is turned inside out, reversed, and displaced.

Derrida says that the more metaphysical propriation and identity assert power, the more powerful the force of expropriative heterogeneity also becomes. For example, in modern theories of meaning in philosophy, the more it is insisted that meaning is ideal, the more recalcitrant seems the graphic element of writing, which resists idealization, as well as the differential referential relations that overflow the bounds of any seemingly self-enclosed text and make the self-identity of ideal meaning seem spurious. In political-economic terms, this law is comparable with Marx's claims that an increasingly appropriative capital becomes by that very token increasingly expropriable. The self-expansion of capital also expands that which can undo it—the proletariat. The intensification of homogeneity implies an equal degree of heterogeneization. By the law of differentials, the more appropriation occurs, the more possible is its expropriation. If you own nothing, you cannot be robbed, but if you own everything, you can only be robbed. In terms of capital-state power, the intensification of subordination, in favor of capital appropriation, also implies an equal intensification of the possibility, through a differential tension, of insubordination. The homogeneity of control and of identity, even in political-economic terms, is undecidable. What completes it also contradicts it. But this contradiction is not of the classical dialectical sort, a negation that can be negated into a more complex, mediated identity. Rather, it is radically heterogeneous in relation to the system it both completes and contradicts undecidably, because it marks an open possibility of extension. The closing off of the system (as philosophical or political control) is equally the sign that it is the closing of an opening.

One gets a better sense of how deconstruction relates to dialectics by comparing Derrida to such modern dialectical thinkers as Sartre, Marcuse, and Adorno. This is not an altogether fair operation. Marcuse, for example, was an essentialist and, therefore, his work falls under the purview of what Derrida calls "metaphysics." Yet one must bear in mind that his political project makes Derrida's academic work seem tepid in comparison. Nevertheless, it is also good to remember that Marx garnered more that was useful for a critical analysis of capitalism from Hegel than from such more politically radical thinkers of his time, as Cabet, Weiterling, and Ruge. We might do well also to bear this historical example in mind.

Isolated quotations from Sartre's *Critique of Dialectical Reason* might lead one to think that he and Derrida are in essential agreement. If context is considered, however, these passages always turn out to be concerned with ideas Sartre considers negative—counterfinality or seriality, or example. Sartre describes the individual in seriality as constituted by differential, other-relations: "But it should be noticed that this constituent alterity must depend both on all the Others, and on the particular possibility which is actualised, and therefore that the Other has his essence in all the Others, in so far as he differs from them." In a note, Sartre adds: "In so far as he is the *same*, he is simply and formally *an other*."[3] Even as seriality, as something to be overcome, Sartre describes the other-relation as an "essence," whereas for Derrida, alterity is precisely that which makes any notion of essence impossible. Also, the other-relation in deconstruction is not added on to a sameness already constituted in it. It is rather that which produces "sameness" as difference, that is, as nonselfsameness. Sartre's adherence to a metaphysical ontotheology that would be alien to deconstruction is evident in the fact that, in the *Critique,* alterity is at least à function of the reciprocal recognition of sovereign subjects for whom the Other (with a theological capital) is constitutive, not subversive. The difference between the two thinkers becomes aggravated when one considers that many of the basic concepts of the *Critique* would be put in question by deconstruction, for example, legislative Reason, apodictic unification, identity, and voluntarism. Given the deconstructive critique of such notions as presence, ground, property, and knowledge as mastery, the following quotation from the *Critique* should speak the difference for itself: "In its most immediate level, dialectical investigation (*l'experience dialectique*) has emerged as *praxis* elucidating itself in order to control its own development. The certainty of this primary experience in which *doing* grounded its consciousness of itself, provides us with one certainty: it is reality itself which is revealed as present to itself" (*Crit,* 220).

Marcuse's critical theory and Derrida's deconstruction are compatible in that each promotes a negative thinking that destabilizes the apparently stable positivity of the world—its facticity. Each thinker conceives the world as being constituted by an inherent negativity or contradiction. To dissolve the hegemony of common sense, which is enslaved to facticity, Marcuse believes one must flush out the immanent contradictions of reality. For this project, it is necessary to develop a logic and a language of contradiction. Derrida might agree with Marcuse's strategy, but he would probably find the goal of Marcuse's logic of contradiction—the making present of an absent, true essence—less acceptable.

Whereas the Marcuse of *Reason and Revolution* (1941) remains faithful to the hegelian telos of introreflected self-identity, Derrida's entire undertaking has put that notion in question. The goal of the dialectically negative attitude toward positive existence in Marcuse is the restoration of the true content of existence, its essential being, which lurks as an unrealized potential restrained by facticity. The dialectical method unearths contradictions for the sake of producing a proper identity of existence and essence, of realizing an adequation of existence to its true content, of transforming negativity, through mediation and sublation, into something positive. The dialectic is a Doctrine of Essence, and the essence of existence is reason and freedom. The rational freedom of each individual subject is attained by negating alterity. To be other, for Marcuse as well as for Hegel, is to be unfree. Because truth lies only in the subject/object totality, true self-identity occurs only when the subject becomes independent of the objective other, masters alienation, and maintains itself while being other than itself. Freedom, therefore, is the appropriation by the subject of exteriority, the integration of otherness into its proper being, the attainment of power over its own self-determining movement, the incorporation of external, determining conditions into its own nature, the positing of the other as one moment in the subject's emergence, the negation of the negation the other poses and its reflection into the essential self-identity of the unified subject. Freedom, in other words, is power over the other, the self-assurance of appropriation—property. All the potential of essence is summoned to existence, and cognition masters the estrangement of objectivity.

Marcuse retains Hegel's equation of absolute knowledge with absolute freedom. Derrida, I suspect, would criticize this apparent welding of an epistemology of power and appropriation to a politics of liberation. For a deconstructive dialectic, alterity could never be fully reduced; indeed, deconstruction is a questioning of the metaphysical desire to reduce alterity, to gain proper identity. Even in its proper selfsameness, the subject is hollowed out by the trace of the other it has appropriated. It is as much other as selfsame subject, and hence, never properly selfsame. To invert Marcuse's law: the other maintains its alterity even in the subject.

A deconstructive logic would also question Marcuse's notion that one universal principle dominates the whole, the principle of proper self-identity. Deconstruction posits the undecidability of identity and nonidentity. It defuses the sublating mediation and rejects the synthesis that would conflate nonidentity into identity. By placing nonidentity on a par with identity, deconstruction makes clear that Marcuse's universal principle, that is, identity, is a particular that has been generalized to the form of a universal. In deconstruction, nonidentity could just as easily be raised to the level of the universal, but that would mean that there could no longer be a single, universal principle as such, which dominates the whole. The status of the whole as a unified totality would itself be questioned.

This is the kind of problem deconstruction engages. By stopping mediation short, that is, by refusing to conceive of the other as reflected into the subject, deconstruction promotes a notion of interminable mediacy that undoes the circle of property that appropriates nonidentity and posits it as a moment of identity. It would not conceive the subject as an autonomous entity detached from eternal conditions whose only relation to the subject is one of oppressive determination and expropriative alienation, conditions that must be sublated and appropriated if the subject is to return to its true self. Because the ultimate goal of the hegelian dialectic is to describe the constitution of a sovereign and autonomous (bourgeois liberal) subject, one could be tempted to say that deconstruction, like marxism, is a dialectic of unfreedom and dependence. The resignation to necessity and the impoverishment of action are certainly two rallying cries of the right-wing users of deconstruction. But deconstruction may also be interpreted as a critique of the limitation of the concept of freedom to individual subjective freedom.

From a deconstructive point of view, then, one would say that individual freedom is a concept that needs to be redefined in relation to the constitutive alterity of the subject. Because the opposition of subject and object is undecidable, a deconstructive concept (or Marx's, for that matter) of freedom could not be limited to the subjective pole. The subject is as much the historical world of objective social institutions in which it lives (and which it has constructed) as it is "subject." One cannot therefore privilege subjective cognition as the sole instrument of liberation. The objective institutionality of the subject—the complex of language, custom, social role, and history in which it is immersed and the traces of which constitute its "self-possession"—must also be "liberated" if something resembling subjective freedom is to be attained.

Feminist emancipation, for example, is not only the emancipation of the subject woman, but also the transformation of a world of oppressive social institutions and of a set of institutions which define and constitute subjectivity, not always consciously—language, self-concept, role models, habitual thought patterns, customary reactions, cultural mind-sets, and so on.

Marcuse's concept of revolution as liberation, therefore, needs to be rewritten. Freedom can no longer be defined in terms of property, the negation of alterity in the name of the subject's self-possession. A deconstructive concept of freedom would preclude conceiving liberation as simple independence, autonomy, self-ownership, or nonalienation. Positing emancipation as a general concept whose limits are defined in terms of the subject programmatically marginalizes the multiple institutional or social structural "liberations" that would have to occur before the subject could be sufficiently "free."

It would be unfair to limit consideration of Marcuse's dialectics to *Reason and Revolution*. In his later writings, especially *Counter-Revolution and Revolt* (1972), he revises his earlier association of freedom with an appropriate subject. And he criticizes the "hubris of domination" in "Marx's notion of a human appropriation of nature." "Appropriation," he writes, "no matter how human, remains appropriation of a (living) object by a subject. It offends that which is essentially other than the appropriating subject, and which exists precisely as object in its own right—that is, as subject."[4] That the other must still be conceived as a subject indicates that his new version of nonappropriative liberation is still based on a concept of homogeneous autonomy, rather than one of deconstructed dialectical heterogeneity.

In *One-Dimensional Man* (1964), Marcuse criticizes repressive objectification in the form of positivist science and analytic philosophy. Therefore, he champions subjective individual freedom. Social institutions appear as infringements upon a naturally autonomous, unalienated subject, instead of as the dialectical counterparts of a subject primordially alienated in objectivity and alterity. If the problem is formulated as a dialectic, Marcuse's subject becomes the negation of the dehumanizing objectivism of modern technological society. The negation of that simple negation will be Adorno's *Negative Dialectics*. Already in *One-Dimensional Man*, one senses how Marcuse's dialectics differ from Adorno's. Marcuse says that more is always contained in a universal like "freedom" or "beauty" than is realized in a particular form of freedom. The desire to realize the full essence, therefore, is the springboard of progress. Adorno provides the necessary dialectical inversion of the equation: there is always also, he says, an excess of the particular in relation to the universal. Each individual's unconscious, his or her inscription in personal as well as general history, implies a perpetual deviation from the norm or the essence of universal reason. There is therefore no identity of the universal apart from each particular deviation from or nonidentity with that universal.[5]

Unlike the early Marcuse's neohegelian dialectics, Adorno's negative dialectics bear strong affinities to deconstruction. But to say that the two undertakings are the same would be to betray the spirit of each. I shall first outline the similarities between the two. Then I shall suggest some ways in which they depart from one another.

Both negative dialectics and deconstruction are immanent critiques of philosophies of identity and transcendence. These philosophies must be undermined from within, on their own ground and using their own principles. Both Adorno and Derrida see this strategy of subversion as an imposed necessity. Derrida says that the language of metaphysics is the only language available to him. He has no choice but to place it under erasure, effaced yet legible, so that it can be used against itself. For this reason, the postcritical text will be almost indistinguishable from the precritical one. Adorno makes a similar claim about the concepts of the philosophy of identity. One must use the concept, which for Adorno is an instrument of repression, in order to transcend the concept. Because there is no other language at our disposal, we must break out of the context of delusion and identity from within. This entails a double strategy. Dialectics requires but also departs from the coercive logic of identity. The purpose of this method is to turn conceptuality toward nonidentity by resorting to a deliberately irregular, fragmented, and inconclusive mode of thought, while at the same time avoiding absolutizing the method or hypostatizing nonidentity.

Anyone familiar with Derrida's *Glas* will probably recognize in Adorno's program a version of Derrida's project — to elaborate the origin of literature "between the two," that is, between Hegel's seminar of absolute knowledge and Jean Genet's saturnalia of fragmentary dissemination. That "in-betweenness" marks the unstable, differential limit between spiritual idea and material body (the human body or the body of the sign). The hegelian "concept" (which is the model of all concepts in metaphysics) would lift the body of language up into a spiritual idea, but the inscription of language, its spatiality and its differentiality, draws ideality or subjective spirituality as meaning down toward the objective other which fragments its identity. This counterspiritual force of inscription leaves an irreducible remainder that can never be idealized. The logocentric model of homogeneous conceptual meaning, because it must pass by way of rhetorical figuration and heterogeneous syntactic fragmentation in order to be constituted "as such," is cut and let fall at the very moment of its erection. Derrida, like Adorno, admits the necessity of having to inhabit rationality in order to turn it against itself, to study the philosophy of identity in order to flush out the nonidentity that constitutes it.

For both thinkers, the concept is not a purely subjective construct. For Adorno, it is inalienable from objectivity and, therefore, from nonidentity. For Derrida, *Glas* has no meaning apart from the differential shuttling back and forth between columns. A conceptual identity of meaning cannot be detached from and elevated above that constitutive nonidentity. Similarly, for Adorno, the crux of his book is the ceaseless self-renewal of its texture, not a thesis but what happens in the text. Philosophy, he says, is not expoundable. (There is, clearly, an elitist bias in each. But all forms of critical thought, including marxism, which begin with the premise that things are not what they seem to "common sense," run this risk.)

Both philosophers attack the idealist privilege of identity over non-identity, universality over particularity, subject over object, spontaneous presence over secondary rhetoric, timeless transcendence over empirical history, content over mode of expression, self-reassuring proximity over threatening alterity, ontology over the ontic, and so on. The point of each of their critiques is not simply to reverse the hierarchy in each case, but to displace it as well. For Adorno, this leads to the emergence of a more radically dialectical concept, one given over to nonidentity. For Derrida, it leads to a questioning of the concept of conceptuality—not a more complicated notion of the concept which would include nonidentity, but a questioning of the very grounds of metaphysical identitarian conceptualization, inasmuch as that is founded on the model of the concept as a subjective, ideal institution.

The primary target of each is the logos or ratio, the principle of rational domination through conceptual identity whose operation denies dialectical mediacy and differentiation. For each, the logos represents the desire for a primary substructure and for an absoluteness of the concept which would rest on the autonomy of the subject. Adorno calls this stabilizing of invariants as transcendence "ideology," and his critique of Husserl's version of it—the formal logic of transcendental subjectivity detached from tradition and history—follows closely the lines of Derrida's early critique of phenomenology.

Phenomenology, according to Adorno, relegates rhetoric to a secondary position because rhetoric threatens to usurp what cannot be directly obtained from presentation. Although he does not question the status of "presentation" within phenomenology, Adorno does, like Derrida, criticize the husserlian and heideggerian privileging of vision and of Being as presence. Negative dialectics rescues rhetoric from being a mere flaw and promotes the necessary link between thought and language. It places rhetoric on the side of content, and therefore it sees the phenomenological desire for substance in cognition as doomed. Adorno joins Derrida in suggesting that consciousness might not be constitutive, but instead derivative.

Each one did a thoroughgoing critique of Husserl early in his career. Certain parts of Adorno's *Zur Metakritik der Erkenntnis-Theorie*[6] parallel Derrida's statement about phenomenology: that the absolutism of phenomenology becomes indistinguishable from empiricism (180); that there is no pure, singular meaning uncontaminated by relation [*Beziehung*] (104); that the necessity of an example puts the purely ideal status of essence in question (130); that idealism is truth in its untruth (242). Adorno makes one very important point that Derrida neglects. He relates Husserl's monadology of consciousness to a social world in which private interest reigns. When a more politicized (post-1968) Derrida finally does get around to making the connection between the ideology of consciousness and economics, it is less based on Adorno's moralism than it is an institutional critique, an attack, for example, on the philosophical bases of the conventions of property, and an analysis of the relationship between philosophic scientism, the assumption of a supposedly disinterested neutrality, and the methodology of capitalist crisis management:

> An economics—even "welfare" economics—is not one domain among others or a domain whose laws have already been recognized. An economics taking account of effects of iterability, inasmuch as they are inseparable from the economy of (what must still be called) the Unconscious as well as from a graphematics of undecidables, an economics calling into question the entire traditional philosophy of the *oikos*—of the *propre*: the "own," "ownership," "property,"—as well as the laws that have governed it would not only be very different from "welfare economics": it would also be far removed from furnishing speech acts theory with "more elegant" formulations or a "technical terminology." Rather, it would provoke its general transformation. . . . Or *Limited Inc* [the title of the piece from which this quote is taken] which aside from its use value in the legal-commercial code that marks the common bond linking England and the United States . . . *condenses* allusions to the internal regulation through which the capitalist system seeks to limit concentration and decision-making power in order to protect itself against its own "crisis." . . . If the police is always waiting in the wings, it is because conventions are by essence violable and precarious, *in themselves* and by the fictionality that constitutes them, even before there has been any overt transgression. [LI, 216, 226, 250]

Here, Derrida's deconstructive argument consists of showing how a phenomenological ideology of consciousness relates to values of ownership and of property. Those values are constituted by "iterability" (repetition and difference), which undermines their supposed "natural" status and allows them to be shown to be conventionalized institutions or fictional constructs.

Adorno's readings of Heidegger and Kant in *Negative Dialectics* can be characterized as protodeconstructions. One key to deconstruction, I suggested, is constitutive negation (that identity is limited by what makes it possible). In positing itself, a concept like idealism necessarily betrays itself. The idea or concept must pass by way of rhetoric and differentiation, that is, a detour that renders no presence and a differential relation that disallows property, in order to realize "ideality" as presence and property (the selfsameness of consciousness). Its proper presence, therefore, is haunted by a constitutive alterity; from the outset, it is given over to absence and nonidentity. In the case of Heidegger, Adorno shows how the hierarchy of ontology over concrete ontic existence, of Being over the entity, comes unraveled. An otherness inhabits the identity of Being, because a philosophy of primacy always becomes a dualism. The primacy of Being implies a derivation whereby something else becomes heteronomous to Being. Identity, in this case the self-identity of the primordial ground of Being, is thus marked by nonidentity. Adorno concludes in a derridean spirit that the concept of origin or primacy is ideological.

Kant's system of ethics also sabotages itself by a constitutive negation. Kant wishes to make the human subject transcendent, but he nevertheless describes how the antonomous subject is dependent on objectivity. In order for the subject to objectify itself in action, it must already be objective. The subject's ethical freedom, therefore, is always entwined with society and history. Whenever Kant defines freedom, he must also declare the necessity of repression and law. Unfreedom is the premise of freedom. In Kant, freedom and determination coincide because they both proclaim identity, that is, coercion. In perhaps his most derridean moment, Adorno points out that Kant contradicts himself by using an empirical metaphor—the word "mainspring" [Hauptfeder]—to name extratemporal freedom. In positing freedom, Adorno concludes, Kant takes it back.

For Adorno as well as Derrida, such specific critical readings feed into a more general critique of logocentrism. Derrida's project entails showing how the timeless universality of the logos becomes dependent on that which it excludes—contingency, errancy, spacing, alterity, representation, difference. In its very constitution as something infinitely repeatable, the idea includes that which it excludes in the form of representation—repetition in difference. For Adorno, it is the principle of identity which proves to be self-contradictory. All-governing, universal reason subsumes particularity, but in so doing, it constructs itself by installing itself above something else. When reason is unity over something, then unity becomes division.

The two thinkers often reach surprisingly similar conclusions. Adorno's idea that there is no transcendence, no outside to mediation, and that causality, when one tries to pin it down, withdraws to the totality (interminable mediacy, in other words) resembles Derrida's notion that alterity and, hence, filiation (the attempt to pin down an origin, an "absolute ancestor") are irreducible. Both see pure identity as death. Its mechanism is appropriation, the principle of denial. The fullness of presence and plenitude implies subjugation and violence. Against the appropriative foreclosure of nonidentity, both thinkers strategically promote the trivial over the essential, the constellation of particulars over the universal. And both locate an affirmative moment in the negativity of rational domination. Even as it identifies, the concept bears the mark of the nonconceptual. As Adorno puts it, the cognition of nonidentity lies in the fact that this cognition identifies.

In The Jargon of Authenticity, the book in which Adorno most closely resembles Derrida, the differences between them become most clear.

Here, their points of contact include, in Adorno's phrasing, the denial of the possibility of a nonderived primary ground, of a nonexchangeable self-identical entity which is not a member of a class or a type, of a starting point outside the texture of thought and culture, of an essence not subject to immanent mediation, of a transcendent philosophy not bound to a language of empirical figures, of an identity founded on pure self-possession, of a nature free from cultural and historical determination, of an ontology that would remain after the subtraction of all ontic elements (that is, a "Being" still there after all living things are removed), of the elimination of all mimesis, play, and sophistic arbitrariness by enlightened reason. Adorno seems most deconstructive when he argues that Heidegger declares the immediacy of Being while involuntarily describing its mediation. As if he were following Derrida's early program of undoing metaphysical oppositions, Adorno shows how, in Heidegger's text, *Dasein* and death pass into each other.

A difference between the two emerges around the question of language, and it is a difference of style or execution (which for each is also a central philosophical and political question). Derrida would agree with Adorno's argument that the objective context of words precludes establishing a singular meaning, that there will be something accidental in the nature of the most precise words, and, finally, that the element of objectivity in words struggles against those intentional acts which subjectively give meaning. But the undecidability which Adorno locates on the conceptual level, Derrida works out in language and style. Thus, he not only criticizes the metaphysics of identity, he also forges word-concepts (neither simply words nor simply concepts) like supplement and pharmakon, whose undecidability pushes against the logocentric closure of metaphysics.

The greatest difference between the two emerges around that point where they most converge—the critique of identity. Derrida much more successfully executes the critique on philosophic grounds; Adorno more successfully articulates the critique with a critique of capitalist society. Like Adorno, Derrida has read Nietzsche. Therefore, he, too, criticizes identitarian philosophy on the grounds that all unitarian concepts derive from division. All philosophical concepts lose what they seem to retain. On the basis of this insight, Derrida calls for a nonconceptual concept of the concept. I am immediately reminded of Adorno's notion of "the preponderance of the object." Derrida will speak in an analogous way of the necessity of the world as a prephilosophic "already there," a necessity that detracts from idealism's pretensions to constitutive spontaneity and primordial originarity. The world, Derrida points out, is primordially implied in transcendence; the major difference is that the critical lever for Derrida is logical (or philosophical-historical), whereas for Adorno, the lever is social. The next item on the agenda of the critique of identity is the principle of exchange, and at this point, Adorno and Derrida part company. Exchange implies equivalence, that is, a principle whereby different things are made equal and opposites are established as equivalent, antithetical poles. The homogeneity of opposition and equivalence allows exchange. Adorno sees a heterogeneity at work within the homogeneous system of equivalence, pointing toward a utopia of nondomination. Yet he distrusts action, and he provides no method for practically realizing that utopia. Derrida, in contrast, does provide a method for unbalancing the metaphysical system of equivalences. Deconstruction is an aggressive act of reading which subverts the grounds of metaphysics in general and of idealism in particular. And the kingpin of those grounds is the principle of exchange whereby difference is reduced to identity.

Adorno limits himself to plotting the emergence of nonidentity within identity; Derrida posits a more radical dissymmetry, heterogeneity, or alterity—supplementarity, differentiation, trace—which includes as one of its determined orientations the metaphysical conceptual system Adorno attacks. Derrida's seemingly "limited" concern with language in fact points toward this broad, underlying structure of differentiation. Within his critique of property or selfsameness, the critique of language (that no proper name, for example, can be a pure appellation subtracted from differentiation or a relational system) is bound up with the critique of ontology (that no natural, proper, substantial thing can ever be lifted out of the system of other-relations that mark a lack in its selfsameness and make the supplementary addition of something else an irreducible and interminable necessity; every event is an issue, every fact an effect). Derrida goes beyond Adorno's own critique of ontology by suggesting that not only does difference emerge within ontology, but also ontology is derivative with regard to differance and the trace (the other-relation within the selfsame).

In his early essay "Thesen über die Sprache des Philosophen," Adorno points out that any critique of idealist philosophy must be *Sprachkritik* because concepts are inseparable from language, and thus from history. Here again, however, Derrida's critique, at least regarding the logical operations and the linguistic-conceptual material practice of philosophy itself, goes further. He says that language is only one region of the process of differentiation and that absolute meaning in language is analogous to the idealist notion of absolute essence detached from empiricity. Within the circular system of metaphysics, essence supposedly passes through the world to return to itself intact. In a similar way, the precipitation into signification or language is always retrieved by semantics. No scraps and bits are left lying around which cannot be accounted for by essence or meaning. This, for Derrida, is the essence of speculative philosophic production. Nothing escapes having an origin and therefore also an identity. Nothing escapes the idealist language police, who are also an ontology or epistemology police, because to be able to secure a meaning for every bit of language is akin to being able to know everything's identity, its proper place, what it is in itself.

Derrida's answer to idealism is that if all language and all "being" are constituted as a differential trace structure, then the passage of a stable and unique meaning or of an unalterable and selfsame essence through language and through the empirical world might be more risky than metaphysics gives out. Meaning and essence always run the risk of going astray in the passage through language and history which is imposed on them. Meaning requires signification in order to be, as essence is essence only in that it is conceived as the essence *of* the empirical, historical world. If language and the world are given over to differentiation and alterity, then the metaphysical notions of absolute meaning, knowledge, and essence might not so much be the truths of language and the world as antidotes against them. Metaphysical epistemology represses differentiation and establishes self-identical entities. Adorno joins Derrida in characterizing epistemology as a process of making identity, but he falls short of an affirmative (and alternative) insight into the differentiation against which epistemology works. Although both thinkers use language to criticize metaphysics, then, Derrida more successfully links that critique of meaning to a critique of ontology and of epistemology.

Derrida's arraignment of the metaphysics of property and presence marks an extension of Adorno's indictment of the metaphysics of identity. As a critique which is more logical than social, deconstruction more successfully undoes the bases of bourgeois philosophy from within, on its own terms. But this implies equally that deconstruction falls far short of Adorno's description of the relation between philosophy and the political violence of capitalism. Yet, whereas Adorno remains pessimistically bound to conceptuality, troubling it somewhat through complex locutions, Derrida more radically and optimistically attempts to break down the way in which philosophical ideas are produced. Whereas Adorno suggests the possibility of a model of truth as nonadequation, Derrida takes this as his starting point. And Derrida's sense of the differential nature of the unconscious would probably make him skeptical of the limits of Adorno's dialectical self-reflection.

The two thinkers reconverge in their sense of what good action would be. Both perceive a positivity emerging from the negativity of their methods. For Derrida, deconstruction is affirmative; it produces a new way of thinking which takes undecidability and alterity into account without appropriating them. For Adorno, dialectics would maintain difference and refuse to annex alterity. The good society would entail the subject's nonidentity without sacrifice. Utopia would be the togetherness of diversity. Extrapolating from his work, one could say that for Derrida, a good society would maintain difference without hierarchy (the inverse of which is the origin of nationalism, racism, sexism, and classism).

One could say that what Marx did to Hegel, Derrida does to twentieth-century neoidealism. He turns it on its head. Marx pointed out that supposedly ahistorical ideas must take place in concrete history. Similarly, Derrida points out that no systematic or methodic explanation of what "is" or "is true" can be ahistorical. Our own linguistic and conceptual practice is historical, and therefore, heterogeneous, unavailable to the idealizing desire of a supposedly sovereign subject to decide absolute truth as valid meaning and to direct action solely as conscious intention. For marxist dialectics as well as for deconstruction, the historical moment is the only absolute, which is to say that there are no idealist absolutes outside of the differential movement of history. The differentiation of historical situations does not allow a concept of truth which claims transcendent or absolute validity. Nor does it allow a concept of action which delivers the complex of conditions and effects of action into the control of a single subject. One can make one's own history only through history. Similarly, one's systems and methods are equally out of one's control. The mind is too much in history ever to master it absolutely through ahistoric taxonomies or nomenclatures. Hegel dreamed away this limit. Marx restored it in terms of politics. Thinkers like Derrida point to it in terms of philosophy.

Deconstruction, therefore, as much as dialectics, does not disallow analysis or revolutionary action. It does offer certain cautions: not to think of truth in absolute, transcendent, ideal terms; not to act with the assumption that theory controls and subsumes practice, that consciousness can fully account for the unconscious, that cause and effect always coincide. Deconstruction corrects classical dialectics on two counts: there is no closed totality conceivable by rational thought which is not an effect of a nontotalizable differential system that remains irreducibly open; there is no absolute to guide action which is not historical, that is to say, provisional.

❧ 4 ❧

The Limits
of *Capital*

$\mathbf{M}$arx's text can be reread in light of
the deconstructive critique of classical dialectics. Such a rereading has
more than merely scholarly or theoretical consequences. Marx's text is
the subject of a debate in which the contending interpreters seek justification for differing political positions. Whether Marx is himself an
evolutionist or a revolutionist, whether he privileges necessary economic
development or contingent political force, decides the issue. Soviet scientific marxists use the evolutionist argument to justify a prolonged
"transition" to communism. So-called "objective" laws of economic development, rooted in productive forces, are working themselves out
beyond human control, and questions regarding the rearrangement of
productive relations (between workers and owners or managers) are
secondary and tangential to this primary process of necessary development. Radicals such as Antonio Negri argue that Marx's dialectic is not
geared toward a neohegelian model of necessary economic development,
but instead toward a conflictual model of antagonistic forces and ten-
dencies that mark a break from all developmental continuity.[1] This argument emphasizes Marx's point that capitalism is essentially a production
relationship between wage worker and capitalist that communism must
break by abolishing wage labor. I will reread Marx's *Capital Volume One*
as it relates to this debate over economic development and political
force.

My conclusion will be that politics and economics, political force and
economic development, rather than being different or exclusive poles of
an opposition, in fact are differential, that is, undecidably intertwined.
The philosophical opposition that permits their separation in theory is
between nature and its others—history, technology, institutions, production, artifice, and so on. The opposition requires that economic development be conceived as something natural, and therefore prior to political
force, which is bound to history as a form of technical or institutional ar-

tifice deriving from and secondary to nature. Engels made a classic statement of the view that promotes this opposition: "The whole process can be explained by purely economic causes; at no point whatever are robbery, force, the state or political interference of any kind necessary."[2] Engels, however, says elsewhere that for strategic reasons, he was obliged to overemphasize the economic in relation to the political.[3] But although this statement may exculpate him, it does not exculpate an entire tradition of scientific marxism which autonomizes the economic, effaces the role of subjective labor in constructing the objective world, and thereby neutralizes Marx's description of capitalism as a coercive political relation of force. The model of "interaction" between "base" and "superstructure" still adheres to the classical metaphysical scheme of the dialectic by retaining the structure of opposition. Some other model, beyond the dialectic, would be required to compute that *limit* at which there is only interaction and no separation of homogeneous entities like base and superstructure. As Negri points out, Marx places productive relations (political) within productive forces (economic):

> The "agents of production": here we are from all evidence at the heart of the analysis. The general concept of production breaks the limits of its materialist and dialectical definition in order to exalt the subjectivity of its elements and their antagonistic relations. This antagonistic relation runs through the entire concept. "But before distribution can be the distribution of products, it is: (1) the distribution of the instruments of production, and (2) . . . the distribution of the members of the society among the different kinds of production. (Subsumption of the individuals under specific relations of production.) The distribution of products is evidently only a result of this distribution, which is comprised within the process of production itself and determines the structure of production." . . . Identity is split into difference, and difference is acknowledged as antagonism. . . . Difference, differences, antagonisms. We do not see how to read these marxian passages otherwise. The category of production—like that of value—in its generality and its abstraction carries living within it possible scission.[4]

More "original" than the so-called primary law of the economic development of productive forces is the antagonistic differential of productive relations, and that difference of course does not have a homogeneous origin. It is rather a limit, a line of interaction without possible separation or distinction.

I will argue that Marx's *Capital Volume One* disallows the categorial binary opposition between economic development and political force and that the two, rather than being homogeneous instances that "interact," are constituted as an undecidable limit or differential relation of force that cannot be described as an ontology of interactive, yet distinct, things or homogeneous entities. Each one is the other, undecidably. Each is a limit that is both economic and political, neither one exclusively, but in between both. Economic development (in the capitalist mode of production) cannot occur independently of political force, and capitalist political force is never exercised for its own sake, but for economic reasons. The second is an accepted insight of most marxisms; the first is an object of debate between critical and scientific marxists. Scientific marxists would like there to be an economic development independent of political force, and this theoretical postulate has practical consequences. If the work form characteristic of current modes of economic development (both in capitalist and so-called socialist countries) can be isolated as a purely economic form that in no way entails political force or the coercive imposition of work, then the Soviet Union's strategy of development is justified. And its maintenance of the capitalist work form, within the context of a transfer of titles of ownership to "society," can be legitimated as "socialist." Marx's argument in *Capital Volume One* is that the work form itself is coercive or political. Indeed, capitalism can be simply defined as the "command over unpaid labor" through the coercive imposition of wage labor.

The notorious "confusion" of the categories of politics and economics in Marx's political journalism can thus also be located in the supposedly purely scientific description of the formal laws of capitalism. This confusion is negative only from the point of view of the classical dialectic of scientific marxism's dialectical materialism, which would order categorically all differences and differential limits into strict opposition, rigorous identities, and unilinear causalities. From a deconstructive point of view, that confusion of the categories is positive because it discourages simplistic oppositions, and it encourages a more careful analysis of the complexities of a force field like that of capitalism in which it is not possible to separate political force from economic development. Read from a deconstructive point of view, *Capital Volume One* allows one to rethink the boundary that supposedly defines the opposition between economic development and political force. Marx's critical appropriation of Hegel's dialectic is not entirely alien to the deconstructive critique of classical dialectics.

The classical hegelian dialectic resolves difference into identity, inequality into equality, contradiction into continuity, heterogeneity into homogeneity, dissonance into unity, and so on. The seriality of history is subsumed under a logical paradigm that orders that seriality into a successive and teleological linear development. The paradigmatic meaning and logic of the dialectic is an antidote to the possibility that history may be only a seriality without paradigm or transcendental meaning. Marx shifted the dialectic into history without referring it to an ideal paradigm. Rather than a logic of opposition mediated as synthetic unity on a progressively grander scale, he saw in history a difference of force called class struggle. In capitalism, that difference is made up of the order capital attempts to impose through the law of value and the resistance of labor to that imposition. The law of value is implicitly coercive; it is predicated upon the ideal equivalence or exchangeability of unequal or different entities. It makes equal or identifies what is different. That operation can only take place ideally and with the help of a transcendental paradigm (money). Capitalism, therefore, requires an idealizing operation that abstracts from inequality, identifies difference, and resolves seriality into a paradigm. That operation is a concrete version of the classical speculative dialectic. The aspect of the dialectic which Marx saw as being more helpful emphasizes the heterogeneity or scission internal to capitalism which breaks the logic of capital and the law of value. "In its mystified form," he says, the "dialectic . . . seemed to transfigure and to glorify what exists." But as Marx uses it, it includes a recognition of the "inevitable destruction" of "what exists."[5] In *Capital Volume One*, Marx implies that the inevitability of this breaking up is due not to a transcendental objective logic of economic development, but to the differential of force inherent in the economy.

In *Capital Volume One*, Marx demonstrates that the capitalist economy is political, that is, structured by the imposition of force (either directly through the state or indirectly through economic laws) and resistance to that force. All the economic categories are points at which coercion, resistance, force, and struggle intersect. Marx's analysis proceeds by locating the structural and historical origin of the capitalist mode of production.

That analysis begins with the phenomenal form of capitalism, the commodity, and leads to an insight into the way capitalism is constituted as an antagonistic differential and as the coercive appropriation of unpaid labor. As a system, capitalism has its origin in the division between property owners or capitalists and workers:

> A division between the product of labor and labor itself, between the objective conditions of labor and subjective labor-power was therefore the real foundation [*Grundlage*] and the starting-point of the process of capitalist production. . . . The worker himself constantly produces objective wealth, in the form of capital, an alien power that dominates and exploits him; and the capitalist just as constantly produces labor-power . . . , in short, the capitalist produces the worker as a wage-laborer. This incessant reproduction, this perpetuation of the worker, is the absolutely necessary condition for capitalist production. [*Cap 1*, 716-17; *MEW*, 23:595-97]

But how did this structural division, this difference of force between classes, come about? The question leads Marx to plot out the historical origin of the capitalist relation:

> The capitalist relation presupposes [*setzt . . . voraus*] a complete separation between the workers and the ownership of the conditions for the realization

of their labor. . . . So-called original [*ursprungliche*] accumulation, therefore, is nothing else than the historical process of divorcing the producer from the means of production. . . . The immediate [*unmitterbare*] producer, one worker, could dispose of his own person only after he has ceased to be bound to the soil, and ceased to be the slave or serf of another person. . . . Hence the historical movement which changes the producers into wage-laborers appears, on the one hand, as their emancipation from serfdom and from the fetters of the guilds. . . . But, on the other hand, these newly freed men became sellers of themselves only after they had been robbed of all their own means of production. . . . The starting-point of the development [*Entwicklung*] that gave rise both to the wage-laborer and to the capitalist was the enslavement of the worker. The advance made consisted in a change in the form of this servitude, in the transformation of feudal exploitation into capitalist exploitation. . . . The expropriation of the agricultural producer, of the peasant, from the soil is the basis [*Grundlage*] of the whole process. [*Cap 1*, 847-48; *MEW*, 742-44]

The *economic* foundation of capitalist production is thus a coercive division produced through the exercise of political force: "These methods depend in part on brute force, e.g., the colonial system. But they all employ the power of the state, the concentrated and organized force of society, to hasten, hothouse fashion, the process of transformation of the feudal mode of production into the capitalist mode, and to shorten the transition. Force is the midwife of every old society pregnant with a new one. It is itself an economic power" (*Cap 1*, 915-16; *MEW*, 779). Marx describes the essence of capitalism not as an economic law but as an exercise of force, "command over unpaid labor" (*Cap 1*, 534; *MEW*, 556). The reproduction of capitalism is also the reproduction of this coercive relation of force: "The capitalist process of production, therefore, seen as a total connected process, i.e. a process of reproduction, produces not only commodities, not only surplus-value, but it also produces and re-produces the capital-relation; on the one hand the capitalist, on the other the wage-laborer" (*Cap 1*, 724; *MEW*, 604).

One cannot, therefore, isolate something like an "economic development" to which political force would be appended in a merely secondary or instrumental fashion, just as one cannot, in any mode of production, isolate "productive forces" from "productive relations." The primacy of that development is predicated upon a sustained exercise of political force, either directly by the state or indirectly through the political-economic system itself. Before capital can "secure its right to absorb a sufficient quantity of surplus-labor," it "must be aided by the power of the state. . . . Centuries are required before the 'free' worker, owing to the greater development of the capitalist mode of production, makes a voluntary agreement, i.e. is compelled by social conditions, to sell the whole of his active life" (*Cap 1*, 382; *MEW*, 296-97). The most characteristic "economic" law of capitalism, according to Marx, is the political force that coercively imposes a command over unpaid labor on workers.

To understand the famous passages in *Capital Volume One* concerning the dialectical "negation of the negation" as meaning an automatic *economic* development, free from political force, is to misunderstand the dialectic Marx locates in capitalism for a hegelian dialectic of continuity, purely necessary development, logical succession, and identity. There is, for Marx, no autonomous continuity, objective necessity, or identity of economic development. Arguing against pinning one's hopes on factory legislation, Marx writes: "The development of the contradictions of a given historical form of production is the only historical way in which it can be dissolved and then reconstructed a new basis" (*Cap 1*, 619; *MEW*, 512). One of these contradictions is that the greater expropriation of labor requires centralization of capital, but "with this there also grows the revolt [*Empörung*] of the working-class. . . . The centralization of the means of production and the socialization of labor reach a point at which they become incompatible with their capitalist integument" (*Cap 1*, 929; *MEW*, 790-91). When, therefore, he speaks in the next paragraph of the inexorable negation of the negation which capitalist property represents, he is not describing a purely economic or a purely necessary, objective, logical development. Centralization is a means of exercising greater coercion over labor, and it produces greater "revolt" on labor's part. Both lines of political force are "inevitable" given the antagonistic and divided class structure of the mode of production, and this contradiction leads inevitably to a transformation in the mode of production. What Marx described is not an inevitable economic development, but a political-economic development, which he defines not in terms of transhuman or objective economic laws, but of the category most important to his analysis—human labor. Centralization leads to greater socialization and to working-class revolt: "But with this there also grows the revolt of the working-class, a class constantly increasing in numbers and trained, united, organized by the very mechanism of the capitalist process of production" (*Cap 1*, 929; *MEW*, 790-91). In the interesting passage that follows, Marx describes the mode of production and the means of production as separate from the "monopoly of capital" which "becomes a fetter upon the mode of production, which has flourished *alongside and under it*" (*Cap 1*, 929; *MEW*, 791; my italics). In other words, within capitalism, a centralized and socialized means of production springs up which is antithetical to capitalist private property. What is significant is that this increasing socialization is identified with the growing "revolt of the working-class." It is not a purely "economic" development, both because it is itself predicated upon the exercise of force ("The capitalist mode of appropriation, which springs from the capitalist mode of production, produces capitalist private property. This is the first negation of individual private property, as founded on the labor of its proprietor" [*Cap 1*, 929; *MEW*, 791]) and because the transformation of that first negation into the second necessarily requires a counterforce of "revolt" exercised in

terms of the object of the first negation, that is, ownership of the fruit of
the labor of the producer: "But the capitalist production begets, with the
necessity of a natural process, its own negation. This is the negation of
the negation. It does not re-establish private property, but it does indeed
establish individual private property on the basis of the achievements of
the capitalist era: namely co-operation and the possession in common of
the land and the means of production produced by labor itself" (Cap 1,
929; MEW, 791). The "necessity of a natural process" is worked out as the
resolution of a political differential of class subjects (capital and labor) in
relation to the objective structures of property and production. The
development does not occur according to a logic of necessity entirely
immanent to and operative solely on the basis of purely "objective"
structures and laws.

Marx describes a capitalist system that is politically coercive, not purely
economic, a transformation to socialism operated not as a purely economic
development, but through the revolt of workers against their political-
economic coercion, and a resulting system that assumes workers' control
over what they produce. The category of productive labor and the relations into which it enters are essential for deriving these three points.

Capitalist ideology presents capitalism as a homogeneous entity;
Marx's text is deconstructive of that ideology in that it demonstrates the
fissured structural and historical origin of the system. Any stasis that it
attains is merely the provisional stabilization of a differential of antagonistic force. That differential is defined less by a systematic interrelation of distinct entities than by *limits* of force and resistance. A fissure
runs through the capitalist system, and it delineates the limit where the
differential of power between capital and labor is determined by the law
of value and the wage. In the nineteenth century, the crucial limit in this
regard is the limit of the work day:

> The establishment of a normal working-day is . . . the product of a pro-
> tracted and more or less concealed civil war between the capitalist class and
> the working-class. . . . If machinery is the most powerful means for raising
> the productivity of labor—i.e., of shortening the workingtime needed to
> produce a commodity, it is also, as a repository of capital the most powerful
> means . . . of lengthening the working-day beyond all natural limits
> [*Schranke*]. . . . Because it is capital, the automatic mechanism . . . is animated
> by the drive to reduce to a minimum the resistance offered by man, that
> obstinate yet elastic natural barrier. [*Cap 1*, 412, 526-27; *MEW*, 316, 425]

The question of the limit of the working day, then, is also a question of
the limits of power, the differential of force between the classes. That
limit is important because it determines the "economic" limits on how
much surplus value can be extracted from labor. Capital wins through
the medium of the law of value; the diminution of the working day

cannot exceed certain limits at which the production of surplus value, the purpose of capitalism, would no longer be possible. A systemic economic goal can thus be achieved only through the exercise of political force, the reduction of the resistance of labor, and, likewise, that political force can be exercised through a seemingly objective economic systemic constraint—the length of the working day.

The wage is an example of another limit where a differential of political force, as much as an objective economic law, defines itself:

> As soon as this diminution [of the amount of unpaid labor in proportion to paid labor] touches the point at which the surplus-labor that nourishes capital is no longer supplied in normal quantity, a reaction sets in. . . . The rise of wages is therefore confined within limits [*Grenzen*] that not only leave intact the foundations of the capitalist system, but also secure its reproduction on an increasing scale. The law of capitalist accumulation, mystified by the economists into a supposed law of nature, in fact expresses the situation that the very nature of accumulation excludes every diminution in the degree of exploitation of labor. [*Cap 1*, 771; *MEW*, 649]

Here again, the law of value assures capital political domination through the workings of an apparently objective or natural mechanism. If wages rise too high, they encroach upon the proportion of unpaid labor, hence surplus value, extracted from labor. Capital retracts automatically, forcing workers out of work and reducing wages. But that seemingly objective economic mechanism is in fact the exercise of political force within the economic system. It imposes discipline on labor and assures submission to a properly proportional extraction of unpaid labor. But for that very reason, it is a locus of antagonism and a site of potential scission.

The law of value imposes "continuity, uniformity, regularity, order" upon the labor process. In its very structure, value unifies by homogenizing difference. In order for commodities to be exchangeable, their differences from all others must be effaced, and their inequalities must be mediated by a general equivalent (money) which abstracts from all their distinct forms and is identical with each. Labor is one such commodity: "Equality in the full sense between different kinds of labor can be arrived at only if we abstract from their real inequality, if we reduce them to the characteristic they have in common" (*Cap 1*, 166; *MEW*, 87-88). The common denominator of all commodities is the general equivalent, a commodity like all the rest, which is extracted from the relational system of commodities and transcendentalized as the equivalent of all. As if taking a lesson from Derrida's analysis of metaphysical philosophy, Marx points out that without the general equivalent, which is abstracted from the series of commodities as its paradigm, the series becomes potentially interminable: "Different simple expressions of the value of one and the same commodity arise according to whether that commodity enters into a value-relation with this second commodity or another kind of commodity. The number of such possible expressions is limited only by the number of the different kinds of commodities distinct from it. The isolated expression of A's value is thus transformed into the indefinitely expandable series [*Reihe*] of the different simple expressions of that value" (*Cap 1*, 154; *MEW*, 76). Marx goes on to speak of this series as "interminable," "infinite," without any "single unified form of appearance." There is, then, within the structure of value a radical heterogeneity. The exchange of commodities with each other on a relational value basis serves the end of use, but it cannot be regulated according to the needs of capital exchange. That system requires a general form of value that unifies all the different commodities in a single value equation: "The general relative form of value imposes the character of universal equivalent on the linen, which is the commodity excluded, as equivalent, from the whole world of commodities" (*Cap 1*, 159; *MEW*, 81). The next step is to insert money in the place of linen. Homogeneity of the sort required for capitalist production is attained through a transcendental structure of universalization and identity which limits the potential interminability of the series of relative value relations, where exchangeability is defined by differentially related uses rather than by a paradigmatic exchange equivalent. A general or universal paradigm operates the containment, but the potential for disorder and infinite seriality remains contained within the system as a structural possibility. If the universal equivalent loses its social credibility, if it is recognized as merely one more commodity in the series whose paradigmatic status is socially constructed, then a heterogeneous seriality erupts from within the system, breaking its boundaries and the order it imposes. Abstract value accumulation would no longer be possible.

To a certain extent, it never is possible in an absolute sense, as a closed, stable, self-sufficient system. The mechanism that allows the heterogeneity of the potentially interminable series to be arrested—the money form—also inserts capital accumulation into another series that promises to be equally interminable, not for reasons of infinite possibility or richness, but because the initial structure of accumulation is such that an absolute closure is never possible:

> The repetition or renewal of the act of selling in order to buy finds its measure and its goal (as does the process itself) in a final purpose which lies outside it, namely, consumption, the satisfaction of definite needs. But in buying in order to sell, on the contrary, the end and the beginning are the same, money or exchange-value, and this very fact makes the movement an endless [*endlos*] one. . . . The simple circulation of commodities—selling in order to buy—is a means to a final goal which lies outside circulation, namely the appropriation of use-values, the satisfaction of needs. As against this, the circulation of money as capital is an end in itself, for the valoriza-

tion of value takes place only within this constantly renewed movement. The circulation of capital is therefore limitless [*masslos*]. . . . The unceasing movement . . . this boundless drive for . . . exchange value. [*Cap 1*, 252-55; *MEW*, 166-68]

The structure that initiates this interminable process without closure is the extraction of surplus value from labor:

This increment or excess [*Überschuss*] over the original value I call "surplus-value". The value originally advanced, therefore, not only remains intact while in circulation, but increases its magnitude, adds to itself a surplus-value or is valorized. And this movement converts it into capital. . . . It is a law, springing from the technical character of manufacture, that the mimimum amount of capital which the capitalist must possess has to go on increasing. In other words, the transformation of the social means of production and subsistence into capital must keep extending. [*Cap 1*, 251-52, 480; *MEW*, 165, 381]

There is, then, a skidding inscribed in the very rationality (in the sense of a proper ratio of surplus value) of the capitalist system which situates the system in an interminable seriality it cannot arrest or close off. That skidding is initiated in the structural division or differential disproportion between capital and labor; what makes the system possible can equally make it impossible as a self-sufficient machine which is not pushed beyond its own limits by its very own operation. The *ratio* of the system is possible only as the generation of irrationality, imbalance, and scission. The law of value subordinates workers through the rational proportions that place limits on wages. But the flow of force in that differential relation can also be reversed. Because of their position, workers can exert pressure on the law of value, pushing it beyond its proper proportion, furthering the skidding that is structurally inherent in the system. Increased pressure or resistance in the determination of the limits of power in the workplace (such as wages and working day) have direct effects on the economic structure that push capitalism beyond its proper limit. The potential for its dissolution is thus *both* part of its economic laws of development and a matter of political force.

At this point, a deconstructive argument would need to be brought to bear on the subjectivistic tendency in critical marxism. Like economic development and political force, which form an undecidable limit in Marx's text, necessity and subjective will are also undecidable. Neither one is exclusively original in determining the course of events. Scientific marxists excessively emphasize necessity as objective economic law, but in relation to this metaphysic, such critical marxists as Negri excessively privilege subjectivity and fall into an inverse metaphysic. Marx's argument is more problematic than either of these positions. A structural necessity, he argues, is built into capitalism and cannot be willed away:

"If Russia is tending to become a capitalist nation after the example of the West European countries—and during the last few years she has taken a lot of trouble in this direction—she will not succeed without having first transformed a good part of her peasants into proletarians; and after that, once taken to the bosom of the capitalist regime, she will experience its pitiless laws like other profane peoples."[6] But, equally, contingency and subjective will cannot be denied a role: "World history would indeed be very easy to make if the fight could be taken up in terms of unerringly opportune chances. On the other hand, world history would be of a very mystical nature if 'contingencies' played no role. These contingencies themselves of course fall into the general course of development and are compensated for by other contingencies. But acceleration and delay [of the course of development] are very much dependent on such 'contingencies'—in which figures as well the 'accident' of the people's character who stands at the spearhead of the movement."[7]

One cannot justifiably claim that Marx believed in either objective necessity or subjective will exclusively. In his text and in the world, the relation between the two is undecidable; neither one exclusively can be privileged as the origin of historical change. The structural logic of capitalism does necessarily tend to develop toward greater automation. But that development is predicated upon subjective action; technology is the human mind working up the natural world into machines. And, as I have argued, it is motivated by the desire of a class of subjects—capitalists—to maintain power over another class of subjects—workers. Similarly, workers revolt and bring about revolution, but their will to do so operates within an objective structure that supplies its conditions outside of the will of the agents. Neither is revolution a matter of subjective will purely, because the desire for revolution is itself an effect of structural constraints that make that desire possible in the first place and place limits on its extent.

Marx says that contradictions within capitalism develop and push the system beyond itself into another mode of production. That process is not purely or only automatic, that is, *natural*; it depends on the development of economic laws, but only inasmuch as those laws are defined by a differential of political force operative in the workplace, in the structure of value, and in all the other limits where force meets force throughout the social factory:

> For the transformation of money into capital, therefore, the owner of money must find the free laborer available on the commodity-market. . . . Nature does not produce on the one side owners of money or commodities, and on the other hand men possessing nothing but their own labor-power. This relation has no basis in natural history, nor does it have a social basis common to all periods of human history. It is clearly the result of a past historical development, the product of many economic revolutions, of the

extinction of a whole series [*Reihe*] of older formations of social production. The economic categories already discussed similarly bear a historical imprint [*Spur*]. [*Cap 1*, 273; *MEW*, 183]

The point of bearing the imprint of history is to be inscribed in a series for which there is no paradigm, that is, in this case, no natural basis. The economic categories are not the result of nature conceived as an objective process of economic development. To conceive things thus, according to the ideology of scientific marxism, is to provide a trans-historical paradigm of necessary or inevitable economic development which reduces the seriality of history to an instance of nature. Scientific marxism naturalizes history by reducing political force to a secondary aspect of inevitable, objective economic development. The positing of such a natural origin or paradigm is ideological. But to emphasize seriality and the role of force is not to discount necessity altogether. It is simply that the necessity at work in historical development is not transcendental and independent of the actions of human agents. The objective laws are intertwined with subjective processes. This is the point of Marx's concept of productive labor, which radically deconstructs the binary opposition between nature and history, nature and technology, in such a way that the development of an economy can no longer be conceived as an inevitable objective mechanism. Economic systems do not arise naturally; they are the work of a technology of political force, as of productive forces. That force is never reducible to subjective intention or will; it is molded by systemic constraints, situations, and contexts. Like the economy, it is itself never purely "itself," but instead a differential limit of impetus and resistance, of subjective action induced by objective structures constructed by subjects.

Marx's description of history as seriality without paradigm, of economic development as being intertwined with political force, and of the skidding inscribed structurally within the system which precludes its ever attaining self-identity or closure places him closer to the deconstructive critique of classical dialectics than to classical dialectics itself. This is not to say that Marx does not locate dialectical processes in the world that are not derived hegelian schemes. Striking among these is the interrelation of presupposition and effect in the process of simple reproduction:

A division between the product of labor and labor itself, between the objective conditions of labor and subjective labor-power, was therefore the real foundation and the starting-point of the process of capitalist production. But what at first was merely a starting-point, becomes, by the mediation [*vermittelst*] of the continuity of the process, by simple reproduction, the characteristic result of capitalist production, a result which is constantly

renewed and perpetuated. . . . The capitalist . . . produces the laborer, as a
wage-laborer. This incessant reproduction, this perpetuation of the worker,
is the absolutely necessary condition for capitalist production. [*Cap 1,* 716;
MEW, 595-96]

For Hegel, in order for something to become independent and free, it
must become self-reproductive; this implies that all external presuppositions or conditions of its makeup must be internalized and posited as its
own products or effects. In other words, the separation between labor
and its product (originally the work of force, something "external" to
economic law) must be internalized and reproduced automatically by the
mechanism of capitalism. Capitalism does not require external political
coercion (say, from the state) because the very system of production
operates that coercive separation of labor from its product. Political
force is internalized and posited by capitalism as an economic law. Where
Hegel would have described a developmental process that adheres to the
closure of logic (presupposition becomes a posited effect, and the self-
identity of autoreproduction is achieved), however, Marx describes an
apparently logical mechanism that resides upon a differential of force
and whose objective logic is in fact *also* subjective coercion. Capital is not
a logical category, but the forced imposition of wage labor which is
reproduced "logically" by the coercive political mechanism of capitalist
production, by the necessity of maintaining a proper *ratio* of value. And
any historical modification of that situation will not be the result of a
logical development of objective economic laws, but rather of the exacerbation of that differential of force beyond the limits it currently defines,
to the extent that the homogeneity of the system is ruptured by the
heterogeneity it harbors, not to give rise to a transcendental or universal
synthesis, but to a mode of production, which, as much as capitalism, is
inscribed in the seriality of history and in which the tyranny of the
"objective" economic law will give way to a free regulation of production
by producers themselves.

Marx's definition of the capitalist economic mode as a system of political coercion is nowhere more clear than in the last chapter of *Capital
Volume One* dealing with the colonies. It is also a place where the dispersive heterogeneity which the capitalist system contains and arrests
breaks the bounds of the system. The structural kernel of that heterogeneity is contained in the very capitalist relation—between labor and capital—that makes the system possible.[8] Marx privileges the colonies because
there incipient capitalism (both historically and structurally) is on dis-
play. Only just beginning, the system has not yet developed to a point
where it is self-reproductive. Something similar to the process of original
accumulation in western Europe can thus be observed in action. The
relationship between capital and labor is only just being established, and
it appears not as an objective economic development along rational or

logical lines, but, rather, as the reduction of heterogeneity to homogeneity through the forceful imposition of wage labor: "The only thing that interests us is the secret discovered in the New World by the political economy of the Old World, and loudly proclaimed by it: that the capitalist mode of production and accumulation, and therefore capitalist private property as well, have for their fundamental condition the annihilation of that private property which rests on the labor of the individual himself; in other words, the expropriation of the worker" (*Cap 1*, 940; *MEW*, 802). In principle, therefore, capitalism will always contain a potentially dispersive, disruptive, and heterogeneous force pushing against its bounds and limits, simply because the system is established as a repressive homogenization; where there is coercion, there will be resistance; where there is forced closure, there is the possibility of a rupture.

Marx begins the chapter by describing the ideology of classical political economy which reduces difference to identity: "Political economy confuses, on principle, two different kinds of private property, one of which rests on the labor of the producer himself, and the other on the exploitation of the labor of others. It forgets that the latter is not only the direct antithesis of the former, but grows on the former's tomb and nowhere else" (*Cap 1*, 931; *MEW*, 792). In the colonies, however, the two modes of property and of production exist side by side. The forced separation between labor and land has not yet occurred: "There the capitalist regime constantly comes up against the obstacle [*Hindernis*] presented by the producer, who, as owner of his own conditions of labor, employs that labor to enrich himself, instead of the capitalist. The contradiction between these two diametrically opposed economic systems, has its practical manifestation here in the struggle between them" (*Cap 1*, *MEW*, 931; 792). The establishment of the capitalist mode of production is thus impossible as a "natural," "objective," or inevitable development:

> So long, therefore, as the worker can accumulate for himself—and this he can do so long as he remains in possession of his means of production—capitalist accumulation and the capitalistic mode of production are impossible. The class of wage-laborers essential to these is lacking. . . . We have seen that the expropriation of the mass of the people from the soil forms the basis of the capitalist mode of production. The essence of a free colony, on the contrary, consists in this, that the bulk of the soil is still public property, and every settler on it can therefore turn part of it into his private property and his individual means of production, without preventing later settlers from performing the same operation. This is the secret both of the prosperity of the colonies and of their cancerous affliction—their resistance to the establishment of capital. [*Cap 1*, 933-34; *MEW*, 794-96]

Because of free land, the workers can become free landowners. That "indispensable requisite" of capitalist production—a surplus population of laborers to regulate the laws of supply and demand of labor—disappears into the landscape. The workers are constantly transformed into independent producers. For them to be self-sufficient and autoreproductive, capital must incorporate independent producers as wage laborers; it must contain and regulate the "dispersion" they represent: "A 'barbarising tendency of dispersion' [*Zersteuung*] of producers and of the wealth of the nation, fragmentation [*Zersplitterung*] of the means of production among innumerable owners, working on their own account, annihilates, along with the centralisation of capital, all the foundations of combined labor" (*Cap 1*, 937; *MEW*, 798-99). The only solution to such "dispersion" is political force and the manipulation of artificial economic pressure. The colonies provide an example both of original accumulation and of the necessarily political or coercive nature of the "economic" laws of capitalism:

> Where the capitalist has behind him the power [*Macht*] of the mother-country, he tries to use force to clear out of the way the modes of production and appropriation which rest on the personal labor of the independent producer. . . . In the interest of so-called wealth of the nation, he seeks for artificial means [*Kunstmitteln*] to ensure the poverty of the people. . . . Let the government set an artificial price on the virgin soil, a price independent of the law of supply and demand, a price that compels the immigrant to work a long time for wages before he can earn enough money to buy land. [*Cap 1*, 931, 932, 938; *MEW*, 792, 793, 800]

Marx concludes the chapter by pointing out that what happens at the margin of capitalism in the colonies reflects upon the nature of capitalism in the home countries; it rests upon the expropriation of the laborer and the forced imposition of wage labor. The margin, then, inheres in the center of the system. What happens at the boundary is essential to the system's laws. The margin is always a place where the inside of a system articulates with its outside. In the colonies, the margin is a place of undecidability because they are both within capitalism, yet outside it. They satisfy the economic axioms of the system—production is taking place; private property exists—but they also demonstrate the incompleteness of the system if its axioms are purely *economic*. There, economic law requires political force, and Marx argues that this supplementary necessity is no accident, that it reflects a structural necessity of the system in the center, as much as at the margin. Capital is power and domination operating as "economic laws."

The law of capital value is not, therefore, a scientific description of an objective mechanism; it is a law in the juridical sense, a matter of enforcement. As such, it must be defined to allow for the possibility of a transgression. In the colonies, at the margin of the system, that transgression consists of the worker refusing wage labor and becoming an independent producer. Because the margin reflects upon the structural center of the system, that outside or transgression defined at the margin also inheres in the center or inside of the system. The system is internally opened up to its outside. The possibility of the refusal of what constitutes the system's interiority, its self-sufficient autoreproduction—wage labor—also is contained in the system. The law of value is not a description of an objective mechanism, beyond human control; it is something that can be either obeyed or disobeyed, heeded or displaced. Disobedience at the center is made difficult by the fact that the force of political coercion required at the margin in the colonies has become a functioning part of the "objective economic" mechanism. This is the secret of modern libertarian fascism. The coercive function of the political state can be performed by giving free rein to free market forces, so-called independent and objective economic laws that must follow the requirements of value production, an imperative that necessarily imposes limits on wages and worker discretion. Value, we have seen, is constituted as the suppression of the heterogeneity of relative use values. So also, the mode of production based on exchange value requires the suppression of use value production. An economic law is itself a political force, just as, Marx points out, political force is an economic power.

Capital contains transgression of the law of value, both in the sense of harboring and of regulating. The colonies show that capital harbors the possibility that its offer of wage labor will be refused and that possibility must be regulated through political-economic force. What is also proved is that the possibility of transgression, of a resistance to the force of enforcement, grows from the conditions of capitalist production themselves; they do not have to be imported from the party office: "The working class movement on both sides of the Atlantic . . . had grown instinctively [*instinktiv*] out of the relations of production [*Produktionsverhältnissen*] themselves" (*Cap 1*, 415; *MEW*, 319). Thus, one can articulate those two seemingly absolutely exclusive strands in Marx's thought: that which emphasizes the instinctive political resistance of workers and that which emphasizes the inevitable economic sublation of capitalism into socialism, seemingly independent of any political action. Economic development is inevitable, but only through productive relations necessary to the system, which constitute a differential of political force, a disequilibrium of value (the constantly renewed need for the excess of surplus value), and a never fully closed possibility of scission. The condition of possibility of capitalism—the *difference* between capital and labor, a disequilibrium that must be maintained in order for surplus value to be extracted—is also that which makes the system impossible *as such*, as an automatically self-sufficient and self-reproductive mechanism. It drives the system beyond itself. Seemingly instinctive political resistance through economic means by workers is inevitable given the constraints of surplus value extraction which require the exercise of force against workers in the form of limits on wages and other benefits that cut into surplus value. That force produces "instinctive" resistance, which leads necessarily to adjustments in the structure of capitalism if surplus value is to continue to be extracted at a "just" proportion. Those economic adjustments, in wages, prices, and so on, will in turn result in the exertion of more pressure on workers. The "inevitable" economic development of capitalism according to the law of surplus-value extraction on an expanding scale is produced by the differential of force and resistance between capital and labor. Resistance to the demands of labor leads "logically" to inflation (maintaining a ratio of disproportion merely at a higher power, on an expanded scale) and to automation. Both imply economic developments that are necessary, given the structure of the system, and both constitute forms of political force exerted against labor to enforce compliance to the laws of surplus-value extraction. All this leads to further "instinctive" resistance, until a *limit* is reached at which the ratio of disproportion can no longer be maintained in accordance with the axioms of the system. The law of undecidability here intersects the marxian theory of necessary revolution. The margin where the system itself overflows the limits set by its axioms, thus rendering them incomplete and inconsistent, is a point of revolution. The necessity of reconstructing new axioms imposed by the law of undecidability also applies to political-economic systems.

Like political force and economic development, "spontaneity" or instinctive resistance and inevitability form only a binary opposition in metaphysical thinking. Considered deconstructively, the two form a differential that cannot be resolved into the form of an opposition; they form part of a chain or a seriality without paradigm. A paradigm would decide which of the two is primary, which ethically or logically prior. A deconstructive argument would point out the undecidability of the two in history.

For scientific marxists to claim, then, that "the economic" is "determinant in the last instance" is to ignore the always already political nature of the so-called "economic."[9] To isolate something called "the economic" in this way, which precedes such "relatively autonomous instances" as "the political," is to play into the hands of capitalist ideology, which would also like to conceal the coercive political force inherent in the relations of production, that is, in production itself. (It should not be surprising that it is scientific marxists in both cases — French [Althusser and others] and English [Hobsbawm and others] — who are responsible, on the one hand, for making a metaphysical paradigm of "the economic" and, on the other, for eliminating "productive relations" from the marxist vocabulary by translating *Produktionsverhältnisse* in the new English edition of the *Complete Works* as "conditions of production.") The "economic" is not an ensemble of productive forces (determinant in the last instance) which exists prior to and *without* productive relations, that is, without the political relations of force between, say, capitalist and laborer.

"The political" and "the economic" cannot even be considered as separate categories for the sake of theoretical exposition. This is the significance of Marx's confusion of the two categories in his political journalism, which can thus be said to be deconstructive of the metaphysical opposition. The political "determines" the economic:

> The revolutionary crisis intensified the commercial crisis. And if private credit is based on the confidence that bourgeois production . . . and bourgeois order are inviolable and will remain unviolated, what sort of effect must a revolution have which calls into question the basis of bourgeois production, the economic slavery of the proletariat . . . ? The revolt of the proletariat is the abolition of bourgeois credit. . . . The financial aristocracy, which ruled under the July monarchy, had its high church in the Bank. . . . Thus, the February revolution directly [*unmittelbar*] consolidated and extended the bankrocracy. . . . Thus, long after the democratic representatives of the petty bourgeoisie had been repulsed by the republican representatives of the bourgeoisie in the National Assembly, the civil, real [*burgerlichen, reelen*] economic significance of this parliamentary split became manifest in the sacrifice of the petty-bourgeois debtors to the bourgeois creditors.[10]

The economic "determines" the political:

> But in reality [the new tax] hit *the peasant class* above all, that is, the great majority of the French people. *It was they who had to pay the costs of the February revolution,* and among them the counter-revolution found its main material. . . . The Provisional Government had succumbed to the old bourgeois society by honoring the bills which it has drawn on the state. . . . Credit became a condition of its existence. . . . And nobody was more fanatical about the alleged machinations of the communists than the petty bourgeois, who tottered helplessly on the brink of bankruptcy. . . . The workers were left with no choice; they had either to starve or to strike out. They answered on 22 June with the gigantic insurrection, in which the first great battle was fought between the two great classes which divide modern society. [CSF, 51, 52, 54, 58; *MEW*, 25, 27, 31]

The text invalidates any decidable distinction between even "relatively" autonomous levels such as the "economic" or the "political." The positioning of subjects as workers and owners and the lines of force necessary to maintain each class in that position through the mediation of the structural law of value cut across such categorical distinctions.

To say that "the economic" is "determinant in the last instance" is to hypostatize something beyond human control, and for Marx, at least, communism meant human control over human life, that is, over the production of life. The determination of the "economic" "in the last instance" is the theoretical equivalent of a productive force economism which coercively imposes wage labor in the name of (scientific) "socialism," claiming the necessity of following "objective" economic laws that only party scientists, but not mere workers, can know, and of a bureaucratic politicism that constitutes the party-state as determinant in the last instance. A deconstructive analysis of the grounds of scientific marxist methodology would ask what is primary and what made secondary by seemingly neutral categorial distinctions; and it would ask what interests are served by the method? Marx's method serves the interests of the working class by denying the categorial distinctions (between political force and "objective" economic development) which, in the method of scientific marxism, legitimate a division of labor that preserves the coercive work form and the enslavement of the working class to wage labor and the law of value.

His founding category—material production—is much more radical in its implications than the scientific marxist category of "the economic." "Material production" calls to mind human labor, the ability to produce things, to fashion nature (within certain limits) to satisfy human needs. It implies human activity, the ability to control the manufacture of goods for need satisfaction; there is no hint of a transcendental, quasi-metaphysical system into which humans plug their labor. What is primary, for Marx, is the process of productive labor, which is, after all, merely one aspect of the productive technology at work in the natural (that is, non-human-made) world. It is not subject to "objective" laws that determine it; rather, it is the characteristic of subjectivity embedded in objectivity to the extent that it cannot be categorically separated from it, to act and to produce.

The category of material production also implicitly legislates against the patriarchy, and scientific marxism is patriarchal. The rigidity of the "objective" law, sanctioned by an absolutist concept of "science," is merely a theoretical version of the unquestioned self-empowerment of the male. Production includes the production of human life, of human beings. The category of "the economic," on the other hand, makes sexual production secondary to the "real issue," "the economic," which, when one gets down to locating it as such, in its essence, cannot be isolated from politics or the patriarchy. Starting from the wrong categories explains the recalcitrance of many male marxists to the socialist-feminist issue; political-economic radicals are sexual-political reactionaries in part because their initial categories are wrong, and this conservatism is reflected in their choice of political and economic categories.

From a marxist materialist and a deconstructive point of view, there is no origin or foundation, a "last instance," that one could go back to that would be outside the series or field which is supposedly determined "in the last instance." As I have argued, "the economic" cannot be made prior to what it supposedly determines—"the political." Material production includes the possibility that institutions, which would be secondary or determined from the viewpoint of the primacy of the "economic," can themselves be determining. Material production emphasizes the role of subjective human labor in the technological construction of a social world.

Even when considered philosophically, the matter of the last instance becomes problematic. The probable reason why Marx used material production instead of "material life" is that he wanted to emphasize its nature as an activity. But it also emphasizes the fact that life, in order to continue, must reproduce. Human production takes place because humans need to satisfy the requirements of sustained physical existence. To do this, they need to reproduce themselves. Production is inseparable from reproduction. Production is always in terms of reproduction. Speaking deconstructively, one could say that a certain doubling or repetition is inscribed in its apparent singularity. Production reproduces. Without reproduction, there would be no production. Reproduction is the effect of production, but it is also its condition. There can be no singular origin here, of the sort that would lend itself to categorical description as a "last instance," because production is itself an effect of reproduction, itself conditioned by its own effect. Reproduction is nonoriginal, secondary, but it retroactively induces production from a nonprimordial position of origin. What comes first is an effect of what comes after. The point of origin is split by what makes it original, the necessity of reproduction. This is a trace structure.

That structure or force of differentiation or original repetition operates without "being" anything present which one could know through empirical observation. It acts, producing effects, while remaining outside the field of presence, or of a localizable "instance," just as the relational structure or force of exchange value exists nowhere concretely except as the effects it produces.

The possibility of a last instance has once again flitted away, at least as something homogeneous or self-identical. In its place, one finds a relation or a differential (production-reproduction). This differential cannot serve as a principle of authority; indeed, it questions the sort of authority (theoretical, as well as socio-political) which emerges once "the economic" is made determinant in the last instance. Like the idealism that makes the mind determinant in the last instance, the simplistic, premarxian materialism that absolutizes "the economic" in a similar way also supplies the ideology for an unequal division of labor. And it implicitly sustains currently existing structures of sexual domination. The determination in the last instance of "the economic" implies something durable and hard, a sort of bedrock, an authority. I think of it as a characteristically phallocratic notion: the male produces, is the authority, and determines in the last instance. The determination in the last instance of the economic is itself a determined effect of a metaphysical and patriarchal culture, which institutionalizes both philosophical and sociopolitical points of authority.

When, therefore, both Marx and Derrida speak of the necessity of reconsidering the way we fashion categories—through what procedures, on what grounds, for what ends—it is because such categories as "the economic" falsely represent the world by positing nonexistent homogeneous grounds that reduce out complex relations and forces that are not amenable to simple categorical representation as homogeneous entities and that require what Marx calls a different mode of exposition. The fabrication of categories is a political act. Just as any act of periodization periodizes the person doing the periodizing, so also, categorization politically categorizes the person categorizing. The choice of "the economic" over material production since Marx is indicative of the conservative turn marxism has taken in its "scientific" form. The positing of a final, founding, authoritative category like "the economic" is not inseparable from an authoritarian politics. An approach like Antonio Negri's that emphasizes the role of difference, tendential antagonism, and scission inside capitalist production, rather than so-called transcendent structures and laws that make a cohesive working class a necessity for any "economic" system, including a socialist one, leads to a more open, less authoritarian, more autonomous, and self-directional politics.

Marx radicalized the dialectic in a way that moves toward the deconstructive critique of classical dialectics. That radicalization has been recuperated by scientific marxism, and any critical pertinence deconstruction might have in this regard seems best attained through applying it to that metaphysics. This is not to say that there are probably not areas in Marx's text that could benefit from deconstructive analysis; what political interests such an analysis would serve would need to be laid out in advance. My interest here has been to read Marx in such a way that the implicit opposition his text offers to the metaphysics of scientific marxism becomes evident. And, ultimately, because I believe Marx and Derrida, critical marxism and deconstruction, are on the same side, I have not tried (nor do I see the value of trying) "to deconstruct" Marx's text. The critical validity of marxism does not depend on the sanctity or inviolability of that text. And the relation between deconstruction and marxism can take more critically helpful (less scholarly) forms, as I shall now argue.

❧ 5 ❧

From Derrida
to Habermas and
Beyond, via Lacan

That a small number of marxists use deconstruction as a method of political critique would seem to suggest that it has exercised limited influence on the left in the fifteen years or so during which it has been current. This is not quite the case. In France especially, Derrida's work has had a tremendous subliminal impact on the thought and writings of such overtly politicized intellectuals as Julia Kristeva, Gilles Deleuze, and Michel Foucault. One need only compare the work of these thinkers before Derrida entered the French intellectual scene with their work immediately after to notice Derrida's influence. From Deleuze's rhizomatics to Foucault's microsphysics, the imprint of deconstruction is unmistakable.

In the English-speaking world, deconstruction has been used more for conservative than for politically radical ends. This tendency results in part from the depoliticized and aestheticist propensities of the importers, most of whom are literary critics interested in "applying" deconstructive methodology as a form of conventional literary criticism for the sake primarily of rejuvenating a jaded elitist canon of great, male Western books.[1] It is unfortunate that the conservatism of these critics has provoked hostility toward deconstruction in general on the part of leftists. It is even more unfortunate that these leftist detractors have almost unanimously misrepresented Derrida's work by interpreting it in relation to its American literary critical progeny. The most telling example is the misunderstanding of the concept of "textuality" as a privileging of literature or of a self-sufficient writing, instead of as the name for radical heterogeneity. At Yale, "textuality" does indeed boost "the literary" to a status it has not enjoyed in years, and it helps resuscitate a profession that is witnessing a secular decline in the value of its treasured fetishes, in the face both of the politicization of the canon by women's and black studies and of the inevitable coming to the fore of media and popular culture studies. Yet "textuality" in Derrida's work has very little if anything to do with an idealist concept like "the literary," and its implications for political and sociocultural analysis far exceed the survival imperatives of a generation of salaried aesthetes, anxious to restore a book culture terminally eroded by electro-media and translating, through a curious reaction formation, a sense of disciplinary hopelessness into an exaltation of the profession of literary critic. Even in domestic deconstructive literary criticism, however, something of the potential radical use to which deconstruction can be put shows through; it at least manages to raise the hackles of the neohumanist right wing of the literary academy.

Given the literary critical port of entry of deconstruction into the United States, it should not be surprising that one of the first attempts to articulate deconstruction with a brand of leftism should come from a literary critic. Rainer Nagele argues[2] that Frankfurt School critical theory and such recent French developments as lacanian structural psychoanalysis and deconstruction can be brought together. Although I support the general outlines of the attempt, I think Nagele tends too much to equate deconstruction with its American subset. In addition, he accepts Jacques Lacan's sexism without so much as a qualm, and he overlooks the fact that deconstruction invalidates many of Lacan's more metaphysical presuppositions. Here, I will offer a critique of lacanism from a combined marxist and deconstructive perspective and then turn to a consideration of Nagele's use of deconstruction in relation to the work of Jurgen Habermas. My point will be that deconstruction has political implications that exceed even the use Nagele finds for it in critical theory.

Nagele seems to give unreserved approval to Lacan, without ever raising the question of what in the theory does or does not lend itself to progressive political use. In undertaking an articulation between a nonpolitical theory and a political project, it is necessary to distinguish between derivative and immanent radicalism. A radical theory of the human subject or of ideology can be derived from Lacan's work; this effort has been pursued for some time by film theoreticians and by althusserians. But the claim that Lacan himself is a radical is subject to debate.

Despite his maverick status within the profession of psychoanalysis, Lacan has always struck me as being a clever fundamentalist, rather conservative, clearly antimarxist, roundly antifeminist, and theocratic. Marx suggests that the materialist philosophic tradition necessarily leads to a radical political position. Method and mode of action, theory and practice, conjoin in mutually determining ways. Lacan's rejection of historical and social etiologies to account for psychic disorders, his Leo Straussian method of returning to Freud's text, his heideggerian ontology (the famous "future anterior" is nothing more than the existential project in grammatical form), his deconcretization and abstract formalization of psychic life, subtracted from historical society and limited to intersubjectivity, and his idealist hypostatizing of the "Other"—the "locus of the signifier"—as a metahistorical instance all would seem to program a conservative politics. The ex-centricity of the unconscious does radically undermine the sovereignty of the ego, but it also programs submission to forces beyond the human subject's control. This conception of the subject subjected to a Symbolic Order differs from the marxist hypothesis that subjects make history only on the basis of what history provides. Rosa Luxemburg formulated it thus: "The unconscious comes before the conscious. The logic of the historic process comes before the subjective logic of the human beings who participate in the historic process."[3] Political forms that privilege conscious decision, Luxemburg argues, fail to take into account historical situations and processes that may not be consciously controllable. Lacan is not concerned with political organization, but a politics is implied in a theory that prescribes submission to a paternal "Law" and describes the resolution of the oedipal situation as accession to a Symbolic Order, the formal nature of which seems to deny specific historical or social content.

This is why Nagele is wrong to dismiss any link between Lacan and the "new philosophy." The "new philosophers'" brand of antiprogressive, individualist pessimism (transmitted via the work of Pierre Legendre to Christian Jambet and Guy Lardreau, the authors of L'Ange, a less popular, untranslated, but nonetheless essential text of the "new philosophy") nurtures the new philosophic justification of acquiescence to the powers that be and the sense that to try anything is to show that one is duped. They share Lacan's taste for abstract idealist categories, the Master, for example, to name the inextinguishable instance of Power in human life. The abstract generality of the term makes power seem so diffuse as to be unassailable. And this sense of tragic inevitability is conducive to the rejection of all progressive action by both Lacan and the "new philosophers."

The passive role Lacan assigns the subject in relation to the Symbolic Order and the paternal function is similar to the role he himself assumes before his own intellectual father, Freud—one of grateful prostration. He makes the same gesture toward Heidegger: "When I speak of Heidegger, or rather when I translate him, I at least make the effort to leave the speech he proffers us its sovereign significance."[4] The sacred oracle must be translated intact (and the conservative value of preservation plays itself out particularly clearly in methodologies), just as the sacred "truth" of the unconscious must be allowed to speak without interference from the analyst: "For it is clear on the other hand that the analyst's abstention, his refusal to reply, is an element of reality in analysis . . . founded on the principle that all that is real is rational, and on the resulting precept that it is up to the subject to show what he's made of. The fact remains that this abstention is not maintained indefinitely; when the subject's question has taken on the form of true speech, we give it the sanction of our reply, but thereby we have shown that true speech already contains its own reply and that we are simply adding our own lay to its antiphon" (*Ecrits,* 95). The rationality of reality[5] is hardly a principle upon which a revolutionary psychoanalysis would be based. The seemingly innocent gesture of returning to Heidegger's or Freud's words as to a scripture contains an implicit conservative value that what "is" is reasonable and what is natural is good. The same value is at work in analytic practice. To unveil the "truth" of unconscious discourse is sufficient for success, because that truth is both real and rational, and it already contains within it the analysts' reply. The unconscious constitutes a good nature a return to which guarantees "cure." The gesture of prostration before the Master's text is replayed in the stance of the analyst, as well as in the position of every subject in relation to the "rational" and "real" unconscious, which takes on the aspect of an exogenous destiny.

That the unconscious might be framed and contextualized by other instances — historical and social — is rejected by Lacan. The unconscious is the bearer of a truth which is real, rational, natural, and good. That unconscious truth, however, may be characterizable in specifically historical and social terms. The cornerstone of Lacan's theory is the bourgeois family and bourgeois intersexual power relations. The male child (and that is the only subject Lacan treats) discovers that he exists in anguished alienation from himself, subjected to a theocratic Order, and that his only recourse is to submit to the Father's (absent but legal) censoring authority and to the mother's obedient withdrawal. In a gesture typical of bourgeois ideology, Lacan declares this historically produced power situation to be nature:

> And if the somatic *ananke* (necessity) of man's powerlessness for some time after birth to move of his own accord, and *a fortiori* to be self-sufficient, ensures that he will be grounded in a psychology of dependence, how can that *ananke* ignore the fact that this dependence is maintained by a world of language . . . whether in relation to the subject or to politics? . . . The Father may be regarded as the original representative of this authority of the Law. . . . But it is not the Law itself that bars the subject's access to *jouissance* (pleasure) — rather it creates out of an almost natural barrier a barred subject. . . . The true function of the Father, which is fundamentally to unite (and not to set in opposition) a desire and the Law, is even more marked than revealed by this. [*Ecrits,* 309, 311, 321]

Lacan provides a "natural" reason for the "necessity" of submission to the Father in the bourgeois family. One can better understand the "new philosopers'" use of this natural necessity to justify a general politics of capitulation by focusing on Lacan's own linking of political submission in the above quotation to the subject's constitution in a familial system of desire regulated by the Father's Law, that is, the law of castration.

The value of nature underwrites Lacan's suspicion of therapeutic technology. But technology or construction is already at work in the value of "nature" he attributes to the bourgeois family. The familial system, which provides the axes (Father, mother, and so on) for the signifying conventions that constitute the unconscious, points to a wider social and historical textual (in the deconstructive sense) system in which it was produced and from which it cannot be disarticulated. Lacan stops short at the presently existing definition of bourgeois family roles, without seeing them as themselves a form of second nature, produced in history and active in maintaining the power relations necessary for a determinate socioeconomic system. That system requires reversal, simply because the rationality of bourgeois sexual power relations which Lacan finds so appealing is itself a form of pathology. That change will indeed be a technology; it cannot occur through a recourse to a value of nature that pretends to be prior to, hence above, history. The technology of revolution would need to begin by questioning all values of nature which claim that the best future is a return to the past (and nature is always in the past, logically prior to history) and that the subject is tragically inscribed in a "rational reality" (itself usually, as in the case of Lacan's bourgeois family, a hypostatized or frozen historical product that is declared to be "nature"), which is beyond the subject's control and to which he must reconcile himself.

Lacan's theory, then, may be of value to marxists because, by radically questioning conventional psychology's privileging of the ego as a norm, it promotes a reexamination of the subject's placing in ex-centric social and linguistic structures, but it offers little that would enable collective action to transform oppressive social institutions and relations. This lack in part is caused by Lacan's failure to perceive these institutions and relations as oppressive; indeed, the patriarchal family constitutes the norm of his system. In addition, the theory has little to say on the issue of collectivity because, despite all its attention to extraconscious forces, its focus remains the individual subject. Consciousness is subordinate to the unconscious, language, desire, and the social relations in the bourgeois family sublated into a formal structure, but the point of the analysis of these ex-centric determinants is to argue that the subject is subjugated to instances that result less from society and history than from the very nature of Being.

Nagele's essay is a review of Samuel Weber's *Ruckkehr zu Freud.* Weber has written a clear and informed account of Lacan. Ultimately, he tends, I think, to read Lacan through derridean eyes, and, consequently, he gives Lacan more credit than he deserves. Weber does at least raise the problem of the central place accorded the phallus in lacanian theory. But he excuses Lacan's sexism through an unconvincing equation of the "differential" nature of the phallus with deconstruction. Nagele writes: "In the sign of the phallus, which as Weber correctly notes implies a phallo-

centrism which aims 'the deconstruction of every "centricity," insofar as
the phallus represents and misrepresents (*dar- und entstellt*) nothing but
the differential feature of the signifier within the intrasubjective economy'" (*NGC*, 22). For Lacan, the phallus is the signifier which is at stake
in the intersubjective dialectic of desire (which can only be so inasmuch
as woman's desire is defined in rigidly freudian terms as the desire for
the phallus). To that extent, the phallus can be called "differential." But
given that Derrida, who, after all, still holds copyright on deconstruction,
criticizes this very centrality of the phallus as a "transcendental signifier,"
one has reason to doubt the deconstructive status of the term.[6] The
phallus is a centralizing instance in that it erases the difference between
the sexes and subsumes them both under the norm of male sexuality.
Lacan says he chose the term because it is the "privileged signifier" of the
"play of displacement" to which "man" is "doomed in the exercise of his
functions." The one function he offers as an example is the male's insemi-
nation of the woman: "It can be said that this signifier is chosen because it
is the most tangible element in the real of sexual copulation. . . . It might
also be said that, by virtue of its turgidity; it is the image of the vital flow
as it is transmitted in generation" (*Ecrits*, 287). Here, the phallus is no
longer differential; it is quite simply an ideological imposition of the
model of male sexuality on female sexuality and the definition of the
latter in reference to the former. All of human sexuality is reduced to an
erect penis. The vagina, as William Vollmann points out, becomes a
"special case."

In Lacan, the woman's "phallus" is always discussed from a man's
point of view: "the phallus of *his* mother . . . that eminent *manque-à-être*
[lack in being, a quasi-Heideggerian phrase meaning that the attribution
of a phallus (Why not say erect penis, which is what is meant? The word
is itself a ruse of male self-protectiveness.) to the mother reflects an initial
sense of lack or castration anxiety]" (*Ecrits*, 170). The woman's phallus is a
male attribute; her sexuality is defined by what the male possesses: "Such
is the woman concealed behind the veil: it is the absence of the penis that
turns her into the phallus, the object of desire" (*Ecrits*, 322). Woman, then,
is a proletarian within phallocracy; she is defined by her lack of ownership, yet her assistance as the disowned is required to substantiate male
ownership. By defining her condition as one of lack, the phallocrat reassures his own possession. This, for Lacan, is "the equivalence maintained by Freud of the imaginary function of the phallus in both sexes"
(*Ecrits*, 189). The phallus should indeed be associated with the principle
of equivalence, because it represents the equating of two different things
—male and female sexuality—in a single term. Such an equation can be
produced only through idealist abstraction because, concretely and materially, the two are unassimilable. At least, most women would have
difficulty accepting a turgid penis as the "privileged signifier" of their
sexuality.

The continuity of male power demands reproduction, but the female is a moment of discontinuity in the line of direct descent from man to man. From this point of view, phallocentrism appears as a form of centering, not of "decentering," as Nagele suggests. I am reminded of Bertolucci's *Luna*, a recent example of what Deleuze and Felix Guattari might call the "oedipalization" of woman. The wayward son, who has almost been seduced by his mother, is straightened out in the end by a slap from his father, who has been absent, himself a "victim" of his own mother's love. Male bonding is reestablished through punishment, and in consequence, the mother, an opera singer, regains her voice. Potency is restored on all levels. The last scene has the men sitting in the audience smiling complicitly at each other, while the mother, once powerful, now looks debased and vulnerable, singing on stage with her mouth grossly distended, her deep throat exposed, and her arms outstretched — an allegory of feminine sexuality as seen from a male perspective.

I mention the centering power of patriarchal genealogy and of male bonding because there are traces of them in Nagele's essay. It is not insignificant that his opening paradigm is Hamlet and his ghostly father, or that his essay ends with an emotive reference to Walter Benjamin, depicting him as Saturn ("the sower"). And one must keep in mind that the subject of his essay is another male's presentation of another male's "return" to another male (who is the absolute father of the chain) — all on the occasion of a theory that posits the centricity of the penis and the marginality of woman. A consistent sign of male bonding is the in-group joke at the expense (and exclusion) of women. Should we be surprised, then, when Nagele remarks that when "the subject is the phallus," "jokes and amusement lie close at hand." Men at play with themselves — it might stand as a definition of phallocracy.[7]

Dominant classes, whether sexual or economic or both, always monopolize the value of truth to buttress their claim of legitimacy. The phallocracy is no exception. A metaphysical value of truth, as Derrida argues, dominates Lacan's discourse. Nagele/Weber say the unconscious "misspeaks," but in Lacan's text, the unconscious speaks nothing but the "truth" through the "mis-utterances" of the conscious ego: "If from having heard its message in this inverted form, you could not, by returning it to him [the patient], give him the double satisfaction of having recognized it and of making him recognize its truth. . . . By which we can also see that it is with the appearance of language the dimension of truth emerges. . . . We are used to the real. The truth we repress. . . . This Other, which is distinguished as the locus of Speech, imposes itself no less as witness to the Truth" (*Ecrits*, 130, 172, 169, 305). Now, given Lacan's assumption that the unconscious and the Symbolic Order which emerges through its emissions are governed by the Law of the phallic father and the intersubjective dialectic of desire in the bourgeois family, the value of truth is here being appropriated for a highly questionable sociopolitical structure.

which is thereby naturalized, because Lacan never questions its historical derivation. Such formalism is unavoidably conservative because the non-historical concept of truth always evokes a value of nature to which the statements that possess truth value correspond or are adequate. In other words, to characterize a patriarchal Symbolic Order as "truth" is to make the familial power structure seem natural and, by implication, insurmountable. It would be unreasonable to attempt to change it, because to do so would be to assume it is a social and historical construct instead of an essential part of human nature.

Lacan runs the risk of being a semiocentrist. Rosalind Coward and John Ellis describe the model of constitution in this way:

> The emphasis on language provides a route for an elaboration of the subject in the social process, the subject demanded by dialectical materialism. It suggests a notion of the subject produced in relation to social relations by the fixing of its signifying chain to produce certain signifieds. ... Without the signifier, there would be no subject. ... The unconscious is constructed in the same process by which the subject acquires language. ... The claim that the phallus is a signifier the symbolic function of which produces the desiring subject in the place of the structure which already included him or her becomes clearer. ... This conception of desire simultaneously situates the process of the subject across and beyond needs or drives. It is the movement which skips the limits of the pleasure principle and invests in a reality which is already structured as signifying. ... Desire results from the process by which the subject is produced in a system of finished positions, that is, signification. ... The play of combination and substitution in the signifier ... determine the institution of the subject.[8]

The first part of this passage points in the direction of what I think would be the most productive marxist use of Lacan, that is, "the elaboration of the subject in the social process." But that social process extends far beyond the play of signifiers between agents in the bourgeois family. Those signifiers are not endogenous to the family. The father's authority, which results in the penis becoming the privileged signifier, is a symptom of a wider cultural phenomenon of male domination. The placing of familial agents (the submission of the wife, the power of the husband) whose positions are significant in the symbolic order of bourgeois oedipalization[9] and which constitute the signifying matrix that determines the subject are themselves culturally and historically determined.[10] They could not signify without the controls and constraints provided by that broader social text.

I would not deny that semiology plays a determining role in the constitution of subjectivity. To emphasize semiology (and culture and ideology) in the determination of material history is to make a necessary and significant gesture against orthodox marxist economism, which is itself produced by semiological manipulation—the deft rhetorical honing of certain phrases ("the dictatorship of the proletariat"), which then become the ground for a social arrangement that unjustifiably claims another word ("socialism") for its legitimation. But signifiers are effective only in certain controlled contexts. The bourgeois family, for example, offers a perfect situation of control, regulation, and coercion in which signifiers can become effective. The queen, as Austin points out, can christen a boat only on a certain ceremonial occasion. If a communist grabs the bottle of champagne from her hand and names the boat "Generalissimo Stalin," it does not count. The contextual constraints will not permit it. Similarly, in the bourgeois family, only the authority of a father can declare the law of the threat of castration which severs the male child's desire from the mother.

Given all this, one can ask if Lacan, by his semiocentrism, is not guilty of metalepsis—a reversal of cause and effect. Signifiers can act to determine the subject only by virtue of determinants that lie outside the process of signification. The position of the father becomes significant for the male child only because of a cultural and historical context that extends beyond the walls of the bourgeois home. Lacan's "cause"—the locus of signifiers—is itself an effect. Semiology determines social structure, but only inasmuch as it is itself determined by that structure.

Rather than revert to a naturalism in opposing Lacan's semiocentrism, I would argue that language and conceptuality do act upon human life in a determining way. But to describe how they are determining in the world, instead of in a formalized model of the bourgeois family which makes a norm of culturally determined power structures, one has to work with social, political, and economic history. Fortunately, Nagele seems to be pointed in this direction: "I find in conversations with students and colleagues who come from Lacan and Derrida that here a confrontation with Habermas and Critical Theory means a progressive step to the degree that for Lacan, and especially for the Lacan students, the public sphere which Habermas problematized remains either excluded or undeveloped" (*NGC,* 29).

Nagele speaks of structural psychoanalysis and deconstruction in the same breath, but the two discourses are not compatible. I have suggested a deconstructive critique of certain essential(ist) notions in Lacan's theory—semiocentrism, the use of idealist concepts such as the "phallus," the subsumption of the unconscious under the normative instance of "Truth," and the unquestioned acceptance of the oppressive political model of the patriarchy. Nagele seems to equate deconstruction with an emphasis on "the form of presentation," "discourse praxis," and the search for "contradictions" or "aporias" in texts. This scenario reflects the influence of the domestic literary critical methodology of deconstruction. This methodology concentrates on producing technically complicated (though redundant) readings of texts which manifest the brilliance of the critic, while reinforcing the academic and ideological institutions of literary criticism, an institution that, were the political implications of deconstruction pursued rather than ignored, would be fundamentally questioned by deconstruction. Much of the fault for this lies with the institution of literary criticism itself, which measures work done outside the discipline, especially revolutionary intellectual work, only as it is useful for literary criticism.

Nagele deconstructively reads Habermas's *Knowledge and Human Interests* by locating a contradiction in the text. Habermas uses the concept of emancipation in two mutually exclusive ways: "Unexpectedly, the act of emancipation becomes indistinguishable from the act of repression" (*NGC*, 9). Domestic deconstructive literary criticism usually ends with the location of such an aporia or contradiction. Why such a contradiction arose or what political implications it has are questions that are rarely if ever addressed. For example, the "unexpected," and hence seemingly purely formal, confusion of the categories of emancipation and repression in Habermas may not so much be the result of the autonomous operations of rhetoric, as a domestic deconstructor might contend, as of Habermas's reliance on concepts, values, and discursive strategies—reflexive subject, identity, the marginalization of distortion in relation to an ideal speech dominated by a value of juridical truth—which characterize the metaphysical tradition in philosophy. French deconstruction would point out that the binary oppositions at work in Habermas are not peculiar to Habermas. This decentering situates Habermas within a broader historical frame, that of the inability of metaphysics to realize in practice what it claims for itself in theory. For example, Habermas would desire a ground of ideal speech communication between integral subjects, in relation to which distortion by institutions stands as a nonessential event that can be remedied in order to restore ego and group identity. (Clearly, I am collapsing several of Habermas's arguments here; more discriminating readers of Habermas will, I hope, excuse this heuristic device.) A French (as opposed to an American) deconstructor would argue (in a way I will only sketch here) that the fact that distortion is possible implies that it is a necessary part of the structure of ideal speech. The concept of ideal speech is, for Habermas, an ideal limit, a border marking a within of distortion and a transcendental beyond free from distortion. Ideal speech is primary, original, and good, whereas distortion is secondary, derived, and bad. Politics must consist of restoring the original, removing distortion. But if distortion can pertain to ideal speech, then it must already be part of its structure, as a necessary possibility within ideal speech. That necessary possibility puts in question the rigor and purity of the concept of ideal speech.

Even French deconstruction would stop at this point, and one could say that this marks a shortcoming, a failure to pursue the political implications of its insights. For one can argue that the deconstructive critique of

Habermas's concepts also necessarily changes the political agenda pro-grammed by the concept of ideal speech. Politics can no longer be guided by a desire to restore an original if the purity and rigor of the original can be questioned. Of what would a politics taking its cue from the deconstructive rewriting of Habermas's concepts consist then? Let us pursue the analysis of Habermas a bit further before trying to answer that question.

Anyone who has practiced speech communication recently is aware of the error and misunderstanding to which speech is liable. An argument similar to the one made above could be made concerning the necessary inscription of the possibility of error and misunderstanding in the struc-ture of ideal speech—if it is to be possible at all. More important, to be pure, ideal speech must exclude error and misunderstanding. An ideal speech situation is one of mutual understanding, shared meaning, and the undistorted communication of truth. It is at this point that Habermas's goal of emancipation (ideal speech freed from distortion) begins to operate through a procedure that can be called "repressive." A speech in which error and misunderstanding, the possibility of nontruth, are purged entirely could function only by establishing absolute univocal meanings for words and by rigorously determining contexts so that a displacement of truthful meaning by a contextual shift would no longer be possible. Without these constraints, a displacement of the originally intended meaning through misunderstanding or decontextualization will always be possible. The establishing of the conditions necessary for ideal speech (as the ideal goal of the removal of all distortion) requires measures that contradict the emancipatory impulse of Habermas's project. Ab-solutely undistorted truth is possible only on the basis of absolute con-straints.

The problem is Habermas's starting point, that his theory depends on a normative starting point that constitutes an assumed, self-evident axiomatic origin around which the rest of the theory is built. What if Habermas's starting point, the human subject conceived as the conscious, self-identical ego or cogito, is itself possible only as an *effect* of other struc-tures, other networks of events and relations? What if the cogito, putative possessor of conscious meaning that can be communicated intact to other conscious subjects without interference or distortion, can function only on the basis of an unconsciousness that is radically other and a structure of repetition and citation that is not part of the structure of the cogito, but makes its function of communicative intention possible while at the same time, consequently, making impossible a cogito that would be absolutely self-identical in its meaning giving acts of communication? These sup-positions tend to displace the originality of Habermas's origin or starting point. Derrida argues that no conscious meaning intention is original because to operate at all it must "cite" a context, a code, and the entire structure of signification which is, therefore, "prior" to it. Conscious communication is always nonoriginal, derived. A nonconscious, nonsubjective structure of repetition allows a consciously intended sign to signify, as the repetition of a previously given sense of the meaning and function of the sign and as the repeatability of the sign beyond the moment of enunciation in the mind of the addressee or in other contexts. To function at all, the sign must be given over to repetition, which, as Derrida points out, always implies alteration, a difference or becoming other. The same sign, yes, but only inasmuch as it is also different, other. Its identity is inseparable from difference. The identity of meaning is thus internally or constitutively fissured, and the identity and originality of intention are displaced by the necessity of citing or repeating previously given, nonconscious structures.

Habermas's normative starting point in identity would thus be criticized from the point of view of French deconstruction. Deconstruction displaces the metaphysical centrality and primacy of consciousness, meaning, and identity in Habermas's discourse. It would point toward a decentralized theory of communication which would see the traditional centers and grounds of metaphysical theories of communication (consciousness, meaning, intention, and so on) as *effects* of complex structure-movements which they do not regulate as transcendental instances. The result is a theory that attends to the preconscious, presemantic constituents of communication, as well as to the necessarily nonideal, nontranscendental, contextually inscribed, situationally differential nature of all communication. If consciousness defined as self-identity and meaning conceived as an integral substance that can be communicated intact (without necessary alteration or difference) from one homogeneous subject to another are both effects of more complex, problematic, micrological processes, then they cannot serve as transcendental instances or norms that permit a hierarchical binary between good original speech and bad derived distortion to be established. The deconstructive argument suggests that there may be no transcendental instance. If all speech is given over to the possibility of distortion as a necessary part of its structure, if difference and repetition structure identity and permit it to assume the status of origin, then the concepts of integral meaning and intact conscious intention, which characterize undistorted speech, may themselves be distortions.

What are the political implications of all this? Perhaps, that absolute truth, defined as the adequacy of language to conscious intention, without any unconscious remains or side effects, is not a justifiable norm of political theory and practice. If intentionality in politics is governed by the same necessity as intention in communication, the necessity of the possibility of unintended side effects, deviations, and missed targets, then it, too, would be questioned by the deconstructive argument. Not that one cannot "intend" politically, but one always runs the risk of having one's intention go astray. This possibility cannot be reduced out without recourse to an absolutism which, the more it tries to secure meaning and intention against deviation and distortion, leaves itself more open to that possibility. The possibility that intention and effect might not coincide is inherent to political action, as to political communication. The most "secure" (though far from absolute) antidote to this possibility is the "correct line" of party discipline, which assigns undeviating meaning and prescribes right actions. Is there an alternative to the leninist "solution," one that affirms, rather than denies or flees from, the problem of the ever-open possibility of the nonalignment or inadequacy of intention and effect, theory and practice? Deconstruction, as it exists and is practiced, does not provide an answer, but it does permit the preliminary formulation of a politics that would heed the lessons of deconstruction. Such a politics could not, like Habermas, privilege conscious subjectivity, nor could it place all its stakes on assumptions concerning the absoluteness of truth in communication between conscious subjects. If such a politics has a starting point at all (in the sense of an axiomatic, self-evident first premise that aligns all further developments), it would be those historical, social, institutional networks that produce consciousness and truth-as-meaning-intention as determinate effects, networks characterized by their resistance to axiomatic foundationalism. Such a politics would not have a center in the sense of a consciousness in command of its intentions, a singular subject (the urban industrial proletariat) which excludes all other possible subjective centers, or a Party office, the ultimate arbiter of truth and the source of decreed political intentionality.

To return to Habermas, the deconstructive critique of the normativity of ideal speech is implicitly a critique of the positing of the reduction of all extrinsic institutional distortion in the name of (hope of restoring) ideal speech as a political goal. If there are only distortional communication situations, unregulated by any ideal situation and structured by forces that are prelinguistic or preconscious, then the politics that addresses them cannot be univocal or homogeneous, that is, it cannot operate in pursuit of a single goal (restored communication) that mirrors the ground of the theory (the model of an ideal speech situation). All such teleological-archaeological isomorphism would be abandoned in favor of multiple, situationally defined, complexly mediated, differentiated strategies. In other words, the "decentering" of the metaphysical assumption implies a decentering of the political project. This decentering would be applicable not only to Habermas's centering of a metaphysically conceived speech communication, but also to a leninist metaphysics that centers "the idea of the party." And it would leave open the possibility of additional situational centers forming—in and around socialist feminism, for example—that normally would be marginalized by a more centered approach. The multiplicity of centers will inevitably produce contradictions that will seem problematic only to theories founded on principles of identity. Habermas's goal of restoring ego and group identity would no doubt be challenged by socialist feminists who would point out that existing models of social group identity deny validity to those who see their political interest as lying in the breaking of the coercive identity the group imposes on them, by assigning them a place defined by the rationality of the group. The breaking of group identity can be more crucial to emancipation than the restoration of group identity. And it is the metaphysical idealists, those who find such contradiction intolerable because it denies the rational categories of identity, binary opposition, and archaeo-teleology, who will brand it as "irrational" and call for its resolution in the name of rational efficiency and clear knowledge, and at the expense of those such as socialist feminists who have little to gain from the restoration of either categorical or political group identity.

What is at stake, then, is a politics of multiple centers and plural strategies, less geared toward the restoration of a supposedly ideal situation held to be intact and good than to the micrological fine-tuning of questions of institutional power, work and reward distribution, sexual political dynamics, resource allocation, domination, and a broad range of problems whose solutions would be situationally and participationally defined.

Only part of the above "program" finds expression in Derrida's work.[11] The question is not even raised in the dominant mode of deconstructive literary criticism in the United States. That lack can be supplemented by German critical theory, with certain sectors of which deconstruction shares a great deal. And critical theory itself requires the kind of anti-metaphysical differential analysis that deconstruction offers. Both together still lack the concrete anchoring in current struggles which American neomarxist political economy, European and North American socialist feminism, and Italian autonomy theory have to offer. And even then, we are still working only with western Europe and North America. How do we relate even this already discontinuous network to problems of popular power in Mozambique, of the antifeudal peasant movement within the context of a democratically elected communist government in West Bengal, and of the liberation struggle in El Salvador? Epicenters without a *primum mobile*—the fields of struggle are complexly fissured and heterogeneous. No one theory or system accounts for all of them adequately, in a way that subsumes situational difference—not critical theory, not leninism, not deconstruction—just as there is no such thing as a "phallus" or an "ideal speech situation." Deconstruction comes closest to theorizing (and discursively practicing) this decentered plurality, but the nature of the object described defuses any potential centering privilege this theoretical insight might bestow.

✣ 6 ✣

The Metaphysics of Everyday Life

The terrain of political, economic, social, and cultural struggles is plural; it cannot be subsumed by one school or system. Deconstruction is privileged (but immediately undermined) to the extent that it theorizes this inconclusivity and indeterminacy —what it calls undecidability, one implication of which is that any political theory of radical transformation must include the assumption that further work, on more than one plane, will always be needed, work which exceeds the axioms of the theory. Within the field of multiple struggles on separate but related fronts, one can at least articulate different strategies from diverse domains. Here, for example, I will articulate deconstruction with political criticism and the critique of ideology. Such an articulation is helpful because very often political criticism deals tactically with capitalist ideology and social policy without disturbing their conceptual infrastructure. And in large part, that infrastructure is the target of deconstruction.

The deconstruction of metaphysics can be integrated with the critique of ideology because metaphysics is the infrastructure of ideology, and until that infrastructure is deracinated, ideology will reappear, against the best intentions of revolutionary activists, with the regularity of weeds to a garden. One caution deconstruction offers is that deracination can never be completed, either *at one go* or *once and for all.* The work involved is constant and repetitive, like, as Gayatri Spivak puts it, keeping a house clean.

Metaphysics, Derrida shows, is not a historically periodizable school of thought; it is, rather, a permanent function of a kind of thinking which overlooks (that is, theorizes away) its own historicity, differentiality, and materiality (its anchoring in language, among other things): "The reproduction of contemporary capitalist society is tied not simply to specific categories, but to the very way we categorize."[1] The metaphysical belief that the mind is a domain of pure thought removed from the historical

117

world it observes and categorizes survives in the dominant paradigms of the bourgeois social sciences. Closely related is the belief that the world of practice can be understood using coherent, complete theoretical systems that can be computed apart from the world of practice (Parson's sociology). Metaphysical assumptions become ideologically effective when they are institutionalized or woven into the habitus of a society. For example, metaphysical categorical distinctions between private and public, interior and exterior, would be used to justify the division of labor between women in the household and men in the public domain. Consequently, women's work is rarely, if ever, counted in Gross National Product. The omission has ideological, political, and economic consequences: "Because of the vital elements of economic life that national accounts often leave out, great skepticism should be attached to the use of GNP as a measure of well-being."[2]

Ideology is the political use of metaphysics in the domain of practice. Ideology always legitimates a division of labor; metaphysics supplies the categories and modes of categorization that define and legitimate the form of division. That division necessarily gives rise to fissures, contradictions, and tensions, because it relies on an unequally distributed differential of power and force. Metaphysical thinking is important to ideology and to its function of legitimating dominance and guaranteeing hegemony because metaphysical thinking homogenizes contradiction, dissonance, and heterogeneity. One could say that what Derrida criticizes in, for example, the metaphysical hierarchy of speech over writing is the philosophical equivalent of the division of labor between mental and manual. His discussion of metaphysics in terms of differentials of *force* (writing is not simply outside speech; it is a historical materiality repressed and expelled by a force attached to an idealistically conceived speech) is helpful to marxist analyses of ideology, which often assume that ideology has to do with an autonomous cultural arena of consciousness and ideas. Ideology is always inscribed in material structures of force. So-called "false consciousness" is always bound up with powers that threaten hunger, privation, and death, and it results from the forceful exclusion of certain messages from the public domain.

My point, then, will be that metaphysics is not simply a question of knowledge confined to the philosophy classroom. Metaphysics is in the world, as ideology, in those unconscious presuppositions and categorical foundations of social practice.

Gerard Chaliand, not a deconstructionist, writes: "The term *Third World* envelops in a semblance of unity what is in reality a multiplicity of worlds."[3] Such semblances of conceptual unity would be the target of a deconstructive ideology critique. They permit and simultaneously prevent thought. By binding thought to linguistic and logical categories of unity and identity, they can serve an ideological power function. As Falstaff put it: "What is honor? A word." Perhaps more important, concepts and doctrines based on values of homogeneity or unity can also orient action: "Early hegemonic designs are visible as far back as 1823, when the Monroe Doctrine, with its neo-colonization and non-intervention clauses, proscribed the Old World from meddling in the affairs of the New. The growth of North American power is reflected in the transformation of the Doctrine from rhetoric to reality."[4] Economic power requires political force, which in turn requires legitimation by a conceptual-rhetorical apparatus that can also serve an instrumental or performative function. That is, a doctrine can justify as well as promote imperialism.

The word "people" works to occlude power relations in the ideology of practical politics. A deconstructive reading of the logic of political representation would argue that, under bourgeois democracy, what apparently has the structure of metaphor—the substitution of a sign or representative for another whole entity, the "people"—actually conceals a metonymy. The relationship is in fact part for whole. One class—the technocratic, corporate elite—comes to stand in for the whole country or "people." The illusion must be maintained that all the "people" thereby gain representation. A deconstructionist might describe such representation as being the logic of the sign. The "people" supposedly preexist representation, as meaning supposedly preexists and is expressed by the sign. If political representation is, like the sign, a structure of supplementarity, then one could say that the "people" is not a homogeneous entity that exists prior to representation. Rather, it is constituted retroactively as something homogeneous by the very representation it seemingly delegates and for which it seems to function as an origin. The "people" is a necessary fiction of origin and of homogeneity which allows the part-for-whole structure of political representation to take on the appearance of a system whereby the "whole" populace is represented.

The deconstructive critique of the hierarchical opposition of inside and outside, by which the supposedly pure inside is seen as always already contaminated by its so-called outside, provides a rigorous instrument for undoing such ideological oppositions as that between the private and the public sectors in the economy. The private sector claims pure autonomy; any incursion upon its right by the purely external public sector therefore appears as a violation. But from a deconstructive point of view, the violation has always already begun—in both directions. Once one considers that the private sector depends on a passive and exploitable public sector for its life, then the claim to sovereign autonomy on the part of the private sector becomes questionable. But the undeconstructed, nondialectical opposition between public and private is used to legitimate this exploitation.

Nevertheless, if it is deconstructable, the opposition can exist only as the occlusion of a differential relation. The concept of the private sector is eminently defensible because all human subjects, all private parties, can identify with it. It represents the self-proximity of self. It is a proto-type of that normative ground of self-certain, self-evident, self-present consciousness which, as a first principle, allows concepts connoting distance, alterity, strangeness, and loss of self and of property to take on the aspect of subordination or secondariness, if not outright danger and moral evil. To be "public" is to be outside oneself, other, estranged from the homeland of property and self-possession. The mediacy the public sector represents is reduced to a subordinate position and declared to be an absolute outside which in no way infringes upon the private sector except as an accident or a crisis.

An example of the practical (as opposed to logical) deconstructability of the private/public opposition is offered in the form of money. The object of conservative, free enterprise protectionism toward the private sector is the preservation of the right to make profit or money unhindered by government or public interference. But because money can exist only by being printed, sanctioned, and guaranteed by governments, public interference is constitutive of the process of private accumulation. Public and private form a nonhierarchizable, supplementary differential, not a clear and rigorous opposition.

I suggested above that the privileging of the private sector relates to the priority accorded the conscious subject in our culture and philosophy. The split between subject and object and the privileging of the first underlies the axiological and ethical priority given theory over practice, mental or managerial over manual labor, and ownership over work. The detached, neutral stance of the theoretical, disinterested, knowing subject, balancing all the equations in a proper *ratio*, the owner of his thoughts and the master of his property, is valued by liberal society over the practical assumption of any one-sided position and over the dependence on others (nonownership) which is wage work. It goes without saying that this liberal theoreticism itself represents a practical, political position; abstracted theoretical mastery is the philosophic analog of ownership without work.

Deconstruction subverts the metaphysical desire to detach theory from its practical side—language, society, history. The philosophical concept of theory as a disinterested, neutral, rational activity, elevated above empiricity and history, is reflected in everyday life. As in "high" philosophy, this privilege is always linked to political and ethical value judgments, which place some standard of presence or property at the upper pole of the hierarchy and some "other" at the lower pole. These judgments are assumed to be both neutral and natural. They are sustained by a belief that the privileged standard is exempt from the evil it subordinates in its opposite, which lies outside it as a pure outside. The analog of this attitude in idealist philosophy is the belief that concepts and ideas are uncontaminated by spacing, representation, alterity, inscription, and the like, the practical side which idealist metaphysics overlooks (as *theoria or vision*).

Terrorism, feminism, and liberalism are examples. Terrorism can be judged to be outside the law only if the law is itself deemed innocent and untouched by violence. A short stay in Watts would teach the good Americans, who, in all moral righteousness, condemn the Red Brigades, to what extent their own detached, economically secure position of critical judgment is the product of a systematic terrorism, which differs from anticapitalist, urban guerilla warfare only in that it is sanctioned by law. The recognition that one's own theoretical position is contaminated by the practice one condemns removes the grounds of normative judgment.

For feminism, a similar reversal and displacement of a purely theoretical position is conceivable. Men, Mark Kann points out, tend to detach themselves from woman's violence and "hysteria," especially when it is directed against male rationality and domination. Men know (that is, can theorize, en*vision*, over*look*, and over*see*) what feminine "hysteria" is about. They believe it is an untheorized practice, an unconscious rage that has not been elevated to theoretical consciousness and thereby controlled. Deconstruction would fix on this exclusion of "hysteria" from the male position. Might not the self-monumentalizing paralysis of rational rigor (mortis) itself be an effect of what it excludes as feminine "hysteria"? In other words, the hierarchy of male reason and female unreason could be reversed. Feminine "hysteria," rather than male coercive self-control, then becomes the sign of moral and philosophical goodness. The deconstructive displacement of this hierarchy would entail allowing neither side to have a monopoly on either of the poles. The poles of expressive violence and implosive control would be seen to pass into each other. Male theoretical detachment in the face of feminine "hysteria" is, like all theory that succeeds always in balancing all the equations, simply a less evident form of hysteria and violence. And "female" hysteria might be a "rational," therapeutic, and potentially revolutionary form of violence.

At first glance, the system of liberalism seems inclusive, rather than exclusive. That is, it claims that all political positions are equally valid. The liberal program is in every respect positive; it seems to exclude no one. All negativity is itself negated and transformed into an example of liberal openness. That positive inclusivity has all the appearance of being seamless. No contradiction, no fissure of any kind, disturbs the transcendentality of the system. And it is transcendental because it rises above the specific, antagonistic nature of positional difference and reconciles all differences through the principle of equal exchange. All political positions are equal and therefore equally exchangeable.

Liberalism seems to attain an absolute degree of inclusion. But by that very token, according to the deconstructive argument, it is absolutely exclusive. There is one position which liberalism cannot include, and that position denies the validity of liberal inclusion. It cannot ultimately grant validity to the position that holds that the granting of validity to all political positions is itself invalid. Liberalism's transcendence of difference remains theoretical; it cannot allow any political position to be realized practically that is not itself liberal, in other words, that does not rest upon the celebration of the plurality of positions. It is here that the coercive core of liberal generosity makes itself felt. Liberalism seems to mandate nothing, but in fact it does nothing but mandate itself: one *must* be universally inclusive and accord equal privilege to all political positions. This seemingly general inclusion is at the same time a universal exclusion, excluding any specific position that is defined through a differential, antagonistic relation of force with other positions, because such a position cannot attain to the transcendental generality and distinterested inclusivity of liberalism.

The liberal position seems transcendental because it rises above specificity, antagonism, the differential of force, and self-definition through the negative relation to an other. Liberalism has no outside, because it is itself outside that play, that conflictual scene. But the argument can be made (and this is the point of a deconstructive analysis) that the apparently transcendental position is itself irredeemably caught up in the play of differentially related positions. It cannot stand outside, because there is no outside to those differential interrelations. Liberalism is merely one member of the series, not the paradigmatic endpoint of general transcendental inclusion into which all particular positions are absorbed. In the very absoluteness and generality of its inclusion, liberalism must exclude, and, by that token, immediately become what it seeks to avoid being—merely particular, relative, and part of a series. At the same time that it tolerates all political positions, it finds each political position intolerable. If the transcendental umbrella is itself constituted by the exclusion of everything it supposedly includes, there can be no transcendental position above thé fray. Liberalism is not the benign center mediating between extremes; it is itself extreme. Its paradigmatic trancendentality is defised; its assumptions self-deconstruct.

Here, deconstruction consists of showing how an apparently transcendental position is specific, regional, a member of a series of differential relations which it aspires to regulate from outside. There is no outside, no absolute inclusion which is not the exclusion absolutely of everything it contains. This is a necessary component of the logic of liberalism, not a sociology of repressive tolerance. Liberalism comes apart on its own terms, not only in terms of its repressive effects on radical positions which it supposedly tolerates.

In part, then, the social world is supported by institutionalized concepts and categories, such as the public-private sphere distinction, whose coherence cannot withstand critical analysis, but which play a constitutive role in social construction. The public-private distinction structures legal institutions (property, for example), and it underwrites the philosophy of private enterprise protectionism which orients legislative institutions in present-day America. In a less self-evident way than in theocratic countries, where behavior is structured by religious principles, such categories and concepts underwrite our institutional and behavioral world.

Because of their structuring role, the categories and concepts that prevail in a culture have a significance that exceeds mere questions of knowledge. Or rather, the categories by which one knows the world are merely a subset of the transsubjective institutional conceptual system that underwrites the construction of the social world according to logocentric or metaphysical principles. Deconstruction can be of political use to marxists because it provides a refined philosophic instrument for criticizing this social rationale.

The metaphysical detachment of the conscious subject or cogito from the social and material-historical world has clear ideological implications. It goes hand in hand with a separation of theory from practice and a division between mental and manual labor. Paul Hirst argues for an example of this practical effectiveness of metaphysics when he describes the way the concept of the human subject in seventeenth- and eighteenth-century philosophy acted as a support for "a proprietal theory of right":

> In the natural rights doctrines of this period rights are commonly conceived as attributes of the subject by means of the model of possessions, as appropriate to the subject by reason of a claim or right it can advance. . . . The subject is a locus prior to and appropriative of its attributes. This concept of subject as an *epistemological-ontological point* is given its classic formulation by Descartes in the *Discourse on Method*. The subject is the prior (already presupposed) point of inspection-possession, identifying (and therefore annexing) experiences and attributes as its own. Possession stems from *identification* ("I think therefore I am"): the subject is *possessor of itself*, capable of constituting itself in the moment of identifying thoughts as its *own* (proper-proprietal to it). . . . This concept of subject also makes possible a proprietal theory of right. . . . Rights like experiences can be considered as attributes of the subject-point.[5]

Hirst argues for a version of deconstructive undecidability when he points out that rights are added on as attributes to an already existing subject: "The attributes of the subject are constituted by its (proprietal) identification, but the subject which identifies and claims is prior and *without properties*" (*OLI*, 162). There is nothing in the relation between the subject and its attributes or properties to explain why rights "rather than some other attribute" should be annexed to the subject: "Possession merely establishes a relation between right and the subject. The primacy of the subject, its identification, guarantees this relation but not what is involved in the relation. The ontology of the self-possessive subject ensures the *emptiness* of the point (expelling theories of a given nature in which the subject cannot stand in opposition to its attributes because they constitute it). It also ensures the inexplicability of the attributes it annexes except in terms of its own recognition" (*OLI*, 162-63). Within the axioms of the system of natural rights, there is no law of consistency which would exclude nonrights from being legitimate attributes or properties of the subject. The system, therefore, can be justifiably extended by an element that contradicts the axioms of natural rights and renders the consistency of the system unprovable. "Nonright" is an undecidable, both inside and outside the system at once: "The legal subject . . . cannot be explained prior to and independent of the process of legal definition. To do so is to identify rights and non-rights, to obliterate the specificity of *legal* effects. . . . This priority of the subject . . . supposes the identity-reducibility of legally defined subjects to some category of subject prior to and outside of legal definition. Laws as a specific object of analysis disappear" (*OLI*, 163).

Deconstruction can thus further a critique of the conceptual infra-structure of an ideology such as that of natural rights. A metaphysical concept of the subject, akin to that which Hirst deals with, can also be found in more recent domains of policy and practice. I shall consider two examples—planning and the political theory of the practice of foreign policy.

My example from planning is Andreas Faludi's *Planning Theory*. Faludi's ideal "planning society" is modeled on a metaphysical concept of the decision-making sovereign subject. That conception of a subject, identical with itself and exempt from society, history, and institutionality, is, of course, the centerpiece of metaphysics. Faludi's theory exemplifies the way in which the capitalist mode of production calls forth liberalism, a doctrine of subjective sovereignty and of individual free choice, as a corresponding mode of legitimation. What is interesting about Faludi is the way the ideology provides a model for the further planned development of capitalism. The doctrine of the individual was a necessary adjunct of "free" enterprise. In Faludi, it supplies the philosophic basis for a future "planning society" modeled on the decision-making power of the self-conscious subject. This society will be, according to Faludi's paradigm, more like a "man" who is "master of himself," who makes rational decisions and possesses the willpower to implement them, who is self-determining, who copes with tension by mastering the environment that causes it, who guides his own growth self-consciously—this Faludi calls "meta-planning."[6] He could just as easily have called it "metaphysical planning."

In real historical terms, the growing individual, master of his environment and of himself, who is the model for Faludi's planning society, translates into a point of authority (an agency), a hierarchized command structure, and a police force. The metaphysical concept of subjective consciousness assumes that theory is applied to practical situations, because consciousness is separate from and above the world. It takes for granted that the world is to be "mastered" by rational consciousness through the instrumentality of "willpower." An integral part of such planning agencies will be to assume authority over people and the right to administer them in the name of the ultimate goal of rational integrity and growth: "In the last analysis, therefore, *implementing* programs always involves, for better or for worse, exercising control over people. . . . This may involve physical force" (*PT,* 281-82). Under capitalism, what Faludi calls "balanced planning" for "rational human growth" will of course benefit only one class. Faludi momentarily lets drop the guise of universal rationality and reveals his class interests when he remarks: "*We* rely on the law for *our* protection. . . . This not only reduces the expenditure of force, but makes life tolerable for the majority who can pursue their interests without relying on physical strength for their protection" (*PT,* 136).

Faludi's theory can be said to autodeconstruct. Its practice puts its theoretical presuppositions in question. Planning based on the model of a rational consciousness in full mastery of itself should be able to implement its program and attain its goal without contradiction or impediment, if indeed it is based on a universal rationality and not simply on the ideological rationale of class force. The fact that it does enter into conflict and contradiction, because the social world in which it operates is heterogenous and unbalanced, puts the initial presupposition or "center" of the theory in question. It would seem to indicate that the supposedly autonomous and sovereign consciousness of the subject is already caught up in a social system that produces it and without which its "rationality" could make no sense. All subjects are social, and no single subject can be a model for an ideal planning agency.

The "center" of Faludi's theory—the individual subject—is not only undermined by the practice that follows from the theory, but also by Faludi's own practical working out of the theory. He removes his own normative ground when he argues that the "shortcoming" of the present planning arrangement is that plans are "filtered through the mind of one person, namely the chief planning officer. This is problematic because planning decisions almost invariably advance some causes to the neglect of others. . . . It is inevitable that, as communications are filtered through the mind of the chief officer, these decisions are also influenced by his personal outlook" (*PT,* 246-47). Faludi fails to connect this problem to the cornerstone of his theory—the mind of one person. He inadvertently describes the bankruptcy of his model. Nor does he apply his critique of the single mind filter to himself. A "general theory" of planning will also be subject to the influence of a "personal outlook." Faludi's theory reflects the "personal" (class) outlook of right-wing liberalism, a benign and friendly fascism that is clever enough to deck out authoritarianism and capitalism class domination in the garb of "pluralism" and "rationality."

The "central" symptom of Faludi's metaphysics is the confusion of knowledge and power, as rationalism and authority. If to know were to master, then the scientist who discovers the causes of natural death would master death. At best, science can learn to work with heteronomous substances and forces. The idealist dreams of bringing that heteronomy under the sovereignty of the imperial intellect. This desire springs from the placing of consciousness at the "center" of things. Even Faludi's example of driving a car (as the self-determining mastery of an environment) is not an example of conscious mastery, but of adaptation, mostly unconscious, and of training. It is a dependent, not an independent operation.

Full conscious mastery, which is the condition and goal of Faludi's planning, is impossible. Faludi's approach necessarily works by homogenization, that is, administration and management, that reduces social discontinuity, class antagonism, and political rupture to an accidental, illogical feature of a fundamentally continuous, logical, and self-identical system. According to this rationale, class antagonism merely represents an occasional dysfunction in an equilibrated system, rather than the principle without which the system could not exist. This ideology constitutes the conceptual infrastructure of Faludi's planning theory.

In *The Myth of Marginality,* Janice Perlman examines an ideological thinking similar to Faludi's which serves to justify repression of the impoverished "marginal" population of Rio de Janeiro. Displaced rural poor, the "marginals" come to live in squatter camps on the edges of the urban areas and to seek work. A fully developed social theory has arisen on the occasion of their existence. "Marginality" theory brands the squatters as a "blight" or parasite on civil society; it characterizes them as deviant, criminal, perverse, outside the circle of civilization; it sees them as part of a "culture of poverty" which makes poverty inevitable because the squatters lack the "normal" bourgeois virtues of ambition, enterprise, and hard work which would permit them to raise themselves out of poverty; and it poses them as a threat, a source of radicalism against the bourgeoisie.

The social theory of marginality follows the pattern Derrida attributes to metaphysics—the setting up of norms which are given out to be self-evident (because derived from such unquestionable truths as consciousness, presence, nature, life, and ownership) and the marginalization of anything that puts the norm in question. The reversibility of the norm/

margin opposition demonstrates the instability of the metaphysical system and its ultimate reliance for enforcement not on a basis of "natural" truth, but on social, political, and economic power. Perlman writes: "If the criteria for normalcy were prevalence-determined rather than class-determined, then playing the numbers would be called mainstream, while attending the opera would be marginal. Clearly this is not the case."[7]

Metaphysically informed social theories, in the hands of ruling classes, become social policy. Perlman documents the way the myth of marginality provides the ideological framework that directs and justifies certain political practices. In the 1950s, the theory that the squatters constituted a blight on "normal" society led to a policy of eradicating the settlements. And the theory that the squatters were culturally impoverished justifies the necessity of "external management."

The description of the squatters as "marginal" is accompanied by a projection of a model of society as an integrated whole, in harmonious equilibrium with itself. Referring to Manuel Castells, who relies on Lacan, Perlman calls this model "specular." It is society's ideal image of itself, an image reinforced by the negative image of the marginals who are excluded from it. By making poverty the fault of the marginals, bourgeois society reassures its own values. The model of society as a whole and of the marginals as an outside feeds into a policy of integration. Government policy now calls for an elimination of the squatter settlements and an incorporation of the people into society.

Derrida remarks that the very possibility of a blight lighting upon a supposedly harmonious, self-identical system means that already something is askew in the system. The metaphysical way of thinking (by binary oppositions, norms and margins, insides and outsides, instead of differences and relations) preserves the purity of the social system by making a decisive opposition between the good inside and the bad outside, the good, self-sufficient Brazilian bourgeoisie and the bad, parasitic marginals who come from outside. Here, the deconstruction would consist of showing how the marginals are in fact internal to the bourgeois system, how the purity of society is already contaminated by a blight it would prefer, for its own protection, to consider as external. Perlman makes a kindred argument about the social policy based on the myth of marginality. The squatters are not marginal to a closed social system, she says. They are bound up in it in an asymmetrical way. In deconstructive terms, what is described as "outside" can be shown to be "inside." The squatters are undecidable in relation to the axiomatic system of bourgeois society; the undecidability and the contradiction it poses for the system are repressed. The squatters are *marginalized,* that is, simultaneously excluded and included, by a ruling class whose economic interests are served by the availability of a reserve labor force which keeps wages of workers within the system down and profits up. They are a functional, rather than a dysfunctional, aspect of capitalist accumulation in Brazil.

My next example is the theory of foreign policy. Here, once again, one encounters the presupposition that the conscious mind is detached from the world, that the subject transcends objectivity. And once again, that initial metaphysical assumption contributes to policies of social control which seek to apply "rational" models of homogeneity and equilibrium to the world, often with force.

A very obvious example is Henry Kissinger. In *American Foreign Policy*, he writes: "The west is deeply committed to the notion that the real world is external to the observer, that knowledge consists of recording and classifying data."[8] This metaphysical hypothesis, which separates subject and object, leads predictably to the following idealist conclusion. The differences between East and West are not the result of historically produced differences in socioeconomic and cultural systems, but, according to Kissinger, of different mind-sets: "The instability of the current world order may thus have at its core a philosophical schism which makes the issues producing most political debates seem tangential" (*AFP*, 49). To say that political issues are tangential is to call them secondary, derivative, and accidental in relation to the essential question of mind-set. If the mind is the measure, then it is of course only logical to make rationality the norm. In a profoundly racist way, the norm attaches to the Western mind. "Empirical reality," Kissinger writes, "has a much different significance for many of the new countries than for the west because in a certain sense they never went through the process of discovering it" (*AFP*, 49). It is therefore the Western statesman, who thinks of empirical reality as separate from his mind, who "manipulates reality" in order to attain "equilibrium," the principle of rational balance in the world: "We must construct an international order before a crisis imposes it as a necessity" (*AFP*, 49).

Stanley Hoffmann evinces symptoms similar to Kissinger's—a detachment of the observer from the world, a consequent privileging of theoretical consciousness, and a policy program that calls for the implementation of ideal, rationalist stability models in the world. Hoffmann, in an article fittingly subtitled "The Perils of Incoherence,"[9] laments the "fragmentation" in foreign policy, the lack of "discipline" on the floor of Congress, the absence of a "patriotic *rationale* for yielding leadership to the Executive," and the disturbing "desire of the public to have a greater say in policy formation, and its unwillingness to give carte blanche to the President." Although the relationship is not causal, there is a marked connection between the elevation of the conscious observer above the world, who theoretically orders the world, and the privilege given the authoritative Executive, who through his policies putatively seeks to impose the model of a logic of noncontradiction and rational balance upon the world. That initial idealist detachment of consciousness also implies a cult of expert knowledge which permits professional technocrats to claim that the operations of government are beyond the ken of the public.

Hoffmann demonstrates how metaphysical values of propriety and selfsameness enter the discourse of foreign policy as the declared necessity for "coherence" and "consistency": "To an American observer trying to evaluate American foreign policy with some detachment, the single most striking feature of America's conduct in the world in 1978 was fragmentation. . . . There is an attainable degree of coherence which requires, not the elimination of contradictions, but at least their management" (VH, 463). The separation of "observer" from practical world allows Hoffmann to fail to acknowledge his role as an interested participant and to assume for his particular bias the value of universal, disinterested ("with some detachment") rationality. All the rest, any other nondetached or irrationally committed option, thus becomes "ideological" by comparison.

Two other ideas in the above passage should be noted: first, that the practice most fitting to a world which is addressed from a detached, universalist position is "management"; second, that fragmentation and contradiction are undesirable and should be submitted to order and coherence.

Elsewhere, Hoffmann describes theory as a "principle of order."[10] A "reasonably coherent body of theory" should lead to "a coherent understanding of the data." Although, given his commitment to the separation of theory and practice, Hoffmann would like to maintain the distinction between scholarship and policy formulation, there seems to be a continuity between the necessity of coherence in foreign policy practice and the coherence afforded by theory in general. One could say that the call for coherence in practice is predicated by the norm of coherence in theory. A man committed to the priority of the theoretical ordering of data could not be committed to anything other than the goal of order, coherence, and consistency in the execution of foreign policy. One could also say that the institution of the nation state imposes a bias toward theory — the principle of order — and toward management — coherent ordering of the world as of data — on foreign policy. Foreign policy operates at the edge of the integrated state and relates it to its outside. Foreign policy is therefore defined by the spatial integrity and the conceptual-institutional self-identity of the state. It must privilege integration and coherence over contradiction and inconsistency in the name of the state.

Privileging theory implies, of course, privileging the rational theorizer, the cogito. This initial premise — the cogito or "I think" — gives a centralizing direction to the operations of foreign policy theory which accords with the subjective intentionality a nation state assumes discursively for itself. Hoffmann speaks of the "theoretical center that commands" "the 'policy' periphery" (CT, 11). Along with centrality and command, two other earmarks of the privileging of theory are hierarchy and essentiality. A foreign policy based on the integrity of the state will rank the world according to what serves the essential interests of that integrity: "One of the functions of theory is to distinguish between the essential and the accidental factors in world affairs" (CT, 12). The point of reference for defining essentiality is the central cogito, the subjective "I" which the state assumes for itself—"The United States today agreed to. . . ." What is essential serves its interests; what is accidental does not. The theoretical operation of ordering the world according to essence and accident thus rests on an initial theoretical assumption, or, one could say, on the assumption of theory or of the rational theorizer—the cogito—as the mode of the state. And the state could have no other mode. To come into being, the state must take a proper name for "itself," and with that proper name, a subjective position in relation to the rest of the world; the political is personal. That subjective position is another version of the separation and detachment of observer from world that I have already described. That assumption of a subjective position, that separation and detachment of an "I," even a state "I," from the world, leads to a theoretical outlook that conceives the world as something to be ordered according to the metaphysics of self-identity, that is, the logic of the subject. If Hoffmann's theory is any indication, that ordering will be hierarchical, centralist, essentialist, and command-oriented.

Hoffmann's fear of incoherence goes hand in hand with a call for a strong executive, less popular interference with government, and "a strategic rationale that brings the fragments together."[11] The central cogito, the rational theorizer who legislates the universal truth of the world, translates into the Executive who, elevated above the particularistic mass, carries out the universal rationality of the state in a coherent fashion. Theory and practice do, after all, mesh, and they mesh very neatly indeed if they are initially separated in opposition. The advocacy of theoretical "coherence" is continuous with an integrative political practice that operates teleologically, that is, in pursuit of formal goals of coherence which are more preservative—in that they are defined by the norm of the theoretical or formal integrity of the state which must be preserved and expanded—than progressive—in that they do not consider the material transformations necessary for an expansion of the satisfaction of material needs: "The Administration must explain clearly and steadily to the American people and Congress how the pieces fit, what kind of a world we seek, and the means we want to use to get there" (VH, 491). Theory as a principle of order—"clearly and steadily," "how the pieces fit"—prescribes a practice of teleological ordering—"what kind of world we seek." Theoretical model builders have a predictable tendency (because it is the political practice implicit in the privilege of logocentric theory) to think of the world as something to be modeled according to one's own interests.

The best (or worst) example of this tendency at work in the discourse (and practice) of foreign policy is Zbigniev Brzezinski. When Brzezinski speaks of America's role in "shaping a rapidly changing world in ways congenial to our interests," I detect an unarticulated itinerary of the sort I have just described. The world is to be ordered, managed, and shaped according to an ideal model from a detached subjective position. The hubris of the state-subject and of the theory-making cogito come together in the dream of shaping the world according to a goal (the American model) which is at the same time the subjective starting point of the enterprise (America). "America," Brzezinski says, in a somewhat sinister vein, "is a microcosm of the world," and the world is united by a "common future." The ultimate goal — the subsumption of the world under a central instance, America — is already contained in the starting point. For Brzezinski, America proves that "people can cooperate on behalf of central ideas"[12] — not material needs, or principles of distributive justice, or a decentralized and equal distribution of wealth and resources, but central *ideas*. Foreign policy thus executes a familiar theme of Western metaphysics — the centrality of the logos and the circularity of arche or beginning and telos or goal, all forming a coherent circle of ideal self-identity which is the model for the rationality of central meaning in absolute knowledge we take for granted and which informs even such seemingly aphilosophical institutions as the political state.

❧ 7 ❧

Reason
and Counterrevolution

The question of logocentric or meta-physical rationalism and its consequences invites speculation about the nature of a more radical or social form of reason. Deconstruction points in such a direction, in that it questions the bases and operations of such rationalism. This reconstruction of reason necessarily entails a reconstruction of the institutions of language and of education. Reason is inseparable from the institutions in which it is preserved and passed on, and in the practice of which it has its being. In this chapter, I will describe a current problem in American university education with a view to a possible deconstructive reconstruction of logocentric rationalism.

Two opposed groups—radical teachers and business technocrats—hold the same view of the university, but for different reasons. Radicals argue that the university services capitalism by providing it with trained manpower, technology, and new knowledge. Business technocrats essentially agree, but whereas the radicals deplore this situation, business people recognize its importance, and they do all they can to foster it.

In the years to come, the two groups will clash over the issue of whether or not the classroom should have walls, that is, be immune to manipulation by business, as well as maintain a liberal neutrality toward external politics. Given that these days, the most crucial politics on the agenda of radical teachers are the politics of business, business people are likely to be tempted to seek more of a say than they already have in university affairs, partly as a defense against irrefutable attacks by radical academics on their hegemony, partly as a guard against the "false" education of their trained manpower. The fiscal crisis of the university and the necessity of seeking external funding (one million from South Korea, as the USC dean admitted my first day on the job; later in the year the controversial source would be Saudi Arabia) will enable this breaking down of the walls of the classroom from without.

Radical teachers are equally unconvinced by the liberal ideology of academic neutrality. They break down the walls of the classroom from within, opening intellectual discussion out upon a public sphere of political and economic antagonism. The traditional academic enterprise of stockpiling and communicating knowledge is replaced by a politicized concern for social issues, the most pressing of which is the power of capitalist business in structuring and controlling the economic, political, and cultural life of the United States and of much of the world.

The direct presence of business (and of business-related government enterprises such as defense and research and development) in the university has been amply documented.[1] When a major private university, upon whose board sit representatives of several major pharmaceutical firms, has some of its sizable investments in those same companies, and when one of those companies, the major manufacturer of valium, funds a new department of therapy at the university in which the only method promoted is valium treatment, then one has reason to suspect that such phrases as "academic neutrality" and "conflict of interest" have lost all critical significance. Business schools offer a more striking example of an institutionalized service performed by universities for capital. To put the matter deconstructively, the walls of the business school classroom are not so much lines of strict demarcation between a pure outside and a self-sufficient and autarchic inside as they are margins where inside and outside become interchangeable. Each is structurally dependent on the other. Business could not survive without business schools that teach not only technical knowledge, but also the "self-evident," "natural," and "good" character of capitalism. And business schools depend on business for endowments and for indirect, retroactive financing in the form of guaranteed jobs for their graduates.

Business is aware that its profitable relationship to the universities could be disturbed by the presence of radical teachers on campuses. In *The Crisis of Democracy,* a Trilateral Commission book, Samuel Huntington has expressed concern over an excessively democratic left intelligentsia in the United States. A few years ago, William Simon, a government businessman, suggested that corporations avoid giving money to universities that do not promote the conservative interests of business. More recently, *Business Week* published an article on marxists on campus in which fear was expressed that business might wake up too late to the possibility that American universities were going the way of West European universities—with negative consequences for business.[2] In April 1979, a lineup of conservative ideologues from the American Assembly met at Arden House in Harriman (as in Averell), New York, to discuss the "disorders of the university." The meeting was made possible by "generous support" from parties who may have reason to worry about left-wing critics of right-wing business "order"—"The Ford Foundation,

Exxon Education Foundation, IBM and AT&T." The shared term in their discussion was "integrity": "Disorders" threaten the "moral and intellectual *integrity* of our colleges and universities."[3] "Integrity" usually implies wholeness, purity, and uprightness. According to the *American Heritage Dictionary*, the first meaning of "integrity" is "rigid adherence to a code of behavior," and it is this slightly more sinister definition that the American Assembly seems to have in mind. To assure "integrity," the Arden House conservatives conclude that "our institutions of higher education will do well to rid themselves of unbecoming conduct." As the code word "integrity" probably refers to the way the academy has traditionally served the interests of business, the code words "unbecoming conduct" seem a disguised reference to the marxist presence on the campuses. The message hardly needs to be expounded, although it is couched in the contradictory logic of conservative ideology. The academy must repress "disorderly" internal elements, or else, it is implied, external "government regulations" might be imposed. It never seems to occur to conservatives that they themselves advocate what they ostensibly resist from government—repressive regulation.

Business ideologists conceal the fact that their worries about resistance to government regulation actually serve specific business interests by fabricating general concepts that make their interests seem universal. If they were sincere in their concern for autonomy and self-regulation, they would not make pronouncements about how academics should behave. Frederick Bohm, the director of the Exxon Education Foundation, for example, describes the university's "cohesion of purpose" as consisting of a "new allegiance to the acquisition of knowledge and to new openness to those able to follow." "Naturally," he goes on, "this leaves out any moral perspective." He criticizes the "irrationalism" and "ambiguity" of the 1960s, when "democratic values and rational authority" were "confused" (*DHE*, 6). But Bohm seems confident that order and reason can be restored. Another participant in the conference supplies the probable cause for such confidence: "As money gets tighter, institutions will pressure faculty, and faculty themselves may scurry to do whatever is necessary to get external funds. Outside pressures will accordingly be harder to resist. . . . The balance of influences is clearly tipping toward the donor" (*DHE*, 122-23).

A deconstructive analysis of the concepts and values that inform this discourse would focus on words like "integrity" and "cohesion of purpose" that suggest an institutional identity of being and of will which seems to incarnate the metaphysical model of the logos. The university is given out to be integral and selfsame, proper to itself. This assumption predicates two others: that the university has an essence—knowledge-gathering—and that this essence is defined by a norm—"becoming" or proper conduct. The attribution of an essence ("integrity") necessarily precipitates a norm that defines the exclusion of an outside—"unbecoming conduct." Antibusiness politics will be kept out of the classroom, in other words. As is usually the case in such ideological rationalizations of institutions, the value of reason is claimed as the norm of the institution, and deviation from the norm is characterized as "irrationalism." The political and institutional corollary of the metaphysical postulates of conscious intention is the cohesive purpose that would eliminate all "ambiguity," that is, all that troubles the normative ratio of the institution. Such characteristics of metaphysics as an unproblematic ontology ("integrity"), teleology ("cohesive purpose"), and logocentrism ("rationalism," no "ambiguity," clear and determinable meaning) are summoned as modes of institutional legitimation.

These theoretical rationalizations of the university institution are, of course, undone by the practice of the university. Universities are fields of conflict and force, not integrated wholes with cohesive intentions. Their "reasonableness" is simply the benign face of power, coercion, and the everyday brutality of patriarchal capitalism in America. A professor cited in the American Assembly book as someone who attempts to elevate the "souls" of his students was also recently cited in a university scandal for soliciting sex from female graduate students just before their exams. Cornell University (where this essay was written) itself engages in unbecoming political conduct when it engages in union-busting tactics to counter the UAW's attempt to organize the employees. And without the infrastructure provided by those workers, the neutral gathering of academic knowledge could not continue. The microstructures of university life are crosshatched with political and economic forces. The suggestion that the heteronomous arena is cohesive or integral is mystifying. Universities like Cornell do indeed cohesively service business. The point of ideological generalizations like "integrity," however, is not to name that purpose. Rather, it is to provide a justification for countering any move to introduce "irrationalism" or "ambiguity" into that rationally functioning, cohesively purposeful system, in other words, to counter radicalism that becomes "irrational" and "ambiguous" by a circular argument. By assigning "integrity" to the university, conservatives define their own project as an effort to maintain or restore a spuriously natural condition of purity or wholeness. The postulation of a normative attribute like integrity permits any radical attempt at modification to be characterized as a disintegrative degradation, a falling off from nature. Restoration of "integrity" will consist of curtailing that new development.

From the perspective of both marxism and deconstruction, the notion of integrity is idealist. A marxist analysis would point to the ideological function of the concept, the way it enables the exercise of power through a misrepresentation of the realities of the academic situation. A deconstructive analysis would show how what the conservatives call integrity is itself a form of disintegrity; it would question the conservative habit of thinking in terms of such binaries which make a norm of some ideal model of self-possessed self-identity ("integrity") and treat anything that does not cohere with the model as a derivative deviation or degradation. If integrity names the service universities provide for business, then, simply by shifting criteria, one can say that the business-university channels people into narrow economic functions that are scarcely integrative for them. A different criterion of integrity, a marxist one, for instance, which would demand the full development of all human faculties, makes the business criterion appear obscenely impoverished. Regarding the status of the institution, the deconstructive and marxist arguments intersect in criticizing the "propriety" (selfsameness, wholeness, integrity) of the university. The marxist argument states that the university is bound by social relations to supposedly extraneous instances such as politics and economics. It cannot be isolated as a thing-in-itself from those relations. The deconstructive argument uses the concept of a force field. The university is a locus of forces which constitute the university as a point of intersection in a broad field that defies any single or ultimate determination. The interior or essence of the university is constitutively impugned by what supposedly is "exterior" to it.

The university is a historical product; it reflects and reproduces social stratification by rationing knowledge according to class; it trains "leaders," thus preserving external structures of political authority; it embodies conservative business ideology in its institutional structure by segmenting and instrumentalizing knowledge; it promotes a monopoly of scarce scientific knowledge and technology by business; it trains social agents in the norms and mores of the dominant culture; and so on.

Deconstructive analysis would consider the incredible multiplicity of universities, from the elite country club campuses of the Ivy League leadership factories, with a paradoxical monopoly on elite left culture as well, to the low-prestige two-year community colleges that track the working class away from the liberatory culture and into job training. What is integrative about all this is quite simply the integration of new generations into a business world where their roles will be determined, all apologies for "equality of opportunity" notwithstanding, by wealth and privilege at one end and by the imposition of wage labor at the other. In the name of "integrity," then, what the business leaders of the American Assembly are actually defending is the disintegrity of the university, its specific supportive function in capitalist America.

As far back as 1973, radical educators would have seen the American Assembly-led conservative backlash coming. The Carnegie Commission Report on Higher Education does not bother to camouflage the link between education and business behind a benign vocabulary. "Education," it states, "is the main instrument of opportunity in an industrial society requiring a high level of employment skills from many of its citizens."[4] The commissioners point to academic freedom as the crucial issue for an "industrial society" (read business community) desirous of maintaining unimpeded access to a supply of university skilled labor. The "independent" commission had a duty to issue a warning to the academic left on behalf of business. It takes the form of an indirect threat: "Left faculty members, in particular, may have generally decided, as have several of their most prominent leaders, that campus political neutrality is the best protection of their own individual right to dissent" (*PA*, 55). They then claim, with characteristic flair for self-contradiction, that "the price of academic freedom is eternal vigilance." Vigilance is necessary because those who exercise too much academic freedom are its greatest enemy:

> Academic freedom is now threatened internally as well as externally—by some ideological adherents within as well as by some holders of power without. Thus it becomes more important than ever before that judicial processes on the campus are fully independent of improper internal processes and biases. Processes of faculty hearing established, in part, to protect faculty members from attacks by external powers must now also be capable of protecting the integrity of the campus against those who undertake internal attacks on academic freedom; they must be able to convict internal enemies of freedom.

And they conclude:

> Faculty members, concomitantly, should not be able to plead that their civil liberties as citizens are a basis for not meeting academic standards of conduct on campus. "Free speech" is not an excuse for inaccuracy as a scholar or misuse of the classroom as a teacher. . . . As citizens, scholars should be held to the standards of citizenship, and as scholars, to the standards of scholarship.

Students are also warned that they "need to be guided by reasonable outer boundaries on what they can and cannot do" (*PA*, 61).

The Carnegie Commission raises two questions that will become increasingly more important to radical teachers as the conservative program for the academy is applied: the questions of boundaries and of bias. Radicals, of course, already have answers to those questions, but I want to formulate them in deconstructive terms, because I think deconstructive analysis provides a stronger basis upon which to base a defense of the radical position.

The norm of propriety that defines the boundaries of academic freedom is similar to the concept of integrity, in that it establishes a set of actions integral to the norm, while excluding a body of actions considered external or improper. A deconstruction of this discursive institution points out that the principle of exclusion used assumes a "nature" free from bias. If bias is to be excluded, then what remains is a pure, unbiased position that functions as the norm defining exclusion. Carnegie seems to define those who are biased as "ideological adherents" and "internal enemies of freedom." I assume that to deduce a definition of Carnegie's unstated norm of unbiased teaching, all I need do is generate the opposites of the characteristics of bias: "ideological nonadherents" or "non-ideological adherents" or perhaps "nonideological nonadherents," and, of course, "friends of freedom." The defining terms for Carnegie's unbiased natural norm must also be natural and unbiased, and, given the terms deduced, that cannot be the case. In the ideological lexicon, "ideological" refers to radicals, socialists, progressives, and marxists. And "to adhere," when subtended to "ideological," means to associate oneself with a worked-out, systematic critique of capitalism. A nonideological nonadherent, then, would be someone who dissociates himself from the critique of capitalism, but differently, a liberal pluralist. If I use "anti" instead of "non" to indicate the opposition, his position becomes more markedly conservative — an antiprogressive pro-capitalist opponent of critics of capitalism. Hardly an unbiased position, let alone grounds for establishing a natural norm in relation to which a concept of "bias" could be defined.

The term "friend of freedom" implies a similar pro-business bias. "Freedom" is not a neutral term, and its abstractness conceals a specific history that detracts from its apparent naturalness ("all men are born free" and so on). The word-idea "free" was first used by the thirteenth-century Celts to name members of a household who related to the head or master by family ties rather than as slaves. Its first meaning was economic, and freedom came to be defined negatively as exemption from slavery or bondage, as well as from autocratic control. It was not until the fourteenth century that the word was applied to civil liberties and individual rights. The first meaning of "free" as free labor indicates how the concept was bound up with the onset of small capitalist production. The emergent capitalists first needed unbonded labor "free" from feudal obligation and, later, legal freedom from the power of the feudal lords. More recently, freedom has become almost equatable with pro-capitalism; freedom means free enterprise. Children are taught that the opposite of "free" is "communist." To be a "friend of freedom," then, is to be a friend of capitalism. Again, hardly an unbiased position, unless you accept a definition of capitalist free enterprise as natural, acquiesence to which is itself so natural that it defines the norm beyond all bias, all adherence, and all ideology that permits condemnation of the "ideological" radical anticapitalist position. The Carnegie position, then, seems to rest on a norm of a natural acquiesence to capitalism, one that would be so spontaneous it would transcend all ideological or systematically formulated adherence. The pure state that precedes all bias turns out to be a state of pure bias, that is, of unquestioned, precritical belief.

Carnegie claims a questionable norm of a self-denial, self-possessed nature as the basis for determining the boundaries of academic freedom. The unbiased, natural attitude they propose is itself a form of bias. They are, to a limited extent, aware of this conflict, but they would prefer to have their economic and ideological interests prevail by persuasion rather than force, although a frightening subdued violence underlies their discourse. In fact, ideological coercion is what distinguishes highly developed American capitalism from underdeveloped forms that still require physical force. In one way, they (I use they for the singular Carnegie, because it is a corporation) are faithful to Aristotle's argument that what "contributes most to preserve the state is . . . to educate children with respect to the state."[5] One should not expect people interested (by self-definition) in conserving things, especially things that serve their own material interests, to argue otherwise. "Power within the university," as Edgar Fiedenberg remarks, "aligns itself with power outside it."[6]

The American Assembly uses the word "loyalty" rather than "academic freedom" to describe academic life. It is interesting that the concept of freedom, which originally was used as an ideological instrument against kings demanding loyalty, has with time come to be used as an instrument for enforcing economic fealty. Both Carnegie and the American Assembly demand that academics be loyal to standards of propriety which are supportive of business property and the business ideology of free enterprise. At the same time, they remove the radical academic defense of its position based on academic freedom by branding radicals as "internal enemies of freedom," that is, of free enterprise. And the conservative offensive against government regulation in the name of freedom is used to justify "self-regulation" on the part of university administrators, who, of course, are owned and operated by business trustees. Ideologically and rhetorically, the academic left is cornered. If they choose to defend themselves on the basis of the liberal concept of academic freedom, they become their own judges, because the word "freedom" has been appropriated by business ideologues to name precisely that against which the left defines itself — free enterprise, nonideological nonadherence, freedom fighting, and so on. The Carnegie commissioners make the point with great clarity: academic leftists will retain their right to freedom only as long as they are loyal to the principles of citizenship that identify civic freedom with the economic model of free enterprise. If you like free enterprise, you are free; if not, you are not.

I will now argue for an alternate principle to the liberal concept of academic freedom as a support for the position of radical teachers in the academy.

I will begin with a generalized version of the deconstructive argument concerning boundaries and biases: No boundary is possible that would rigorously distinguish a natural, pedagogic attitude, one that would be unbiased, neutral, and disinterested, from an external arena of unnatural bias. The purity of the internal arena is always already contaminated by what it seeks to exclude, because the act of exclusion itself signifies a bias. Self-identity wrested from heterogeneous relations by an exclusivist reduction immediately ceases to be self-identical. The logical practice that establishes the theoretical possibility of an unbiased natural attitude in teaching at once makes such a thing impossible.

All knowledge operates through acts of exclusion and marginalization similar to the ones that define the proper arena of supposedly unbiased teaching. Rational demarcation bears a resemblance to institutional demarcation. The production of theoretical concepts entails judgments that delimit a field of study and exclude certain unrelated or irrelevant factors. An institutional version of this operation of division by exclusion is the academic disciplines and the professions.

The institutional divisions between disciplines reflect metaphysical conceptual divisions (between the business school and the study of the uses of language, politics and economics, or sociology and formal law) and promote an ideological structuring of the social world. Perhaps the most significant case of such structuring is the separation of economics as an isolated domain of free human activity—business—from politics, which is the area marked off for the struggle for power between various interest groups. That the political struggle is motivated by economic interest and that the economy is structured by political classes puts the conceptual, institutional, and "real" division in question and shows it to serve an ideological function. Certain determinable economic and political interests are served by the maintenance of the division both conceptually and institutionally (in the academic disciplies as well as in the "world"). As long as people think of economics as an isolated instance that entails no force or coercion, in which workers and capitalists exchange "freely," and which therefore is free from "politics," then it is unlikely they will make the connection between their own economic position and political processes. As long as "politics" means elections and government, people are unlikely to see it at work in the marketplace as economics. The intellectual division of labor in the disciplines reflects and reproduces institutional divisions that make economics and politics seem to be autonomous and independent instances. These divisions conceal the relationality of these instances, that they are nothing "in themselves" and that they constitute each other as mutually interdependent determinations or differentiations of a complex system of heterogeneous forces. And they thus prevent the making of effective connections between "economic" and "political" events that might put an end to apathy and lead to a revolutionary consciousness.

Metaphysical categories are institutionalized by the disciplinary divisions of the academy. To study business instead of, say, language or politics is to assume implicitly that the latter have nothing to do with business, which is an independent, isolatable realm, as the singularity of the word suggests. But business could not be carried on if words like "demand," "free enterprise," "labor market," "equilibrium," and "investment climate" were not available to enable its operations. Such words are effective in lending conceptual coherence and legitimacy to the "business world." They also function ideologically by occluding real relations of contradiction, power, coercion, and struggle. Their simplicity, their singularity, and their benign character make a world of incessant battle and suffering seem orderly, noncontradictory, natural, and self-evident.

They also effectively inscribe a disposition in the agents of business to expect the world to be so ordered and to behave accordingly. The vocabulary of business contains embedded in it a theory of the world which, once absorbed by social agents through education, helps produce certain practices that reproduce the objective conditions—the business world —which give rise to that vocabulary. Language, then, is a material force in the reproduction of capitalism, more specifically, of the conceptual system which necessarily accompanies the structuring of the real world so as to serve the ends of capital.

The phrase "stable investment climate" imparts a sense of teleology, of a goal to be reached and of the necessity of attaining it. The model of equilibrium embedded in the phrase accounts for the placing of ends over means which ensues from it. What matters is the goal—stability. The phrase thus helps guide (and also overlook) such actions as the military terror against the left in the southern cone of Latin America. The phrase/concept enables political action, while also concealing an act of political repression under a seemingly innocuous term that limits the description of the situation to purely economic matters. The political function of the language of business is in part the concealment of the politics of business.

The division of the academy into disciplines, then, might not be as apolitical or unbiased as it gives itself out to be. It reflects a metaphysical conceptuality that would classify a world that denies the possibility of such classificatory divisions. In the world, politics, economics, and language overlap; they exist differentially. That is, one can be distinguished only by marginalizing the others and subtracting something from the one distinguished such that it could never be complete "in itself." It is impossible to analyze politics without taking language and economics into account. One cannot determine the function of language in culture and in society without taking into account the political and economic functions and uses of language.

The operations of rational conceptualization—division, exclusion, isolation, concentration, identification, and so on—are institutionalized in the academic disciplines. They help to structure the social world by instituting "rational" dispositions in social agents. It is a commonplace that one's conception of the world is in part determined by one's practice. Academics, for example, tend to see the world according to their disciplinary training—historians as history, economists as economy, and so on. The same can be said for an entire society that has attained a high level of educational homogeneity. From grade school to university, the institutional form and practice of education by rational categorical divisions determines how people think about the world and how they act in it. Disciplinary teaching imparts to students an attitude of rationalization, the tendency of think of the world as consisting of discrete sectors of analysis. This tendency is enforced by the direct linkage between education and employment; there are no jobs for generalists.

The act of knowledge is not spontaneous; it is instituted through training and practice. From the point of view of education itself, then, there can be no natural knowledge that would serve as the basis for distinguishing an unbiased teaching from an external political arena. The practice of knowing is itself already a form of bias, because it entails selecting and excluding, more often than not, according to historically determined institutional norms of what *should* be studied and known. Literary critics, for example, are supposed to know certain things and not others, good style, for example, but never economic theory. The disciplinary segmentation of the world implies imperatives that govern the limits of what can, legitimately, be known.

The conservative law of neutral pedagogy, as grounds for granting academic freedom, requires a model of natural knowledge which exists prior to bias. But if all knowledge is educated or formed, and if that formation occurs through disciplinary institutions, then it is highly unlikely that an unbiased or natural knowledge will be found in the world, even if it were theoretically possible. Education (whether formal or informal, that is, education carried on through the practices of habituation and socialization in the community, the family, the media) enables knowledge, and education, both in the formal and the informal sense, necessarily produces bias. Formal education does so through a disciplinary division that skews knowledge toward an ideal absolute, that would mark the end to partiality and the attainment of impartial neutrality—a positionedness without position. Informal education does so according to a principle of political noncontradiction: if the system is to retain legitimacy and survive, the consciousness of social agents must not contradict the presuppositions of the economy, the social network, and the state. This principle explains the programmatic exclusion of the possibility of a general radical culture in the United States. Informal education is biased by the requirements of social cohesion and political economic legitimation. "Natural" knowledge, then, the normative basis of a disinterested scholarly education, is itself produced and conditioned by an irreducibly biased education. The outside of the university, especially the political outside, is always already internal to the university, in the form of the social and institutional knowledge the university presupposes as having already been imparted if the university is to function at all.

This political deconstructive analysis can be taken a step further, onto the terrain of rationality. The assumption of an unbiased, natural knowledge is put in question by the very process of rational conceptualization. If rational knowledge operates on the basis of a preliminary rigorous distinction between exogenous and endogenous factors, and if the supposedly isolatable object of knowledge cannot in fact be detached from contextual relations and internal dependencies on external factors, then the concepts rational knowledge constructs cannot help but abstract from a world that denies the possibility of a knowledge based on "adequate" conceptual categories. Such categorical conceptualizations are by necessity partial, conventional, and pragmatic (that is, defined by their functional utility, rather than by any claim to absolutely adequate truth). They theoretically represent a world whose practical and material complexity does not correspond to any theoretical or rational model of truth (defined as adequation, indication, correspondence, and the like). No rational knowledge, then, can claim to be "natural," that is, unaffected by bias, convention, and pragmatic considerations.

All knowledge is a form of practice, the construction of categorical representations. The practice implicit in the so-called "natural" or unbiased mode of knowing, for example, is that of manipulation through conceptual abstraction. The semblance of a naturally neutral position can be attained only by the most unnatural extrication of the knowing subject from all social and historical embedding, and this can be achieved only through a conceptual abstraction, the construction of dehistoricized, seemingly transcendental formal concepts. The great model for such abstraction remains science, although "pure" science is becoming increasingly redefined by supposedly "exogenous" social considerations. In literary criticism, Northrop Frye's paradigmatic "anatomy" of criticism reflects the ahistorical urge toward transcendence. Frye weaves together two modes of transcendence through abstraction, pure science and pure theology. When translated back into the society it strives so hard to leave behind, "natural" knowledge, with its rage for the veridical authority embodied in the pure category, becomes categorical and authoritarian. The world that never did mesh with the reasonable concept in the first place is obliged to do so in the reign of authoritative reason. Manipulative technocracy, social engineering, and good business management are the rational products of a "naturally" reasonable attitude toward the world.

Capitalist ideologues may promote the norm of an unbiased, "natural" mode of knowing and teaching for the reason that it coheres so well with the logic of capitalism. Like capitalism, such reason operates under a principle of (cost) efficiency. The best conceptual abstraction is the one that presents the most truth in as little space and time as possible.[7] It has the highest cost-benefit ratio: the minimization of "ambiguity," "irrationalism," discontinuity, and dissonance in conjunction with the maximization of cognitive instrumental mastery.[8] Like a capitalist rationalization, it cannot afford to take all connotational or contextual factors or consequences into account, because that would reduce efficiency. If something is not declared to be exogenous and marginalized, there would be too much complexity to permit rational, balanced understanding, upon which concise decisions and successful, utility-maximizing operations can be based. Capitalism writes off, as exogenous, workers and consumers, and justifies this action in the name of efficient cost-benefit ratios. If the material interests of workers and consumers were taken into account, costs would rise proportionately, and, in consequence, profit margins would decline. Such interests must, therefore, remain exogenous, outside the linear equation that determines the highest margin of profit at greatest efficiency. Similarly, when rationalism isolates a domain of knowledge such as literature, it demands an efficient focus which by necessity reduces out politics, economics, sociology, and other such disciplines as merely "contextual" and secondary.

I will give two concrete examples of this sort of rationality and then discuss how the question of rationality relates to the problem of radical teaching.

I attended a session of an intellectual history conference recently. An intellectual historian gave a brilliant resumé of the West European debates on the relation between language, knowledge, and society. I was familiar with some of the thinkers discussed, though not with all, and I found that I learned a great deal from the lecture. It helped me to save time and economize my own work; in other words, it permitted efficiency. I was struck by how faithfully the method of intellectual historiography followed the pattern of conceptualization as it is found in Western rationality. That method consists of giving a brief synopsis of the arguments of such thinkers. The synopsis in such historiography is analogous to a concept in that it abridges and reduces a complicated, heterogeneous mass to an abstract, homogeneous form. It constructs a reasonable head for a disparate body of information.

This rational operation is normative and hierarchical in that it must create marginal spaces for elements that do not contribute to the efficiency of synopsis. To attain the clarity of a rational resumé, dissonance and discontinuity must be programmed out. Appropriately, a philosopher who deliberately insinuates dissonance into his textual practice, Derrida, was misrepresented by the speaker at the intellectual history conference and accused of "irrationalism," which, you will remember, was also the term used by the Exxon man to describe the campus "disorders" of the 1960s.

From a deconstructive perspective, the greatest dissonance occurs between rationality and the practice that operates and simultaneously undermines its pretensions to theoretical purity. Practice—that "textual" weave, to use Derrida's word, of language, attitude, institutional force and setting, unconscious cause and effect, desire, and so forth—also operates the intellectual historian's reasonable synopsis, but at the same time, it is itself inaccessible to such synopsis. A good analogy for the relationship between rational synopsis and practice is the relation between a television image and the points that make up the image without themselves being images, the electrical circuitry of the set, the systems of networks, transmitters, and stations, the production companies, the historically developed institutions of "entertainment" and fictional representation which define the content, the microstructural system of desire relating audience to screen, and so on out to the entire capitalist system of marketing and mind management. A similar "text" informs the historian's synopsis, but it is precisely the textuality of practice—its heterogeneity—which must be marginalized or filtered out if synopsis is to succeed. Deconstruction usually points toward this heterogeneous domain of practice when it criticizes the hubristic pretensions of reason to legislate the truth of the world as a synoptic rational concept that "corresponds" "adequately" to something in the world that has the same synoptic, abridged, isolated, crystallized, proper form. Synopsis is itself a mode of practice, and reason, rather than being the legislator of truth, might be a region of practice, incapable of transcending that which makes it possible.

I raised this problem with the intellectual historian, and I pointed to the practical fact that at the intellectual history conference, only first world (for the most part white) men were speaking, and therefore it was unwise to speak of "universal reason" or "rational norms" which just happened to be hanging around in midair. I suggested that if a third world feminist attacked his rational assumptions and the institutional rationality of the conference, using nonacademic obscenity, she would have appeared irrational in relation to his universal reason, simply because such individualistic, legislative reason, committed as it is in its very practice to a norm of homogeneous synoptic continuity, uncritical, nonanalytic academic male equanimity, and a well-balanced ratio, cannot tolerate the dissonance and heterogeneity which such deliberately disequilibrating deconstructive criticism introduces.

Fittingly enough, perhaps, the speaker cut me off before I could finish my remarks, implicitly claiming the prerogative (or power) of reason and the chair. I felt the touch of the iron fist beneath the urbane glove of white male liberalism. The rational operation of theoretical exclusion, hierarchization, and marginalization translates fairly consistently into a questionable political practice. This is not the fault of the reasonable man; it is in the nature of the "natural," rational method to assume legislative authority in the knowledge and management of the world.

My second example of the rationality which the conservative promoters of unbiased pedagogy demand comes from the world of business. Reginald Jones used to run General Electric, one of the largest and strongest world corporations, as well as the Business Roundtable, a corporate group that "advises" government and supplies it with skilled professionals to run its financial affairs. William Miller at the Federal Reserve was an example of a Roundtable businessman who is at once above the law and a maker of laws.

Marshall Ledger remarks that Jones's favorite word is "reasonable." Reasonable and realistic are words consistently used by holders of power to describe the limit where what is proper ends and impropriety begins. For someone with Jones's views, reasonable has its original root intact; it refers to a proper ratio or a balanced account of costs and benefits. When GE was held liable for poisoning the Hudson River with toxic PCBs, Jones, after describing the few symbolic gestures of assistance GE made to clean up the mess, concluded: "I don't think it's realistic to ask a corporation to do more than that." Of clean air and water regulations, he remarked: "The cost-benefit [ratio] can get out of line." A former teacher of Jones describes his rational capacities: "There's something conceptual about him, conceptual in the old fashioned sense. . . . It's an abstract way of approaching a problem by a man who is in the middle of it. We'd expect it of an academician."[9]

I cite this brief example to underscore the similarity between the reason academics assume, when they practice synoptic abstraction by isolating themselves in disciplines, and the rationality employed in business to abstract from the complexity of practice and to conceive equations that permit management of the world system so as to guarantee a reasonable cost-benefit ratio. The reason Jones acquired at school and at the University of Pennsylvania is perfectly suited to business. The same operation that allows intellectual historians to detach themselves from a world in which their practice is embedded, to abstract from its heterogeneity, to construct formal synoptic conceptual models and linear histories to account for it, allows a Reg Jones to conceptualize the self-sufficient good of the corporation, to abstract its rational operations from a world of scarcity and need, to define its goals as cost-benefit ratios, and to install a rationally homogenizing theoretical head atop a heterogeneous practical world managed through the implementation of all the decisive operations of "reason," such as division, exclusion, marginalization, segmentation, and hierarchization. In each case, the essential (and essentializing, in the sense of a reduction of the practical and empirical to a theoretically ideal form) operation of detachment and withdrawal to a position of balanced rationality and disinterested contemplation above the fray permits mastery (either theoretical or practical, as the case may be) of the world. The practical consequences of this procedure—the poisoning of the Hudson by the powerful corporation, the exclusion of women by powerful though urbane male academics—appear as marginal in relation to the essential operation of accumulating financial and academic capital.

The university borrows principles of labor rationalization, efficiency, and "sound" management from business. But the rationality of the academy also reappears beyond the walls of the classroom in the world of business. The rational construction of objects of knowledge resurfaces as the intellectual technology that shapes the social world in accordance with the demands of the capitalist economy, itself operated by the law of the ratio, the balance or equilibrium of investment and return. Education is crucial to the inculcation of the needed rationality in capitalized social agents. This might explain Reg Jones's characterization of the University of Pennsylvania: "I still feel the answer to a school such as ours is selective excellence." Business owns and controls universities that, like Penn, provide the rational manpower needed for business to continue existing. The process of rationalization, the production of theoretical concepts, follows the pattern of the development of the human subject as it is rationalized through the educational system, refined and purified until it attains a point of expertise comparable to the point of conceptual synopsis, which economizes heterogeneity by contracting it into a homogeneous unity. Rationality makes unities and identities by sorting out and hierarchizing ("selective excellence"); so also the disciplinary rationalization of social agents in the schools works by sorting ("tracking"), dividing ("disciplinary specialization"), excluding ("career choice"), hierarchizing ("ranking"), and synopsizing ("expertise"). Like a pig who starts out bulky and ends up a slender sausage, the social agent is processed by the schools and told he has "free choice." The Texas bank radio commercial says: "In some countries of the world, you're brought up to think one way, but in the American free enterprise system, you can be whatever you want."

Education within such a context is another form of capitalist technology. As Marx points out in regard to capitalism in general, it turns people into abstractions, one could say, into synoptic concepts. Education is a mode of social production. It forms the supposedly unformed; it converts raw material, through the technological labor of study and teaching, into a commodity to be exchanged on the labor market. The rationality required by capitalism, because it uses abstract labor to produce abstract entities—commodities—is induced not only as the content of knowledge (concepts, technical skills), but also as the practice of the function of knowledge (rational conceptualization) and as the practice of the educational process (incremental abstraction or specialization).[10]

The cohabitation of education and economics is not an altogether recent discovery. Aristotle, in the *Economics,* writes: "Since we see that modes of education form the characters of the young, it is necessary when you have procured them to rear up those to whose care liberal offices are to be committed."[11] Capitalist planners began to notice in the 1960s that economic growth required educational planning. "Human capital investment" was seen to be a necessary factor of capital costs that, for the most part, were shunted onto the public. It was found that education raised the average quality of labor, the amount of qualified manpower, entrepreneurial ability, the marginal productivity of real capital, general economic activity, as well as the gross national product. Education, clearly, was a factor of economic growth.[12]

The business scientists discovered a truth Marx outlined in the past century — the social world is the product of human labor. The economy is not an objective machine; it requires subjective manual and mental inputs. The human mind provides needed technological inventiveness, an instrument of economic calculation, a ready-made machine for decision and management, as well as marketing inspiration. As capitalism becomes more technologically and logistically complex, more dependent on technology, marketing, calculation, planning, and management, industrial production will itself become increasingly more dependent on the production of knowledge.

I would argue, then, that the notion of boundary (between unbiased scholarship and biased world politics) should be replaced by a concept of *economy,* of reciprocal exchange between two instances that have no existence outside of that exchange. The social world "outside" the university permits the university to work by providing the ground for education, both formal and informal. Similarly, that social world would collapse without an educational process of some sort (be it formal or informal) which trains social agents in the skills necessary for the reproduction of that society. The social world is constructed by intellectual labor and intellectually guided technology. Given the high degree of technology required to maintain U.S. capitalist society, one could say with confidence that the dependence of the university on the social world is matched by a reciprocal dependence of the social world on university education. Business, for one thing, has reached such a high stage of refinement that it could not reproduce itself without business schools. And, by creating an artificial environment of scarcity, business exerts indirect economic pressure on schools to turn out more employable M.B.A.s than unemployment-bound Ph.D.s in other disciplines.

The problem of bias, which governs the question of academic freedom, leads, by way of a radical deconstructive analysis, to the problem of social construction, and it is in addressing this problem that academic marxists can begin to formulate an alternate principle to that of academic freedom as a basis for arguing their case.

Traditionally, marxism takes issue with two assumptions of conservative theoretical and practico-institutional rationality: first, that a problematically interrelated social world can be dissolved into isolatable parts (such as economics, politics, and culture), and second, that the "subjective" knower can transcend or separate itself from the "objective" world. The isolation of politics from economics can, I have argued, have pernicious effects. The "disinterested" rational and institutional exercise serves specific class interests. The general process of capitalist formalism, as Marx describes it in the *Grundrisse*, which transforms quality into quantity, human labor into abstract labor, goods into money, use value into exchange value, community into formal administration, real property into legal property, humans into machines, and so on, works as well, it seems, as a formalist rationality whose result is the isolation and abstract hypostatization of concepts like "order" that mobilize action suitable to capitalism. The second critique, however, is more important for what I am considering here. In the Paris manuscripts, Marx, concretizing Hegel's idealist argument, suggests that the objective world is constructed by subjective activity. This becomes the basis for the later theory of labor value, the subjective input that produces capitalist goods and reproduces the capitalist system.[13]

Deconstructive philosophy can add to this argument an insight into the way the social world is constructed by an intellectual technology underwritten by the principles of Western rationality. The domains of mental and manual labor, the academy and the factory, so seemingly separate, are obvious examples of technologically constructed institutions that with time have become increasingly "rationalized," that is, organized according to such principles of Western reason as segmentation, centralization, efficiency, and hierarchy. Institutional and conceptual forms have a comparable morphology.

On the basis of this argument, one might broaden the notion of ideology to include, along with content or a theory of the world, the form or practice of knowing the world "rationally." Education is a form of social technology which shapes minds in such a way that they in turn shape the known world according to rules of rationality compatible with the rationality of the social system. That rationalized social system is itself the sedimentation of past intellectual labor. Its concrete institutions are rational, that is, homogeneous, integral, equilibrated ("the balance of powers"), functional; they bear the imprint of the ratio that guided the technology instrumental in their construction. If ideology works as mystification, misrepresentation, programmed ignorance, and overloaded values ("freedom"), it also works as a mode of metaphysical rational knowledge that merely reproduces as a theoretical operation the practical rationality of the social system. The homology, correspondence, adequation, and compatibility between rational knowledge and the rationalized world is not likely to promote anything but an acceptance of that

150 MARXISM AND DECONSTRUCTION

world as "reasonable." Reason as ideology would be the perfect adequation between the mind and the world. The adequation of rational truth to
the world could also mean the rationalization of social agents in a way
that corresponds to the rational organization and management of the
world. As Adam Smith realized, an education in reason assures social
balance: "The more [the lower classes] are instructed, the less liable they
are to the delusions of enthusiasm and superstition ["the interested com-
plaints of faction and sedition," he adds later], which, among ignorant
nations, frequently occasion the most dreadful disorders. ["Disorders" is
also the word used by the American Assembly.] . . . An instructed and in-
telligent people, besides, are always more decent and orderly than an
ignorant and stupid one. They feel themselves . . . more respectable . . .
and they are therefore more disposed to respect their superiors."[14] A rationally instructed populace is more likely to accept the rationality of the
social system and to conduct themselves according to a norm of ratio or
balance.

In a very real sense, then, in advanced capitalist America, the real is
rational and the rational is real. The injunction to be "realistic" is interchangeable with the call to be "reasonable." And it is no surprise that
those who try to drive a disordering wedge into the order of reason are
accused as much by the liberal academic as by the corporate ideologue of
"irrationalism."

Radicals within the schools teach not only information that contradicts the version of reality constructed by conservative academic ideologues and the capitalist media,[15] but also a different way of thinking
from that required for the functioning of a rationalized social system.
That new way of thinking, in its embryonic form, is negative, critical,
relational, and differential, in the sense that it refuses to isolate and
divide what is interrelated and interdependent.

Even so, dialectical thought has in the past fallen into archaeological
and teleological traps: positing an arche or origin, a pure human nature,
for example, that will be liberated or emancipated by revolution (Marcuse), or positing a telos or goal, the theoretical *idea* of communism
toward which one must move by any practical means available, including
hyperrationalized capitalism (Lenin). Just as education (not simply as
theory or conscious knowledge, but more significantly perhaps, as a
practice and an institutional form that unconsciously habituates students
to rational processes) secures the necessary dispositions for participation
in capitalist institutional life, it must also be the instrument for producing
dispositions suitable to socialism. Humans are not by nature socialist;
such a world must be constructed, not liberated from an oppressive
apparatus that somehow now conceals it. As bias precedes and produces
nature in the sense of the cognitive assumptions of a supposedly neutral
pedagogy, so also it precedes nature in creating the requirements of
socialist construction. A socialist "human nature," which means also so-

cialist intellectual and social institutions and practices, would also have to be "constructed."

If radical teachers accept the marxist and the deconstructive arguments that rationality is a mode of technology that is instrumental in the construction of the world and that knowledge, because synoptic representation is always partial, a theory that can never by definition fully account for practice, never has a "natural" form that is exempt from bias—then they acquire grounds for claiming that the walls of the classroom never strictly demarcate an outside from an inside, "interested" activism from "disinterested" scholarship, or an objective, social world from the constructive, subjective activities of the working mind. The liberal argument for "academic freedom," which assumes the classroom is an enclave where the unbiased and disinterested compilation of truth and the communication of technical or rational skills goes on, loses all relevance. The marxist and the deconstructive positions claim there is never a teaching whose natural, unbiased status could be restored by elimination of all bias. Indeed, each school of thought would claim that the fiction of an unbiased position is perhaps the most ideologically biased of all the possible positions. Neither, they would claim, is there an isolatable realm of "freedom" or self-sufficient autonomy which academics can claim. The academy is constitutively extroverted in that it forms and is formed by the world in contradistinction to which its autonomy is supposedly defined.

Radical teachers, I suggest, might base their arguments for their activities in the academy on a less defensive principle than that of "academic freedom." To accept academic freedom as a rallying cry is tantamount to accepting a definition of the academy as a realm separable from the social world. The clear link between intellectual technology and capitalist business is denied. Instead of emphasizing the fact that the social world is constructed and that therefore it could be constructed in a different form, the liberal philosophy of academic freedom would make that world appear natural, an independent object to be contemplated studiously by the nonactivist, disinterested liberal academic. Liberal academic ideology makes the radical position of pedagogic activism for the sake of an alternate social construction seem a deviation in relation to its apolitical norm. Nevertheless, upholders of the norm are themselves unconscious participants in the structuring of the world by intellectual labor, either as technology or ideology. All pedagogy is a form of activism, and the radical teacher's activism is therefore second degree. It reflects upon the existing activism of the schools in maintaining the mind patterns and the technical levels needed by capitalism, and it engages in its work not as a deviation from a norm, but as an alternative to an alternative.

The very practical problem of the "concern" of business over the disorders in higher education remains unanswered. No amount of theorizing about the constructed "nature" of the social world and the possibility of an alternative reconstruction will dissuade the business technocrats from their belief in (and their power to maintain) the present link between education and business.

Bearing this caution in mind, I will make four suggestions. I have argued that four characteristics of the rationality prevalent under capitalism serve a regressive function: first, the segmentation and division of the world of knowledge into disciplines and the social world into sectors or professsions (politics, economics, health, and so on); second, the essentialist distinction of norms and deviations, endogenous factors (profit maximization) from exogenous factors (ethical and environmental questions); third, the separation of subject and object, knower and known, academic and social world, which downplays the role of intellectual technology in constructing the world; and fourth, the privileging of models of a ratio, an equilibrium, balance, or harmonious order in society (which necessarily ensues from the above practices).

My first suggestion is based on the marxist hypothesis that things are not isolatable, but exist in and as relations, and on the deconstructive thesis that the world is not characterizable by the word "being" if being implies "presence" and "property" or selfsameness. Rather, the world is an unstable, discontinuous movement of self-differentiation, alteration or becoming other, and temporal delay that never freezes as a stable present or selfsame property. I suggest that radical teachers teach not just a counterhegemonic content of knowledge, but a different form, way, or practice of knowing which takes these theses as pointers. This practice is relational in that it combines what capitalist rationality sunders — politics, culture, and economics, for example. And it is differential in that it separates or distinguishes differences which rationalism collapses. Such a practice assumes that the most self-evident and "rational" operations of the mind are fraught with political implications; that the simple, habitual setting up of norms which define out secondary degradations, accidents, or deviations is to be put in question; that consciousness is a material practice inscribed in history (personal and general) and in the world; that, rather than being master of an "objective" world above which it stands, consciousness is instead an effect of social and unconscious processes which it could never fully "know" or control; that all models that provide general explanations of the world are to a certain extent theoretical fictions. A deconstructive practice of thinking would train the mind to treat whatever seems underived, a final cause or ground, as an *effect*, to be wary of the most "natural" desire to locate continuities, to reduce difference to identity, to opt for the reassuring macrocategory in order to avoid the troubling microanalysis. It would teach one to question the most taken-for-granted operations of the mind, as historically derived and politically consequential, to seek "master molecules" where there are instead differentiated aggregates. For example, it would question the "normal" use of broad categories arranged as binary oppositions, and this applies equally to marxist thought (the althusserian binary of "science" and "ideology" or the still prevalent leninist opposition of "politics" and "economics").

Capitalist rationalists teach the world as something which "is," that is, something natural and unchangeable. This is the norm underlying the principle of disinterested scholarship in the liberal academy. Nondifferential thinking isolates a presence (what "is"), as well as a present moment, and this has ideological consequences. For example, such thinking allowed Jimmy Carter in 1979 to call America's intervention in Iran in 1953 "ancient history." What is important, according to this way of thinking, is what is immediately given, not the differential, mediated interrelations between past (the scripting of the present by the events of 1953), present, and the projected future that defines all "present" actions.

The cognitive practice of differentiality applies equally to the interaction of forces that constitutes both the natural and the social world. The initiating gesture of such a practice is the inscription of the other in the seemingly selfsame. Relinquishing the immediate privilege of the sovereign reason which "knows" the world from a singular, selfsame point of view, it takes up the position of the other (for example, Iran, from the viewpoint of American reason), accords it subjective status, ceases to position it as an object in relation to a sovereign subject. To understand Zionism "from the point of view of its victims"[16] is an example of such a differential practice which inscribes the other in the selfsame, upsets the balance of judgment carried out from a singular position, introduces a contradictory force that undoes the one-sided equation or ratio whose logical solution can no longer be taken as a truth whose absoluteness excludes alternatives. The cognitive practices of relationality and differentiality imply accepting contradiction, "irrationalism," and the impossibility of legislating truth solely on the basis of a central logos or ratio. They emphasize collectivity, the irreducible skewing or displacing of "centers," heterogeneity, and interaction; they are inherently anti-individualistic and therefore anticapitalist. This is perhaps why capitalist education, in its rational institutional practice, seems to program out this way of knowing. It is not compatible with the social model of the possessive individual, the economic model of the entrepreneur, and the political model of the nation state. Differential social contradiction can be made compatible with the rationality of the cost-benefit ratio and the linear program only through marginalization and exclusion.

The teaching of a differential and relational cognitive practice serves a positive political function by situating individual reason, with its privileged interiority, in a field where the internal operations of reason can work only in reference to an externality which is equally central, subjective, and internal—both external and internal at once. The tendency in logocentric rationality toward balance is countered by a disequilibrating necessity which is social in character. Such practice generally is also inefficient, time-wasting, and, according to capitalist rationality, unreasonable. The critique of the privilege of the efficient ratio of reason in business and the schools applies equally well to questions of political education and organization. It is worth noting that technocrats on the left demand that organization be conducted efficiently with as much vigor as the business technocrats who argue for an efficiency of management.

To teach an alternative mode of knowing which is differential and relational, then, is to engage in a social practice. For example, by questioning the rational model of essence, one questions the economic model of rational efficiency. The essentializing operation extracts isolatable things or pure entities from differential relations; it marginalizes irrelevant elements until a fine point of selfsameness is attained. Economic efficiency, I have argued, occasions a similar teleology—attaining a goal of purity in which all that is unnecessary is eliminated. Reason and economics articulate not only as ideology but also as economic calculation and social technology.

This leads me to my second suggestion for radical teachers. Logocentric reason, and therefore also an education based on its principles, is by nature asocial. It privileges the individual mind and the individual actor; it legislates, by virtue of the laws of logic, against the contradictions which sociality and difference necessarily introduce into thought; it denies the "sociality" of the world in programming out relations and isolating "things"; and it exempts the sovereign knower from inscription in the social world. By teaching how the world is a relational system, in which the things rationalization institutionally separates are in fact intertwined and interdependent, radical teachers simultaneously teach the principles of mind which would be necessary in a world system organized according to relational and social, rather than isolationist and individual forms.

For teachers, one of the most important "things" that is extracted from relations and isolated is the school itself. That extraction-isolation is accompanied by the assumption that theory is separable from practice. Liberal education is founded on that separation; scholarship can be carried on without any concern for its immediate practical consequences. To mark a break with the liberal ideology which promotes academic isolation, scholarly theory, and academic freedom, the radical teacher engages in popular education. Teaching beyond the walls of the classroom can take place in counterinstitutions (NAM's socialist schools, the University of Massachusetts Center for Popular Economics, the New York Marxist School, Cornell City and Regional Planning's technical assistance center), or through the media (Doug Kellner's public access program in Austin), or through direct educative participation in urban affairs of the sort Alfred Watkins and David Perry engage in.[17] Whatever the form, the important point in a very literal sense (and this is perhaps what has the conservatives worried) is to *publicize* radical teaching. As Bill Tabb pointed out at the Marxist Union conference (New York University, 20 June 1980), the time has come when the economic crisis will permit the word socialism to fall on receptive ears. Barbara Ehrenreich on the same occasion stated that the academicization of marxism in the 1970s has run its course.

Third, if thinking in terms of binary oppositions and of norms and deviations is a characteristic of the rationalism that sustains capitalism, then radicals interested in reconstructing knowledge along lines compatible with a socialist social organization should begin building knowledge practices that work against that characteristic. Beginning with one's own practice of knowing is important in this regard because the thetic style of rationalist discourse (impersonal, universal prescriptive or descriptive statements) itself reflects a separation of subject from the objective world and an abstraction of knowledge from its anchor in social practice. These separations are the basis for the normative oppositional thinking that legitimates inequality (if white males are the norm, then females and nonwhites are lesser, if not deviant) and for the abstraction of mental managerial labor from (and above) the practical world of manual labor. In its very discursive form, rationalist universalism elevates differential specificity and positionality, the place of the subject in a sociohistorical structure and moment, into a transcendental paradigm, an oracle of transsubjective law; it is an operation of power.

Unfortunately, those of us on the left who wish to rework our thinking in ways that reconstruct cognitive practices prevalent under capitalism (and which preexist capitalism in lesser forms, such as theology, platonic idealism, and aristotelian protorationalism) often resort to oppositional thinking and to norm-deviational thinking. For example, we call the New Right a malignancy, thus resorting to an oppositional pathology that recapitulates the rights' positing of a pathology in progressive cultural movements, instead of seeing the success of the New Right as resulting from its ability to address needs and fears which the left itself must find a way of addressing, rather than condemning. The tendency to subsume a heterogeneous series of different positions and interests into a unicategorial monolith—the New Right—disables the plural strategic action that would seek to enlist, rather than oppose, the material needs the right so successfully exploits. Similarly, to call those who promote nuclear warfare "irrational" is to think in the oppositional way, which is the very characteristic of the irrationalism in question (in that it posits the absolute otherness of the Soviet Union), that is altogether rationalistic in form. It is predicated upon a division between knower and known, subject and object, theory and practice, which is the basis of objectivism and which underwrites the ideology of instrumental manipulation implicit in nuclear rationalism. In such objectivism, the world becomes an object regulatable by a subject according to the norms of detached reason, norms of balance and order and ratio, which are made possible by the elimination of the contingency and heterogeneity of the sociohistorical world in favor of the purity and propriety of transcendental, formal universals. (And this is why self-reflexivity on the part of leftists is so important in undermining the power structures of rationalism. Self-reflexivity anchors thinking in living, rationality in social history, ideas in practice.)

Finally, the counter to the current rationalist emphasis on balance, which derives from the separation of subject from object, would be a strategic nonrationalism, a promotion of imbalance through an anchoring of the knowing subject in the objective world and through a defusion of the opposition between nature and culture or technology. Seen as one form of material practice among others, knowing loses the hubris of universalist power over the supposedly objective world it is assigned under the rationalism that developed in the seventeenth century with capitalism. It becomes a part of the technology of nature, not a principle for mastering nature from a position of supposed detachment according to norms of balanced ratios. Relativity, indeterminacy, uncertainty, and undecidability are names for that material and historical anchoring. Such anchoring requires attending among other things to schools and words, the explicitly technological aspects of knowing. Our language limits what and how we know. Schools and reading determine the direction and level of knowledge. Geography and class play a role in elitizing or distributing knowledge. And all of this undermines the pretense to rationalist universalism. The accidental mixture of a reading of Negri with work on Derrida, of a person heeded at twenty with a conference attended at twenty-eight, of a school year spent in Paris with a copy of *Radical America* read on a plane to Austin, can produce results that would not have developed without one or two of the ingredients. I think who I have known and what I have read and seen and heard. And the knowledge I make is not separable or extractable from the natural history and the natural technology within which I operate.

It is necessary to counter the rationalist assumptions concerning the purely ideational origins of knowledge by emphasizing the technological nature of knowledge. This undermines the legitimacy of rationalist norms of legality, balance, harmony, and equilibrium by pointing to the political scene in which knowledge takes place. Knowledge is itself a political arena, a matter of rationing which, at this point of social history, privileges the white and male and well-to-do. The progress of science is bound up with the progress of militarist capitalism led by white males.

The erection of professions and of disciplines is inseparable from a certain sexual political rectitude. The kinds of objective facts discovered through knowledge will be determined by the institutions and the practices that form the social network that makes knowledge possible, down to the linearity of the discursive, written line and of the predicative proposition. In addition, the unbalancing of the rationalist equilibrium of power in knowledge necessitates practices that introduce dialogue and alterity into the centralizing singularity of the discursive voice. Derrida's use of the double column in *Glas*, for example, emphasizes relations between the sides and thereby undermines the rationalist focus on a nonrelational, single discursive line. In this way, the event of reading and the fact read become issues, relational processes.

Why, for instance, do white males discover master molecules whereas female scientists, who have experienced exploitation and who lack an interest in preserving (by projecting as natural) power relations, see nonhierarchical, aggregational, gregarious structures? This does not lead to naturalism, but to an epistemology of the oppressed.

Why are American blacks more prone to understand the epistemology of marxism? Why are former working-class, soon-to-be-middle-class whites like myself less given to violence? Perhaps because white male violence passes muster as science. The call to rational balance is always a symptom.

A socialist rationality, therefore, would necessarily be irrational from a capitalist rationalist point of view. It would distribute according to need, rather than according to "equal" exchange or balance. It would not see the necessity of phallo-centers to enforce homogeneity for efficiency. Situated as a region of broad sociomaterial and historical practice, knowledge loses its regulative, rationalist character and becomes a matter of constitution, construction, natural technology, and material production.

Seen as a form of natural technology (or of cultural nature), knowledge becomes detached from power, from what Derrida calls "phallogocentrism," the power of the white male and of rationalism (that is, the use of reason for the sake of power). The natural world is no longer to be mastered because knowledge is part of that world, a technique of material constitution and of social construction.

Considered materially, knowledge cannot be separated from its institutions or from the practices that operate it. And equally, it cannot be reconstructed without a reconstruction of those institutions—schools, words, professions, and so on. Nor is it an ideal operation that transcends sexuality, or personal power, or physical sustenance. The reconstruction of knowledge cannot be separated from the redistribution of power along sex, class, and racial lines. The myth of professionalized and specialized knowledge, reserved for elites, will disappear only when the imposition of time-consuming work is removed and when education is popular and when an economy exists that does not operate according to an equation of education with labor market viability. Any other reconstruction of knowledge would remain moralistic, elitist, and idealist.

(By the way, Barbara, I do not mean that we would all think differently under socialism. I mean that the prevalent form of reason, especially as it operates in social policy, would need to be reconstructed. Capitalism requires rationalism, and such rationalism is incompatible with the social form of socialism. A good number of leftists already think beyond rationalist limits. They see relations, differentials, and aggregates where capitalist rationalists see decontextualized facts, ideal invariants, neutral methods, purely instrumental techniques, master principles, and so on. They carry on the ideological battle as they must. It will help change minds. But the formation of minds in this society continues to be determined by capitalist-rationalist structures. Ultimately, they will have to be addressed and changed. And ultimately, of course, that depends on changes in power which are institutional, not cognitive.)

A sense of the relation between knowledge and social construction implies that a radical reconstruction of knowledge points not only toward alternative cognitive forms, but also alternative social formations, and, reciprocally, that such social formations require a reconstruction of knowledge.

❧ 8 ❧

Marxism
after Deconstruction

A "political-economic kernel" should by now have begun to emerge from the "philosophic shell." Deconstruction deals for the most part with how we *conceive* the world. And how we conceive the world has broad implications for how we *act* in it. A dogmatic science of dialectical materialism, for example, is unlikely to give rise to anything but integrational and collaborationist politics and a central statist socialism. The question of method or of form or style in thought as in action, therefore, is essential to such more seemingly substantive issues as political organization and socialist construction.

I shall now consider a number of problems in marxism to which deconstruction might make a contribution, as well as certain points of articulation between the two. I will begin with the political implications of Lenin's method of reading Marx's text. Then, I will turn to Marx's analysis of the relationship between credit and capitalist crisis as it relates to more recent institutional developments. Next, I will attempt to bring deconstruction to bear on the question of models of socialist construction. And in the final chapter, I will address the question of the method of political organization in light of recent quasi-"deconstructive" critiques of leninism launched by socialist feminists and autonomists.

Deconstructive philosophy suggests that seemingly neutral and self-evident modes of analysis are fraught with implications and presuppositions which the analytic system can never fully control. The choice of concepts and the strategies of inclusion and exclusion used in the determination of the focus of analysis will reflect preanalytic decisions the examination of which can put in question the self-evident axioms of the system of analysis. Marxists understand the importance of an inquiry into ideological discursive systems, such as capitalist political economy, which strategically exclude, as exogenous to a neutral analysis, such categories as class or exploitation. But deconstructive inquiry can (and should) be applied to marxist discourse as well, if it employs methods inherited from metaphysics without submitting them to critique. Lenin's method of reading Marx, for example, can be said to be metaphysical.

Lenin must be understood within the historical context of the Second International debates over the relationship between economic trade union struggle and socialism. A first deconstructive caution would be that words like "economic," "political," "state," and "democracy" have different meanings within that context than they do now. Yet the leninist left always applies Lenin's terms as if they were transhistorical and in no way shaped by those debates. To a certain degree, these leftists are simply being faithful to their master's own method.

Lenin, from a reductive reading of fragmentary and heterogeneous texts by Marx and Engels, constructs a homogeneous and singular "Marxist theory of the state." The way Lenin's appropriative and manipulative reading of Marx's texts in *State and Revolution* (1917) has become a law instrumental in the oppression of state socialist working classes as well as a slogan for conservative communist parties all over the world is a lesson in why a critical deconstructive disposition has a salutary effect for leftist theory and practice, especially in that, more often than not, that theory and practice derives its working premises from texts and the interpretation of texts, especially the texts of Marx. That tendency to locate a secular oracle in Marx is not condoned here. Yet, to rest content with a condemnation of the practice would be to ignore its pervasiveness. Instead, I will argue that *how* we read a text, in this case Marx's, has political implications. In Lenin's *way* of reading Marx, one finds the outlines of all that is wrong with leninism.

In *State and Revolution*, Lenin polemicizes against gradualist parliamentarianism (Karl Kautsky, Edward Bernstein), which believes the bourgeois state form must be preserved, and against anarchism, which believes the state must be eliminated altogether. Lenin's point, which mediates between the two, is that although the bourgeois state must be destroyed, the state form must be preserved, but controlled by the proletariat. From a deconstructive point of view, Lenin's argument is interesting because it is carried out in the name of the restoration of an absolute truth—"In view of the unprecedentedly widespread distortion of Marxism, our prime task is to *re-establish* what Marx really taught on the subject of the state"[1]—yet it proceeds by a series of interpretive displacements which move Marx's text toward conclusions Lenin himself proposes but Marx in fact contradicts. Lenin reads diverse texts, written in highly different situations for a variety of audiences, as if they merely expressed a preexisting, homogeneous "Marxist theory of the state," which Marx and Engels, without any of the differences that manifest themselves in the difference between their collaborative and autonomous efforts, had in mind, and concerning which they occasionally made statements. Lenin fosters this illusion by beginning with Engels rather than Marx, because he, more than Marx, did elaborate a theory of the state.

Lenin's first displacement is perhaps the most significant. He cites Marx's statement in the *Communist Manifesto* to the effect that "the first step in the revolution by the working class is to raise the proletariat to the position of ruling class" and "to centralize all instruments of production in the hands of the state, i.e., of the proletariat organized as a ruling class" (*LCW*, 402). Lenin uses this quote to argue against the kautskyites that the proletariat does not need the present bourgeois state, but instead a proletarian state: "The proletariat needs state power, a centralized organization of violence . . . to *lead* the enormous mass of the population . . . in the work of organizing a socialist economy" (*LCW*, 404). The crucial displacement occurs in the next paragraph: "By educating the workers' party, Marxism educates the vanguard of the proletariat, capable of assuming power and *leading the whole people* to socialism, of directing and organizing the new system, of being the teacher, the guide, the leader of all the working and exploited people" (*LCW*, 404). After establishing the "marxist" definition of the state as the "proletariat organized as a ruling class," Lenin substitutes the vanguard party for the proletariat. From this point on in the text, it can be assumed that whenever Lenin speaks of the political power of the proletariat, he means the power of the vanguard party.

Marx's own thrust in the phrase "in the hands of the state, i.e., of the proletariat organized as a ruling class" is actually just the opposite of Lenin's. The explanatory apposition ("of the proletariat . . .") is tacked on because Marx obviously did not want the new temporary ruling organization of the proletariat to be confused with the state in the bourgeois sense of the word, that is, a locus of alienated political power. By substituting party for class and by emphasizing statism in Marx's antipolitical statist formulation, Lenin seems set on preserving political power in its alien character, that is, as something external and objective that transcends the subjective will of the participants and exercises a power that is not their power but, rather, belongs to a detached and autonomous elite.

In this section of *State and Revolution*, Lenin limits the application of the notion that the state must be destroyed as such to the bourgeois state. He goes against Marx's argument that not only the bourgeois state but all state formations have to go. Lenin claims that "Marx's theory of the state" posits that the "culmination" of the "revolutionary role of the proletariat in history" is the "political rule of the proletariat" (that is, of the vanguard party). Lenin fails to emphasize that in the passage he cites from the *Manifesto*, proletarian rule is termed the *"first step"* in the revolutionary process, and he does not quote a passage that follows immediately in the text:

When, in the course of development, class distinctions have disappeared, and all production has been concentrated in the hands of associated individuals [*assoziierten Individuen*], the public power will lose its political character. Political power, properly so called, is merely the organized power of one class for oppressing another. If the proletariat during its contest with the bourgeoisie is compelled, by the force of circumstances, to organize itself as a class; if, by means of a revolution, it makes itself the ruling class, and, as such sublates [*aufhebt*] the old relations of production [*produktions-verhältnisse*] then it will, along with these relations, sublate [*hebt . . . auf*] the conditions for the existence of class antagonisms and of classes generally, and will thereby sublate its own supremacy as a class. In place of the old bourgeois society, with its classes and class antagonisms, we shall have an association [*assoziation*], in which the free development of each is the condition for the free development of all.[2]

There is no doubt, given the clear thematic and stylistic resemblances with earlier texts, that this particular passage was written by Marx, not Engels. Its call for an "association," as opposed to a central state power, is in keeping with Marx's statements concerning the Commune, as we shall see. It should be granted to Lenin that he may not have touched on this passage because it deals with an argument that he does mention, in a qualified way as we will see, in later sections. But it should be noted as well that its strategic avoidance (the first of many) permits Lenin to make it appear at this point that Marx supports without qualification Lenin's argument that the bourgeois state must be destroyed and *replaced* by another central state.

In the two sections that follow in the text, Lenin shows an awareness of Marx's more expanded argument: "This proletarian state will begin to wither away•immediately after its victory because the state is unnecessary and cannot exist in a society in which there are no class antagonisms" (*LCW*, 406). Lenin projects the destruction of the state as such into the future. During the period of transition, the dictatorship of the proletariat, that is, of the party, will still be exercised: "The essence of Marx's theory of the state has been mastered only by those who realize that the dictatorship of a *single* class is necessary not only for every class society in general, not only for the proletariat which has overthrown the bourgeoisie, but also for entire *historical periods* which separates capitalism from 'classless society,' from communism" (*LCW*, 413). In the *Critique of the Gotha Program* Marx does indeed speak of the necessity of a transition period characterized by a "revolutionary dictatorship of the proletariat." By proletariat, however, he never meant a vanguard party whose role was to teach, to guide, and to lead. And it was around this time of the *Critique* that Marx spoke out most strongly against the form of vanguardism that was so important to Lenin:

What was new in the International was that it was established by the working-men themselves and for themselves. Before the foundation of the International all the different organizations had been societies founded by some radicals among the ruling classes for the working classes, but the

International was founded by the working men for themselves. . . . When the International was formed, we expressly formulated the battle-cry; the emancipation of the working class must be the work of the working class itself. We cannot ally ourselves, therefore, with people who openly declare that the workers are too uneducated to free themselves and must be liberated from above by philanthropic big bourgeois or petty bourgeois.[3]

If we can extrapolate from Marx's remarks concerning the organizational form of the International to what conceivably might have been a workers' party or even a workers' state, then it is clear that Marx, had he lived, would have repudiated Lenin's claim that he was a centrist: "To talk of secret instructions from London, as of decrees in the matter of faith and morals from some centre of papal domination and intrigue, is wholly to misconceive the nature of the International. This would imply a centralized form of government for the International, whereas the real form is designedly that which gives the greatest play to local energy and independence. In fact, the International is not properly a government for the working class at all. It is a bond of union rather than a controlling force" (*FIA*, 394-95).

It should be pointed out here that most of these texts were not available to Lenin. Therefore, he cannot be accused of deliberately ignoring them when he elaborated the "Marxist theory of the state." It should also be pointed out that, unlike Marx, Lenin was writing in a revolutionary situation. *State and Revolution* was literally written in the middle of the revolution, between August and September 1917. It concludes with the sentence: "It is more pleasant and useful to go through the 'experience of the revolution' than to write about it" (*LCW*, 492). The text (like all texts, and this is ultimately Lenin's failing in regard to Marx's text) is not purely theoretical, a set of ideas detached from history. It is shaped by the material exigencies, constraints, and forces at work in the specific practical situation of its writing. The deconstructive argument applies here: no text is a transparent medium for the communication of theoretical ideas, meaning or a truth, which preexists and is "expressed" in the material practice of the text. No meaning is expressed; rather, it is produced as an effect of the threading together of personal, social, historical, linguistic, and other strands. Therefore, Lenin's "theory" was not produced in an ideal transhistorical realm. If he can be accused of overemphasizing certain aspects of Marx's text in order to generate a much displaced reading, it is because such a prejudiced reading was necessary in the practical historical situation in which Lenin (whose personal life would also have to be taken into account) found himself.

Lenin himself suppresses the heterogeneity that can be used partially to excuse him when he collapses disparate texts of Marx into an absolute theoretical truth—the "Marxist theory of the state." The deconstructive caution here would be that Marx's "text" is not homogeneous, and if one

tries to reduce it to a single theoretical meaning or ideal truth determination, one is being antihistorical and risks being idealist. When Marx
writes with Engels, he says different things than when he writes alone,
and what he wrote in 1848 differs from what he wrote in 1844 or 1871.
That heterogeneity does not lend itself easily to *a* or *the* marxist theory
that does not take into account the practice of the text in the practical
historical situation or the changing political and social class composition
at the different times Marx wrote. The independent craft workers of the
International could organize themselves; the professional workers of
Lenin's time were organized according to the discipline and hierarchy of
the factory. That *difference* makes necessary Lenin's displacement of
Marx's text. The practice of reading is also a matter of material historical
need, not of purely ideal cognition. I am not suggesting that Marx's text
is sacred and inviolable and that Lenin is wrong to manipulate it for his
own needs. The fact that he is obliged to manipulate it in order to derive
a reading suitable to the conditions of his own time confirms the deconstructive hypothesis that interpretation is always a displacement rather
than a restoration of truth (as Lenin believed). And if I point out things
in Marx that Lenin ignores, it is not to restore a transcendental truth of
Marx which can be applied to today's conditions. Rather, it is to restore
the historical situation in which Marx wrote, in terms of a new situation
that obtains today. I am graphing relations between points in history,
rather than restoring a truth that has ideal validity for all three points
— Marx's, Lenin's, and our own. The current social and political class
composition requires different strategies from the ones proposed by both
Marx and Lenin. If I point out how Lenin misreads Marx, it is with the
recognition that his historical situation demanded it. But, now, given the
obstacle leninism represents to the attainment of organizational forms
and socialist institutions suited to the social and political class composition
that now obtains, it is necessary to point out to what extent leninism is
historical. This can be done in part by showing how Lenin's most fundamental "marxist" theses are based on a practice of reading and quotation
which deliberately *displaces* Marx's text. If this displacement is determined
and made necessary by the constraints of Lenin's historical moment, my
analysis of it relying on what Marx actually wrote and taking into account
his historical moment is itself made necessary by the requirements and
constraints of this historical moment.

I have already pointed to texts by Marx which explicitly contradict
Lenin's "marxist theory." To fully demonstrate the deconstructive critique
of the sort of absolute reading Lenin performs, it would be necessary to
take into consideration the context of each one of Marx's statements
concerning the state and to compare it to others that precede, follow, or
in any way relate to it. By tracing such webs, one reduces the chances
for an absolute reading, but one also constructs a more accurate account

of the historicity of Marx's statements. For one thing, Marx consistently revised his ideas. Between his early and his late works, he reversed his position on the classical theory of value. In the mid-1850s, he thought money was the necessary point of departure for an analysis of capitalism. By the early 1860s, after working his way through thousands of pages of notebooks, he concluded that the starting point should be the commodity. That habit of painstaking working through and revision is matched by Marx's opinions on political organization. If the parallel holds, one could argue that Lenin's political opinions are matched by his method of reading Marx, which is hasty to posit a transhistorical "essence," an undistorted meaning, or a pretextual truth, to overlook distinctions and differences, and to fit the text into a preformed intepretive grid of all costs (to the text). The practice of interpretation and reading, in other words, has political and philosophical theoretical consequences. That, it could be argued, is the whole point of deconstruction.

Marx argues against the metaphysical method in political economy, which isolates macroconcepts, like property, and ignores the web of interconnections that lie under the surface of the economic system and give rise to "things" like property. To posit a simple, unitary essence, like property, is to overlook the systematic nature of the system, that it is made up of differentially related parts that have no autonomous existence outside those relations. Deconstruction makes a similar argument about texts. To assign a single unitary meaning or essential truth to a text is to overlook the complex weave of threads which constitute it. Lenin's method in *State and Revolution* is open to attack from both points of view. He cites a letter in which Marx uses the phrase "the dictatorship of the proletariat," and Lenin calls this "the essence of [Marx's] theory of the state" (*LCW*, 411). Locating an essence always involves exclusion; something has to be unessential in order for an essence to be determined. Lenin mentions "class struggle" as something focus on which entails "curtailing Marxism, distorting it, reducing it to something acceptable to the bourgeoisie." Essentialist exclusion in theory implies hierarchical exclusivism in political practice: "Only he is a marxist who *extends* the recognition of the class struggle to the recognition of the *dictatorship of the proletariat*" (*LCW*, 412).

Marx never wrote a complete text on the theory of the state about which one could say "this is its essence." In different situations, at different times, he wrote a series of texts in which he mentions the state, but these do not constitute a fully developed theory. Lenin isolates one point in that series — the thesis of the proletarian dictatorship — extracts it from the series, and transcendentalizes it as the central essence or paradigm of the series. He provides no logical argument to justify this suppression of all of Marx's other theses on the state and their subsumption under this essence. And Lenin hedges on making explicit his own implied argument—the proletariat will exercise rule during the transition period through the party organized as a central state authority—an argument which is itself the result of historical necessity. Like property in Marx's analysis of capital, "the dictatorship of the proletariat" cannot be extracted from the web of contextual relations and historical constraints that give it meaning. It has no meaning outside a context that situates it in relation to other events as a revolutionary moment of reversal leading to a displacement of all state power.

One could make a strong argument, substantiated by more than just a brief quote from a letter, that, had Marx written a full-fledged theory of the postrevolutionary state, he would have given importance to the dictatorship of the proletariat only as a *first step* in the process, and that this "dictatorship" would not have been central statist, but political-economic in character. In numerous texts, some of which were not available to Lenin, Marx places more weight on the *social* character of the revolution; politics (and the state) will cease to lead an alienated existence over against civil society, and its function of power, in its abstract, purely objective form, will disappear and become a subjective activity of the people, an objectification of their will. In the *Critique of Hegel's Doctrine of the State*, the abstraction that would be overcome through revolution takes the form of a separation between the political state and civil society: "The separation of the political state from civil society takes the form of a separation of the deputies from their electors. Society simply disputes elements of itself to become its political existence. . . . In the state constructed by Hegel the *political* convictions of civil society are mere *opinion* just because its political existence is an *abstraction* from its real existence; just because the state in its totality is not the objectification of those political convictions."[4] To delegate a vanguard party to run the state is to repeat Hegel's mistake and to constitute the political state as an abstraction. Marx never revokes this early thesis, and it is reflected in his later belief in an "association" that has shed abstract, statist politics.

At the time of the *Critique*, Marx called for an overcoming of political abstraction through direct universal suffrage and political/social revolution: "There is no doubt about the rationality of a *political revolution* with a *social soul*. All revolution—the *overthrow* of the existing ruling power and the *dissolution* of the old order—is a *political act*. But without revolution *socialism* cannot be made possible. It stands in need of this political act just as it stands in need of *destruction* and *dissolution*. But as soon as its *organizing activity* [*Tätigkeit*] begins and its end-in-itself [*selbstzweck*], its *soul* emerges, socialism throws its political mask aside" (*EW*, 420). This early thesis initiates a refrain we have already seen in the *Manifesto* that also occurs in Marx's later writings, especially *The Civil War in France*, in which he discusses the Commune.

Lenin's treatment of that text in the section of *State and Revolution* entitled "What Is to Replace the Smashed State Machine?" reflects his essentialist method of reducing disparate statements to a self-identical theme ("the essence will inevitably be the same: the dictatorship of the proletariat") and of filtering out statements that contradict his centralizing thesis that Marx was a "centralist." For example, Lenin leaves out explicit statements by Marx supporting the decentralization carried out by the Commune. Lenin cites almost an entire paragraph describing the social policy of the Commune, but skips one phrase—"Instead of continuing to be the agent of the state government [*staatsregierung*] [the police . . .]"—and he leaves off the final two sentences: "Public functions ceased to be the private property of the tools of the *central government* [*Zentralregierung*]. Not only municipal administration, but the whole initiative hitherto exercised by the *state* was laid into the hands of the Commune" (*FIA*, 209; *MEW*, 17:339, my italics). He also leaves out the phrase, "Like the rest of the public servants," before the sentence "magistrates and judges were to be elective, responsible, and revocable," as well as two sentences implying the freeing of public processes from central state, bureaucratic control: "The whole of educational institutions were opened to the public gratuitously, and at the same time cleared of all interference of church and state. Thus . . . science itself [was] freed from the fetters which class prejudice and state power [*Regierungsgewalt*] had imposed upon it" (*FIA*, 210; *MEW*, 17:339). Without these passages, Marx's text would seem to support Lenin's contention that a central bureaucracy will still be necessary under a communal form of society. It seems that Lenin can prove Marx was a centralist only by omitting those passages where Marx explicitly voices support for an anticentrist, antistatist position.

Perhaps the most striking sentence that Lenin deliberately does not cite is the following: "The communal arrangement of things [*Ordnung der Dinge*] once established in Paris and the secondary centers, the old *centralized* government [*zentralisierte Regierung*] would in the provinces, too, have to give way to the *self-government* [*selbstregierung*] of the producers" (*FIA*, 210; *MEW*, 17:339). The sentence lays to waste Lenin's entire argument that Marx's description of the Commune is pro-centralist, and Lenin's omission of it is understandable. It makes somewhat ironic his remark, "Marx was a centralist. There is no departure whatever from centralism in his observations just quoted" (*LCW*, 492), because the anticentrist passages are precisely the ones not quoted.

Lenin also omits through paraphrase. He states, for example, that, according to Marx, the deputies of the National Assembly would be elected by universal suffrage. But the passage he paraphrases contains an explicitly anticentrist theme which he ignores: "The rural communes of every district were *to administer their common affairs by an assembly of delegates in the central town,* and these district assemblies were again to send deputies to the national delegation in Paris, each delegate to be at any time revocable and bound by the *mandat imperatif* (formal instructions) of his constituents" (*FIA*, 211; *MEW*, 17:340).

Through selective quotation, Lenin constructs an argument that depicts Marx's description of the Commune as justifying subordination to the "armed vanguard" of the proletariat, a centralized bureaucratic state, and large-scale production on "strict, iron discipline backed up [read: enforced by] the state power of the armed workers" [read: the party] (*LCW*, 426). Every passage that Lenin leaves out contradicts these claims, especially the following: "Nothing could be more foreign to the spirit of the Commune than to supersede universal suffrage by hierarchic investiture" (*FIA*, 211; *MEW*, 17:340).

The Commune promoted self-government; all the functions of the central state that were not to be transferred to the communes or to be abolished were to be performed by Communal agents, elected through universal suffrage at the local level. The central state was to become superfluous, but the "unity of the nation" was to be preserved by the national delegation. Lenin turns the argument for national unity into an argument for a centralized state. He does so by quoting a passage in such a way that an argument differentiating the nationally unified communes from a federation of separate small states becomes an argument for a central state and by unjustifiably (on the basis of Marx's text) identifying "national unity" with "central authority." Again, Lenin must quote selectively. I italicize the passages he does cite: "The Communal constitution has been mistaken for an attempt to break up into a *federation of small states, as dreamt of by Montesquieu and the Girondins*, that unity of great peoples [*volker*] which, if originally brought about by political force, has now become a powerful coefficient of social production. The antagonism of the Commune against state power has been mistaken *for an exaggerated form of the ancient struggle against over-centralization*" (*FIA*, 211; *MEW*, 17: 340-41). By quoting selectively, Lenin makes it seem as if Marx were arguing for a nonfederal central authority, whereas he is actually distinguishing a decentralized, yet nationally unified, communal social form from the federal political form and distinguishing the new cooperative form from a simple orthodox critique of "overcentralization." That critique would make the issue a question of degree, whereas the issue is a qualitatively different political form, one that, because it defines itself in opposition to all central state power ("the antagonism of the *Commune against the state power*," a line Lenin leaves out, significantly), radically surpasses the critique of overcentralization, which still adheres to a form of centralization.

In addition, Lenin equates Marx's acknowledgment of the necessity of national unity through delegation with a belief in central state authority, a misequation that is contradicted by the passages criticizing central state authority which Lenin strategically avoids. The national delegation would consist not of a "central authority" but of "servants" and "agents" of communally organized producers who would themselves exercise authority over the national delegation. Lenin reverses this equation. Whereas for Marx, the Commune means "really democratic institutions," "free and associated labor," and "united cooperative societies" that "regulate national production upon a common plan" (*FIA*, 211; *MEW*, 17:341-43), for Lenin it becomes an ideological justification for antidemocratic authoritarian centrism that subordinates workers to "strict discipline," administration, and coercive work control.

How does a text that rejects centrist statism and celebrates decentralized communalism become a tool for supporting statist centrism? I have pointed to some unjustifiable equations Lenin makes, as well as to his deft editing job on Marx's text. The polemical situation in which *State and Revolution* was written and the form of argumentation that situation imposed on Lenin must also be considered. He needed to prove that Marx supported his position that the bourgeois state had to be smashed (against the leftists and the anarchists), at least during the period of transition, to "suppress" any remaining bourgeois opposition and to consolidate proletarian power. Whenever Marx speaks of the state in general, Lenin interprets him to mean only the bourgeois state. He then twists the national unity argument (with appropriate omissions) to make Marx appear to be arguing for a new centralized state authority to replace the old. The answer to the question, What is to replace the smashed state machine? then becomes: the state. He speaks of the ultimate "withering away" of the state, but he couples these remarks with such a pertinacious argument for centrism, discipline, and administrative authority that one suspects his sense of a stateless society would have little in common with that of Marx.

The significance of Lenin's suppression of passages critical of state centrism becomes clearer when one considers Lenin's argument that the Commune "only *appears* to have replaced the smashed state machine . . . by fuller democracy." In fact, what occurred was a "gigantic replacement of certain institutions by other institutions of a fundamentally different type." Because "it is still necessary to suppress the bourgeoisie," the state only "*begins* to wither away." Lenin, the great critic of gradualism, transforms the radical rupture with orthodox centrist statism in the Commune into a gradual transition: "The more the functions of state power are performed by the people as a whole, the less need there is for the existence of this power" (*LCW*, 419).

Marx celebrates the Commune's immediate break with centrism; Lenin neutralizes that argument and transforms it into an argument for centrism. By the end of the section, he has turned an antistatist revolution into a "reorganization of the state." By the end of the next section, he describes the "task" of the Commune as "building up the state" (*LCW*, 427). In this same section he speaks of the necessity of subordination to the "armed vanguard" and of workers' discipline "backed by state power."

All of this is a far cry from the suppressed passages in Marx. I suspect there may be grounds for distinguishing between marxism and leninism. In many ways, Lenin is an antimarxist, at least in the sense that the principles of political and social organization which he proposes run counter to those of Marx, especially with regard to work organization, which Marx sees as a free association, but which Lenin sees as a hyperdisciplined central state factory. Lenin excuses the necessity of the centralized state by having recourse to the notion of a "transitional form" of the disappearance of the state in which the proletariat would be "organized as a ruling class." For Lenin, of course, that means a dictatorship of the vanguard party—"the dictatorship of the proletariat, i.e., the organization of the vanguard of the oppressed as the ruling class" (*LCW*, 461). Even though Marx argued that "the proletariat still acts, during the period of struggle for the overthrow of the old society, on the basis of that old society, and hence also still moves within political forms which more or less belong to it" (*FIA*, 338; *MEW*, 18:636), he argues in the same text that "the whole thing begins with the self-government of the commune" (*FIA*, 338; *MEW*, 18:634). Given his remarks against centralization and hierarchical investiture in *The Civil War*, it is highly unlikely that Marx would have been very tolerant of Lenin's disciplinary centrism.

What most pitches Lenin against Marx is Lenin's privileging of the political over the economic struggles. This emphasis leads Lenin to focus his treatise exclusively on political questions and to treat the economic as a neutral sphere that can be left intact in its capitalist form as long as private ownership is transferred into "social ownership." The privilege given the political carries with it a reduction of the economic to the development of productive forces, without any consideration for the socialization of productive relations. Lenin fails to see that the economic is shot through with politics and that it cannot be isolated as a neutral mechanism. That was one of the major points of Marx's analysis of capitalism, and to the extent that he flies in the face of it, Lenin once again falls into an antimarxist position. Lenin thus enthuses over the "splendidly equipped mechanism" of "social management"; it never strikes him that management, subordination, adminstration, and control, as well as the coercive work situation itself may be alien to communism. All the texts in which Marx projects a society free from coercive labor, one in which the revolution is described in economic as well as political terms—especially the *Grundrisse*—were unavailable to Lenin.

Lenin even speaks of socialism as "a purely political reorganization of society" (*LCW*, 421). The contrasting marxist position is reflected in Marx's "Speech on the Seventh Anniversary of the International," in which he states "that in the militant state of the working class, its economical movement and its political action are indissolubly united" (*FIA*, 270). A slightly different version of the same point occurs in *The Civil War*. As one would expect by now, Lenin cites everything up to the beginning of this passage: "The political rule of the producer cannot coexist without the perpetuation of his social slavery. The Commune was therefore to serve as a lever for uprooting the economical foundations upon which rests the existence of classes, and therefore of class rule. With labor emancipated, every man becomes a working man, and productive labor ceases to be a class attribute" (*FIA*, 211; *MEW*, 17:342).

The trouble with Lenin is that his concept of socialism, putting aside the question of social — in fact, state — ownership, is entirely political. Otherwise, his economic projections (and subsequent actions) merely exacerbate capitalist work forms. The concept of transition does not compensate the overemphasis on the political. There is no concept of emancipated labor in Lenin which holds the promise of a posttransitional transformation of the economic process beyond increased discipline for increased productivity. Given his political bias, Lenin could not help but ignore Marx's passage describing the social and economic revolution, the absolute transformation of productive relations, which the Commune marked:

> The Commune intended to abolish that class property which makes the labor of the many the wealth of the few. It aimed at the expropriation of the expropriators. It wanted to make individual property a truth by transforming the means of production, land and capital, now chiefly the means of enslaving and exploiting labor, into mere instruments of free and associated labor. But this is communism, "impossible" communism! [Is it relevant that Lenin chastises students who demand the "impossible"?] Why, those members of the ruling classes who are intelligent enough to perceive the impossibility of continuing the present system . . . have become the obstrusive and full-mouthed apostles of cooperative production. If cooperative production is not to remain a sham and a snare; if it is to supersede the capitalist system; if united cooperative societies are to regulate national production upon a common plan, thus taking it under their own control, and putting an end to the constant anarchy and periodical convulsions which are the fatality of the capitalist production — what else, gentlemen, would it be but communism, "possible" communism. [*FIA*, 213; *MEW*, 342-43]

Lenin's discipline, control, and order in the factory are far removed from freely associated cooperative production. Lenin thinks of the economy in political terms, rather than thinking, as Marx did, of politics in economic terms because he places the political party before and above the economic class. That strategy is, of course, partly a reaction to Second International economism, but it also derives from Lenin's lack of a sense of the significance of labor. Marx recognized that human beings are

active and productive, traits he described philosophically as the intertwining of subject and object, human creative activity and concrete historical materiality. Lenin, in *Materialism and Empirico-Criticism*, describes
the "marxist" concept of materiality as a simple "outside" of human consciousness, and he separates subject from object. He thus demonstrates
an ignorance (understandable, because he lacked access to the pertinent
manuscripts of Marx which explained the "marxist" position that the
social world was a product of past human labor and thus not a simple
objective outside in the feuerbachian sense) of the dialectical relationship,
in Marx's work, between labor and materiality as technology in a historically developed social world. He understands "practice," the word
which in part describes that productive interaction, simply as a means of
validating passive subjective knowledge in an "objective" world.

The point of communism, according to Marx, is the emancipation of
labor, that is, of creative and productive human life activity, from the
capitalist relations of production. It cannot, in other words, simply entail
a transfer of titles of ownership through a purely political revolution.
The process of labor and production must be transformed. Ultimately,
this can be done only by workers themselves, and they are unlikely to
promote a "communism" based on increased work discipline and iron
control in the workplace. The structure of power and the system of coercion in the workplace will be broken only by those oppressed by it. A
nonworker such as Lenin would not be likely to have a concrete sense of
the emancipation needed. Power-under (as opposed to power-over) is a
negative power, but it is the only power on the scene with sufficient
leverage to operate a break of the sort that will reverse and displace the
entire logic of power. Lenin shows that the logic of power needs to be
broken as much on the level of theory—intellectual work—as on that of
practice—workplace, farm, family, school, and the like.

For there is an analogy in Lenin between his practice of reading and
theorizing—locating the center, the paradigm, the master theme, the
essence through exclusion, manipulation, and suppression—and his
theory of socialist practice—order, discipline, central authority, exclusive-
ness. Marx, I think, understood this relationship more than Lenin ever
could, just as he understood that only the oppressed could make their
own revolution. Here is one last passage from *The Civil War*, which, by
now it goes without saying, Lenin ignores:

> The working class did not expect miracles from the Commune. They have
> no ready-made utopias to introduce *par decret du peuple*. They know that in
> order to work out their own emancipation, and along with it that higher
> form to which present society is irresistibly tending by its own economical
> agencies, they will have to pass through long struggles, through a series of
> historic processes, transforming circumstances and men. They have no
> ideals to realize, but to set free the elements of the new society with which

old collapsing bourgeois society itself is pregnant. In the full consciousness of their historic mission, and with the heroic resolve to act up to it, the working class can afford to smile at the coarse invective of the gentlemen's gentlemen with the pen and inkhorn, and at the didactic patronage of well-wishing bourgeois doctrinaires, pouring forth their ignorant platitudes and sectarian crotchets [*sektierermarotten*] in the oracular tone of scientific infallibility. [*FIA*, 213; *MEW*, 343]

Breaking the logic of power in theory (which is also in the practice of reading, interpreting, and knowing) is where the immediate effectivity of deconstruction resides. Deconstruction makes one aware of how theory is determined by practice, as well as of how practice can be produced by theory. The fact that Lenin's theory more or less became the norm for Soviet practice, and that his theory was in part influenced by practical necessities of his historical situation, provides a confirmation of the principle. It also prevents one from too hastily pinning down the decided truth of Lenin's text without taking into account the practical situation of revolutionary Russia. Lenin's own excessive haste in pinning down an absolute truth of (an edited version of) Marx's text must be understood in light of the need for a theoretical anchor in a highly disequilibrated situation. But that deconstructive caution against critical judgment apart from history should also be brought to bear on the leninist movement, which transcendentalizes Lenin's "truths" apart from the historical situation in which they arose. The necessity of a salutary skepsis concerning the possibility of "undistorted" truths, which exist apart from practical historical situations that imply the inevitability of displacement or the impossibility of a purely transcendental, undistorted truth, is demonstrated by the way Soviet practice is based on a theory that claims to restore the absolutely undistorted truth of Marx's text, but is constructed through strategies, displacement, misrepresentation, misquotation, and omission. Soviet practice is leninist but not marxist if *The Civil War* is any indication of what Marx's marxism would have been like in a situation similar to Lenin's.

Deconstruction would, at this point, reach the following conclusion: Lenin's desire for the absolute, undistorted truth of Marx's theory of the state reflects a metaphysical aspiration for a pure theoretical realm, which detaches itself from and pretends to transcend textual practice and historical situational inscription. No ultimately decidable truth of Marx's text can be determined apart from the textual and historical system in which the ideas are embedded. The reconstruction of the "theory" is ultimately only the construction of another text, another practice. There is no realm of purely ideal theory, then, apart from practice, in this case, interpretive practice. And there will always be some distortion in that practice, simply because it pertains to the realm of displacement, change, and alteration in history and can never be the revelation of a purely ideal theory. In the first place, the theory cannot be "revealed" without practice, a textual practice of representation. Therefore, distortion is "original," not an accident that occurs to an already pure theory. Strictly speaking, the theory was never undistorted. To try to restore an absolute undistorted truth of a theory, apart from its practical inscription, is idealist because it overlooks both history and practice.

Lenin consistently overlooks (literally) Marx's text and goes straight for the undistorted truth. But in seeking homogeneous truth, he is obliged to distort the text, which is not of the same nature as an "essence," but instead is crosshatched with strands of reference linked to a specific history (itself highly complex) which do not resolve into an ideal meaning or essence. Lenin reduces out the situation of each text as well as its performative character—the fact that each text was addressed to a different audience and designed to produce different effects. All of this modifies the possibility of a theory, separable from historical situationality and textual practice, which would be purified of all distortions and fixed once and for all as a homogeneous entity. Lenin falls prey to the thematic fallacy: that books reflect homogeneous theories existing apart from and prior to historical situations and textual practices. His aspiration supposes that Marx's finalized version of a theory of the state can be resurrected intact from the textual ruins left behind. It is more likely that Marx constructed bits and pieces of a theory through the practice of his writing. That practice, tied as it was to changes in history and in Marx's life, resulted in inevitable contradictions. What Marx wrote about universal suffrage in 1843 is not compatible with what he wrote thirty years later. And even in "mature" texts, he sometimes praised suffrage, sometimes dismissed it, depending on the situation and the audience. The homogeneous essence becomes difficult to pin down if one begins to attend to these specific differences.

For example, at the end of the Communist Manifesto (1848), Marx emphasizes state centralization as a means of attaining socialism: "5. Centralization of credit in the hands of the state, by means of a national bank with state capital and an exclusive monopoly. 6. Centralization of the means of communication and transport in the hands of the state."[5] In 1872, however, Marx reconsidered this emphasis on state centralization in light of the experience of the Commune. He wrote in a new preface to the Manifesto:

> The practical application of the principles will depend, as the Manifesto itself states, everywhere and at all times, on the historical conditions for the time being existing, and, for that reason, no special stress is laid on the revolutionary measures proposed at the end of section II. That passage would, in many respects, be very differently worded today. In view of the gigantic strides of modern industry since 1848, and of the accompanying

improved and extended organization of the working class; in view of the practical experience gained, first in the February revolution, and then, still more, in the Paris Commune, where the proletariat for the first time held political power for two whole months, this programme has in some details become antiquated. One thing especially was proved by the Commune, viz., that "the working class cannot simply lay hold of the ready-made state machinery, and wield it for its own purposes." [*Rev.*, 66]

It should be clear that it is not altogether legitimate for Lenin to cite the Manifesto, especially the end of section II, which Marx said would need to be revised, as *the* "Marxist theory of the state" or of socialism, for that matter. And the passage just cited demonstrates that Marx himself was aware of the problems of historical specificity and difference Lenin so resolutely ignored.

A politicized use of deconstruction would suggest a link between Lenin's manipulative practice of textual interpretation, with its idealist bias, and the political theory in whose service it operates. The practice and the theory are founded on a privileging of consciousness, hence legislative control, and the decisive, indisputable determination of truth. The world is not internal to the mind in a material continuum of dialectical interrelation, but instead, external as a simple object to be known by consciousness and manipulated from a detached position of contemplation. That attitude of common sense perception reacts against the search after nonempirical *relations* (Marx's method); in Lenin, it proceeds predictably to the ignoring of productive relations and the emphasis on purely "objective" productive forces. If Lenin's practice of interpretation is any indication, a socialist construction based on similar principles is likely to be exclusivist, hierarchial, teleological, so idealist that it dismisses the practical, material domain of productive labor as politically neutral, and objectivist to the extent that the world will not be something in which one is practically inscribed, but something to be manipulated. If one can predict, on the basis of what Lenin ignores in his practice of textual interpretation (in the reading of *The Civil War*), what will be privileged or marginalized in a practice of socialist construction derived from Lenin, then it is clear that the possibility of initiative by workers in the construction of the new society will be disallowed. Anything that contradicts state centrism, especially the possibility of "free and associated labor" in "united cooperative societies" or communes, will be excluded. Marginalized will be such inessential things to the central state as the "antagonism . . . against the state power," "really democratic institutions," and a police that is no longer "the agent to the central government." And finally, there will be no sense of the contradiction between "the political rule of the producer" and "the perpetuation of his social slavery" in the capitalist form of work.

Essential meaning, the proper theory detached from and elevated above the work and the practice of the text as of the factory, will be the property first of the Party and then of the State.

The major point of articulation between marxism and deconstruction is in the analysis of capitalist crisis and its implications. The focus here is credit.

Marx's account of credit reflects a heterogeneous dialectic that in many ways coincides with the deconstructive account of the world. It justifies Derrida's own caution in calling metaphysical only that dialectic operative "from Plato down to Hegel."

Metaphysical dialectics operates on a principle of equivalence, governed by a norm of identity which reduces out difference and the possibility of a radical alterity, that is, of a becoming other which is irreducible to a system of simple selfsameness and simple negation, simple equivalence and simple nonequivalence, and is instead the possibility of plural proliferation. In that system, equivalence and identity are the norms, of which differentiality and alterity are mere derivations or deviations that ultimately resolve themselves back into identity. Contradiction, for example, in Hegel's dialectic marks a merely momentary break with the norm of equivalence which soon resolves itself back into equivalence (the identity of two things which are the same yet different). The self-identity of Mind absorbs all contradictions into its system of self-identity. Contradiction is not characterized by a radical alterity that breaks the circle of identity. Being and Non-Being contradict each other, but only in order to be equated as Becoming, something which itself falls into contradiction, subsequent equivalence, and so on until the entire process is subsumed under the logos, which equates subject and object, ideality and materiality.

Derrida calls this a "restrained economy," because it is defined as equivalence, the identification of difference, and exchange, the law of the return of the same. He calls "general" an economy or logic founded on a heterogeneous dialectic that breaks with the system of equivalence and exchange. Its principle is "expenditure without reserve," that is, without the return of the same which is the basis of equivalence and exchange. It is antilogocentric, because the logos is the principle of absolute self-identity and property; for it, all alterity is merely a moment in its own system of self-equivalence, all other-relations return to the same point of departure in the logos. There can be no loss; exchange guarantees ownership at the end of the temporary alienation of property. The general economy permits conceiving contradictions that do not resolve and differential relations that are not moments of self-identity, but are precisely that which removes all possibility of absolute self-identity once and for all. Rather than logocentric property, the general economy points toward interdependence, interrelationality, and communal nonownership. With regard to political economy, it signals a logic that is "social" or relational.

And it programs a disposition toward social change that would make revolutions interminable, because it would put in question the logocentric desire to resolve all contradictions.

Beyond the logic of equivalence and exchange, then, is a logic more suitable to socialism that takes as its point of departure the principle of expenditure without reserve or exchange. The logic implicit in Marx's analysis of credit already points toward such a principle, inasmuch as it describes the emergence of a radical alterity or difference in capitalism that indicates a crisis for the law of exchange.

Crisis arises because of irresolvable antagonisms within the capitalist system. Marx's notion of contradiction is therefore not theological or resolutive in the hegelian sense. Capital and labor, the antagonistic classes, will not resolve themselves into a third that will move the development harmoniously on toward a telos of self-identity. Instead, according to Marx, the negative power of labor will break open the circle of equivalence (in which, according to the metaphysical dialectic, nonequivalence is merely a moment of ultimate equivalence) that now pits capital and labor against each other in a relation of nonequivalence that is regulated and controlled by an appearance of equivalence and exchange: equal wage for equal work. The system of equivalence is metaphysical; it contains (in both senses of the word—to harbor and to control) a contradiction, an antagonism of differential force, because it always already is nonequivalence. Equal exchange in the market derives from unequal exchange in the workplace (the source of surplus value, because surplus labor is unpaid). A radical disequilibrium inhabits the supposedly selfsame as its very principle of operation. To that extent, the system is "undecidable," that is, it contradicts its own axiom of equivalent exchange, and therefore, it can be extended—as crisis and transition. The restrained economy is always already general, just as mature capitalism is a suppressed, deferred, and delayed socialism.

Absolute logocentric self-sufficiency, translated into ethico-political terms, implies freedom and independence. In political economy, it assumes the form of the capitalist entrepreneur or the corporation. In the doctrine of individual liberty, in ethics as in economics, the contiguity of logocentric metaphysics and bourgeois ideology is perhaps most clear. Equally clear is the necessity of an antilogocentric social and economic philosophy if socialism is to exist fully, as institutions of nonexchange and nonproperty. Such a philosophy would, like deconstruction, need to be based on radical alterity, rather than identity, the possibility of nonequivalence, rather than equivalence, and expenditure without reserve rather than equal exchange. Marx's term for an economy beyond exchange was "to each according to his needs."

His theory of credit both points the way toward such an economy and demonstrates the work of a dialectic of radical alterity, of a becoming other that no longer adheres to the logic of identity, whereby the other is simply the outside of an essentially intact inside, rather than that which disrupts all such selfsameness and equivalence. That dialectic of equivalence would see labor as simply a negative other of capital, a necessary counterpart in an essentially self-identical system, whereas Marx posits labor as a potentially disruptive, antagonistic force within a system that cannot dispense with that radical other and that has to contain its negative force.

Credit operates on a different register. It has none of the antagonistic charge of labor. Nonetheless, it constitutes a condition of possibility for the system, which opens the system to its crisis. It is both necessary and beneficial, as well as dangerous, to capital. It is the condition of the economy beyond exchange value: "If we did not find concealed in society as it is the material conditions of production and the corresponding relations of exchange prerequisite for a classless society, then all attempts to explode it would be quixotic" (Grun, 159; 77).

Credit, Marx argues, is a historically produced result of capitalism, not one of its natural conditions, yet it becomes a necessary condition of capitalist production. Credit thus represents a high degree of social control over natural processes. It is an artificial contrivance that enables capitalism to overcome natural boundaries to production. Yet at the same time, it gives rise to the conditions that bring the downfall of capitalism. Credit is one of those productive forces which, as it develops, shakes the foundations of the productive relations within whose context it operates.

The natural barrier which credit overcomes is the time of circulation. "Economy of time, to this all economy ultimately reduces itself" (Grun, 173; 89). The separation between purchase (for production) and sale (in circulation) contains the "germ of crises," because the value inserted into the commodity in production cannot be realized until the commodity is sold. In the Grundrisse, Marx first mentions credit as something which guarantees that the money necessary for the sale to occur will be in the buyer's hands: "The entire credit system . . . rests on the necessity of expanding and leaping over the barrier to circulation and the sphere of exchange. . . . The English forced to lend to foreign nations in order to have them as customers" (Grun, 416; 319). More important, credit "artificially" shortens the circulation time of commodities by providing the capitalist with the money now that at a future point, after sales will occur, will be his. Credit thus guarantees the continuity of the production process: it enables reproduction of the production process, which would collapse after one cycle if money were blocked or took too long in circulation, and it staves off the crisis that would occur if the potential value of commodities was not realized and transformed into money: "While the necessity of this continuity [of the production and circulation processes] is given, its phases are separate in time and space. . . . It thus appears as a matter of chance for production based on capital whether or not its essential condition, the continuity of the different processes which constitute its process as a whole, is actually brought about. The sublation [*Aufhebung*] of this chance element by capital itself is *credit*" (*Grun*, 535; 434). Capital's recourse to "credit contrivances" in order to achieve "circulation without circulation time" and thus to overcome the "barrier" to the realization of value leads necessarily to an expansion of capitalism: "If we now return to the *circulation time* of capital, then its abbreviation . . . means in part the *creation* of a continuous and hence an ever more extensive market; and in part the development of *economic* relations, development of forms of capital, by means of which it *artificially* [*kunstlich*] abbreviates the circulation time. (All forms *of credit*.)" (Grun, 542; 440). The abbreviation of circulation time through credit extends the market, thus making necessary more credit, because a "more extensive market" means that more time and space must be passed through before the realization of value. Credit combines two undecidably exclusive functions: it abbreviates and it helps expand; it aids and it also produces something that ultimately damages capital — overproduction.

Credit becomes an even more compelling necessity to fixed capital, such as plant, machines, and equipment. Fixed capital necessarily increases as capitalism develops, but "through disuse it loses its use value without passing it on to the product": "Hence, the greater the scale on which fixed capital develops, in the sense in which we regard it here, the more does the *continuity of the production process* or the constant flow of reproduction become an externally compelling condition for the mode of production founded on capital" (*Grun*, 703; 591). Because only credit can provide that continuity, credit becomes a necessary condition of capitalist production.

Marx's most extensive analysis of credit occurs in *Capital Volume Three*. Credit aids the realization of value, extends production, and makes necessary more credit: "Credit is, therefore, indispensable here; credit, whose volume grows with the growing value of production and whose time duration grows with the increasing distances of the markets. A mutual interaction takes place here. The development of the productive process extends the credit, and credit leads to an extension of industrial and commercial operations."[6] Credit becomes a productive force, a motor for expanded reproduction: "The maximum of credit is here identical with the fullest employment of industrial capital, that is, the utmost exertion of its reproductive power without regard to the limits of consumption. These limits of consumption are extended by the exertions of the preproduction process itself" (*Cap 3*, 482; *MEW*, 499). But this "artificial system of forced expansion of the reproductive process" leads inevitably to that which credit was in part designed to avoid — an inability to realize value because too many commodities have been produced:

In the system of production, where the entire continuity of the reproduction process rests upon credit, a crisis must obviously occur—a tremendous rush for means of payment—when credit suddenly ceases and only cash payments have validity. At first glance, therefore, the whole crisis seems to be merely a credit and money crisis. And in fact it is only a question of the convertibility of bills of exchange into money. But the majority of these bills represent actual sales and purchases, whose extension far beyond the needs of society is, after all, the basis of the whole crisis. . . . That is over-production promoted by credit and the general inflation of prices that goes with it. [*Cap 3*, 490-91; *MEW*, 507]

The expansion of credit necessary to capitalist reproduction also necessarily drives "the production process beyond its capitalist limits . . .: over-trade, over-production, and excessive credit" (*Cap 3*, 508; *MEW*, 524).

The crisis which credit helps bring about leads to an increased centralization of capital; some are obliged to sell out, and other capitalists (with credit-giving finance capitalists leading the pack) buy them out. While reducing the number of those who own social property, credit also contributes directly to the increasing socialization of property in the form of stock companies: "The credit system is not only the principal basis for the gradual transformation of capitalist private enterprises into capitalist stock companies, but equally offers the means for the gradual extension of co-operative enterprises on a more or less national scale" (*Cap 3*, 440; *MEW*, 456). Credit, then, is a social form, because the banker lends other people's money to the industrialist, and it permits the formation of institutions which, because they socialize property, become a transitional mechanism that points from within the capitalist system to a socialist one:

Success and failure both lead here to a centralization of capital, and thus to expropriation on the most enormous scale. Expropriation extends here from the direct producers to the smaller and the medium-sized capitalists themselves. It is the point of departure for the capitalist mode of production; its accomplishment is the goal of this production. In the last instance, it aims at the expropriation of the means of production from all individuals. With the development of social production the means of production cease to be means of private production, and can thereafter be only means of production in the hands of associated producers, i.e., the latter's social property, much as they are their social products. However, this expropriation appears within the capitalist system in a contradictory form, as appropriation of social property by a few; and credit lends the latter more and more the aspect of pure adventurers. [*Cap 3*, 439-40; *MEW*, 455-56]

Credit is both "indispensable" to the capitalist mode of production and a lever that works to tip over the immense edifice and send it crashing into another, more social mode. Credit sketches the outlines of socialism within capitalism. Marx sums up his chapter on the role of credit in this way:

The credit system appears as the main lever of over-production and over-speculation in commerce. . . . This simply demonstrates the fact that the self-expansion of capital based on the contradictory nature of capitalist production permits an actual free development only up to a certain point, so that in fact it constitutes an immanent fetter and barrier to production, which are continually broken through by the credit system. Hence, the credit system accelerates the material development of the productive forces and the establishment of the world-market. It is the historical mission of the capitalist system of production to raise these material foundations of the new mode of production to a certain degree of perfection. At the same time credit accelerates the violent eruptions of this contradiction—crises —and thereby the elements of disintegration of the old mode of production. The two characteristics immanent in the credit system are, on the one hand, to develop the incentive of capitalist production, enrichment through exploitation of the labor of others, to the purest and most colossal form of gambling and swindling, and to reduce more and more the number of the few who exploit the social wealth; on the other hand, to constitute the form of transition to a new mode of production. It is this ambiguous nature [*Doppelseitigkeit*], which endows the principal spokesmen of credit . . . with ·the pleasant character mixture of swindler and prophet. [*Cap 3*, 441; *MEW*, 457]

Instead of "ambiguous nature," a deconstructionist might have said that credit constitutes a structure of "undecidability" or "radical alterity." It represents the necessary emergence of what is "outside" or radically other to capital on the "inside" of capitalism. In order to survive, capitalism must remain the same, be self-identical, continuous, absolutely adequate to itself. That is the metaphysical dream as concrete economic necessity. Sameness and continuity, according to the deconstructive argument concerning radical alterity, are possible only by a relay through what is absolutely other to both—difference and discontinuity, or punctuation. Sameness and continuity as such exist by virtue of what makes them impossible "as such."

Credit allows capital to appear continuous, but only at the expense of making it even more discontinuous. And it is precisely the discontinuity of the crisis of overproduction which points toward socialism. That crisis shows plainly that scarcity, austerity, and the obligation to exchange labor for livelihood are all effects of the system of exchange which demands equivalence and forecloses expenditure without reserve. A system that can overproduce can satisfy all needs, but the necessity of value realization through exchange prevents that satisfaction, that socialist distribution, that unreserved expenditure from occurring. The ultimate capitalist fetter that prevents a socialized economy from emerging is the principle of exchange, which imposes wage labor as the necessity of exchanging one's life for the money equivalent in order to live. A production that could put an end to scarcity becomes "overproduction" only because of the necessity of equal exchange and equivalent return. A socialized economic system that fosters rather than forecloses such "over-production" could work only by eliminating the law of equivalent exchange. Because credit, which in itself is already an expenditure without immediate return, encourages such "overproduction," it would be essential to and is prefigurative of that socialized economy.

Credit allows marxism and deconstruction to be articulated in one other way. Credit, as Marx describes it, is in many ways an epitome of certain elements of metaphysics. Marx calls it the most "fetish-like form" of capitalism because "the social relation is consummated as a relation of things (money, commodities) to themselves" (*TSV* 3:455; *MEW*, 447). Capital appears as the "source of its own increase," "money creating money" (*TSV* 3:455; *MEW*, 447; *Cap 3*, 391; *MEW*, 404). "It is therefore especially in the form that capital is imagined" by capitalist political economists (*TSV* 3:455; *MEW*, 447). Capital is imagined as a collocation of material things, not as a necessary system of productive relations. Labor, the real source of surplus value and profit, is thus obscured:

> Thus it is *interest*, not *profit*, which appears to be the *creation of value* of capital as much as therefore from the mere ownership of capital. . . . In this form all mediation [*Vermittlung*] is obliterated, and the *fetishistic form* [*Fetisch-gestalt*] of capital, as also the concept of *capital-fetish*, is complete. . . . In M-C-M' mediation [*Vermittlung*] is still retained. In M-M' we have the incomprehensible form of capital, the most extreme inversion and materialisation [*Versachlichung*] of production relations. . . . Capital more and more acquires a material form, is transformed more and more from a relationship into a thing, but a thing which embodies, which has absorbed, the social relationship. [*TSV* 3:462, 483; *MEW*, 454-74]

The transmutation of a social relation into a material thing sums up the crude materialist, positivist bias that Marx criticizes in classical political economy. That bias embodies the general bias Derrida locates in metaphysics, but he applies the critique to consciousness and ideal meaning, for example, which are fetishized, to use Marx's word, as present and self-relating. What occurs in metaphysics, according to Derrida's description, is in many ways what occurs in the classical conception of credit: "The movement is contracted. The mediating [*Vermittelnde*] omitted. . . . All its specific attributes are obliterated and its real enemies invisible" (*Cap 3*, 393; *MEW*, 406). If we substitute "consciousness" for "capital" and "meaning" for "value" in the following passage from Marx, the relationship becomes clearer: "Consciousness appears as the independent source of meaning. . . . And it is indeed this source in itself in its thingly form [*dinglicher Gestalt*]. It must of course enter into the production process in order to realize this property [*Eigenschaft*]" (*TSV* 3:499; *MEW*, 490). Meaning is dependent on the productive process of language, but metaphysics would obliterate that intervening process and constitute meaning as a "material" thing in relation to itself. Consciousness is then supposed to produce meaning independently of the intervening productive process and of the system of differential relations which gives rise to both consciousness and meaning. Perhaps this analogy helps explain why Marx constantly compares money to the process of conceptualization and why Derrida constantly compares conceptualization to money. The relationship between a metaphysics based on the principle of equivalence and a political economy based on the law of exchange may not, after all, be accidental.

Derrida's concept of fetish differs from that of Marx, but it is coherent with Marx's description of credit as an artificial contrivance that is indispensable in the structuring of the "natural" reality of capital. For Derrida, in metaphysics, there is no pure nature of presence or of property prior to the fetish, which is not produced retroactively by the addition of a fetish. Like credit, fetish occupies the position of an effect, but is simultaneously a condition. Credit is an indispensable addition to that to which it is added on. It is unreal or artificial in comparison to "real capital" (actual money, commodities, or productive forces), but that reality, in advanced capitalism, could not exist without its "indispensable" supplement.[7]

In capitalism, what Derrida calls fetish is clear in ownership. Capitalist ownership is defined by the expropriation of the product of the labor of others. Such property is not natural, nor is it a material thing; it is constituted as the effect of a social juridical relation, something which is supposedly secondary and supplemental in relation to the primary, natural economy. That set of social relations, laws, codes, and institutions precedes property and produces its substance or nature as an effect, a representation, an artificial contrivance, a fetish. It is in the "nature" of something like property that Marx's and Derrida's concepts of fetishism intersect.

It would be possible to continue on this level of analogy and to conclude by being as guilty of obliterating differences as the metaphysicians. My subject here is marxism, not Marx, however, and it is more relevant to ask how deconstruction relates to a marxist analysis of credit as it currently exists.

The world monetary system, which was established after World War II, has moved from domination by a single currency—the U.S. dollar—to an exchange system defined by the differential interrelationship of many currencies. The "natural" material basis in gold has been given up. The system has become increasingly like a structure of relations with no outside, that is, no outside backing that permits conversion from the relational system to something objective and material whose "natural" value is not defined by relations to other elements of the system. Speaking metaphorically, the international monetary system has become increasingly "textual." At least, the concrete applicability of certain deconstructive arguments would seem to be confirmed by the current monetary structure.

There is, of course, an outside to the monetary system which is the capitalist production process. Money and credit, Marx repeatedly reminds the reader, are titles of ownership and tokens indicating command over labor. But he also repeatedly argues that to think of that process as consisting of material "things" rather than as a web of social relations would be to fetishize it. Outside the relational monetary system is not an extrarelational world of "things," but another relational system.

The aspect of the monetary system that most remarkably reflects deconstructive principles in concrete form is the units of account, called Special Drawing Rights (SDR), which were created by the International Monetary Fund (IMF) in 1968 as a reserve supplement to an unstable dollar and to the inadequate supplies of gold. SDRs provide a means of enforcing balance of payments discipline and of controlling liquidity expansion and inflation. They do away once and for all with the "fiction of the central debtor" and the "myth of backing." For SDRs to work, all that is required is credibility, the acceptability or transferability of the unit among all participants in the IMF, so that any country can use its allocation of SDRs in the central account to acquire national currencies to the amount of SDRs transferred. This does not constitute a loan in the traditional sense, although each country must maintain a specified SDR level in the central account. But there is no "corresponding debt."[8]

From a deconstructive point of view, SDRs are interesting because they seem to break the principle of equivalence. Because they are only relationally defined entries in a book, without "material" existence, they open the possibility of a redistribution mechanism that operates without return, or equivalent exchange. The principles of equivalence, return, and exchange would need to be surpassed in a communist society based on the voluntary, noncoercive donation of labor and the distribution of products according to need. That society would have to operate as a diffusion not linked to the maintenance of identity as equal exchange or equivalent return. The notion of a unit of account without material backing and for which no material equivalent has to be given opens the possibility of production without previous accumulation as well as without the necessity of an unequal exchange with labor to secure surplus value. SDRs could lead to an immediate redistribution from developed to undeveloped countries, simply through entries in a book. More important, that power of redistribution through units of account implies that an economy beyond exchange in which surplus labor would be liberated from the present structure of expropriation is conceivable. If the "claims" and "titles" required for production, now available only in money and credit, are available as units of account, then the appropriation of surplus labor without pay (the source of surplus value) is no longer either necessary or possible.

To achieve productivity, Marx placed his stakes on "industriousness," but that would have to be supplemented by a structure for the allocation of products in the manner of the market, but without the principle of exchange. A system similar to that of SDRs would fill that function. In a communist society based on the model of the Commune, one Marx might have agreed to call "marxist," a commune would draw on its units of account to fill its needs and replenish its account through the creation of products allocated to fill other communes' needs. Such an advanced system of "credit" without corresponding debt would alleviate the exchange market, and the absence of a law of exchange to regulate and curtail production according to the expectation of profitable return frees "overproduction" from its current negative status and turns it into a positive attribute.

Such a system, even if possible, is very far off indeed, and a system like that of SDRs, no matter how much subversive potential it has for the exchange principle, will not bring down the economic system based on exchange. Nevertheless, in that SDRs represent the full socialization of finance, its development into a differential system without "material" backing, they represent what Marx called a "condition," posited by capital, of a higher socialist socioeconomic form. In that the SDR system also conforms to deconstructive principles, one can begin to think of the deconstructive emphasis on differential relationality as opposed to natural or ideal backing (in terms of meaning or being) as conforming to the necessities of socialism.

I will conclude with a discussion of the relation of deconstruction to the question of what forms socialist economic and political organizations should take. If indeed deconstruction does promote radically "social" principles in the marxist sense—interrelationality as opposed to positive thinghood and historically and socially constructed institutionality as opposed to the immediate presence of a natural ground—then it should be possible to generalize deconstruction and to apply it to aspects of what passes for marxism to determine if they meet the exigencies of "socialization" in principle, or if they are simply new versions of old corporate political or collectivist economic formalisms, which impose structures of formal communalism or corporatism without working out or constructing a fully socialized network of differential relations within civil society.

Marx, of course, pointed out that such socialization was not possible without the full development of the necessary material conditions. But that would mean that real communism might be possible in his sense only in the so-called first world. At other times, Marx acknowledged the revolutionary imperative and suggested that socialism was possible without fully developed capitalism to serve as a prerequisite. The problem is not merely theoretical, because postrevolutionary third world countries today face the problem of how to develop socialism from underdeveloped capitalist or neofeudal conditions. As the experience of the Soviet Union showed, a high degree of formalization (collectivization without real socialization) is one alternative under such conditions. As the society becomes more capitalistically developed, real socialization can become more possible. But all formal solutions (the party, the collective, the state plan) tend to become ends in themselves—"things."

Deconstruction is relevant here in that it offers a critique of both centralization and formalization. The Paris Commune, as Marx describes it, represents a protodeconstructive organizational form. Communism as Marx foresaw it will be attained only if principles of the sort that deconstruction uses against the principles of capitalization in philosophy —equivalence, logocentrism, hierarchy, axiomatic priority, crude materialism, positivism—are translated into social practice. Deconstruction promotes the social principle of differential relation against the capitalization of hierarchically superior centers, the absolutist totalism of formal systems, and the mediating abstraction of positive nonrelational "things." The differential interrelation of a series of consuming producers and their socialization in communes of the Paris type, without an absolute, nonprovisional, nonfunctional center or authoritative referent outside the series, must take precedence over the extraction of one group of social agents (the party) from the series and their elevation above the interactive process as a source of truth and authority. That formal, transcendental body by definition denies the social principle of nontranscendable differential relation along a series or in a decentered structure, no longer functional, but dominant; no longer differentially related, but a "thing" apart. That political form is metaphysical in the deconstructive sense of the word. Like ideal truth elevated above the concatenated chains of language which in fact permit it to come into being, the party-planning state pretends to transcend and to dominate the relational social system and the mass of productive social agents. But socialization means the dissolution of all antidifferential hierarchy and the merging of all supposedly transcendental instances with the chains that situate "central authority" in a system it can never dominate or control and to which it is subordinate.

The planning of future societies will entail a choice of models, and the concrete significance of which concept or model is chosen is clear today in China, where an idealist maoist model has been replaced by a more pragmatic and technocratic model. Charles Bettleheim is only partially right, then, when he claims: "This [materialist analysis] compels us to renounce any sort of idealistic approach claiming to 'expound' the history of the USSR as the 'realization' of a certain set of ideas.'"[9] He is right to renounce the claim that this approach results *only* from ideas, whether those of Marx, Lenin, or Stalin; however, only a neopositivist materialism would overlook the dialectical relation between subjective activity (including intellectual labor) and objective world structures. The USSR did not develop as it did because of purely "objective" laws of development. Its development was also, to a certain extent, planned, and the orientation of that planning was based on certain concepts of development held by the Bolsheviks. For example, it is possible to predict what Lenin's concept of socialist construction was going to be on the basis of an early text such as *The Development of Capitalism in Russia*. His belief (and his instituted policy) that socialism equals increased productivity was a reaction to the backward condition of the Russian economy, a reaction in the form of a belief in the "progressive" nature of capitalist development (especially of "large-scale machine industry"): "The progressive historical role of capitalism may be summed up in two brief propositions: increase in the productive forces of social labor, and the socialisation of that labor."[10] The move to a conception of socialist construction as a similarly "progressive" increase in the productive forces was inevitable. Similarly, Lenin's metaphysical separation, in *What Is to Be Done?*, between politics and economics already held the promise of what would be done once socialist planning was begun: an autonomous economic development, at the expense of political development, would be equated with socialism.

Conscious socialist construction must rely on consciously conceived models or social plans,[11] and it is at this point of conceptualization that a deconstructive outlook can be relevant. I will now propose some ways in which deconstruction's critique of logocentric metaphysics might be useful in redefining the conceptual basis for model or plan formulation in socialist construction.

Once the centrality of the logos or cogito is deprivileged, the planning models based on the individual mind also lose validity. The planned society would not be conceived as an integrated system with a central nervous system, a homogeneous whole whose unity and self-identity excludes all diversity and difference, but rather as a social collectivity, a heterogeneous aggregate. In the first instance, then, the determination of a plan model would be a collective, participatory undertaking, not the conception of a detached, central planning body whose theoretical knowledge of planning is used to establish a hierarchy of administrative, cognitive center and administered practical instrument, mental and manual laborer. That distinction is essential to the rationality being put in question.

A second logocentric operation, which follows from the hierarchical distinction between mental and manual, theoretical center and practical periphery, is the process of synoptic formal abstraction.[12] This central operation of metaphysics permits the resolution of practical complexity into theoretical purity and clarity, the division of a differentially interrelated world system into determinate, isolated instances, the reduction of heterogeneous multiplicities into exclusive unities. Such processes lie behind the isolation of the synoptic, abstract, and formal concepts of economic good—increase in GNP, utility maximization, Pareto optimality—as the sole telos of the entire social machinery. All qualitative questions are reduced out for the sake of an abstract quantity. The process of idealist sublation—the negation and consequent elevation of substantive materiality into abstract, formal ideality—is concretely institutionalized as the principle that orients an entire social system.

The obvious deconstructive counter to this practical idealism in the rationality of economistic planning would be to privilege substantive material needs and to situate the nonetheless necessary calculating operation of formal abstraction within the domain of that practical, historical concern. This principle is best reflected in the "Basic Human Needs" approach.[13] Such a principle replaces the now dominant model of the single abstract ratio based on exchange (input-output, cost-benefit) with a planning model based on multiple, diverse, differentially related targets, which resist subsumption under an idealist, teleological norm—equilibrium, balanced return, steady growth, an abstractly conceived "development," and the like. Synoptic rationality could never formally conceptualize a single factor model that would fulfill all basic needs. Multiple strategies, policies, and plans would have to be employed, all interrelated, with no one exclusively dominant. A principle of nonexclusion (which would integrate culture, politics, psychology) and nonisolation (which would not privilege economic optimality, abstractly conceived) follows from the deconstructive displacement of abstract formalism from the center of planning.

Soviet planning claims to be multidimensional and participatory. There is space for "counterplanning" "from below" to increase initiative.[14] Nonetheless, the planning is dominated by the rationalist principles of proportionality, efficiency, optimality, and disciplinary management. Social needs are defined, like optimality, as a formal abstraction—"the needs of society as a single entity" (*PSE,* 28). Capitalist rationality claims the good of the whole will be fulfilled by the optimizing of every individual's self-interest. Soviet socialist rationality inverts the capitalist rationale: "What typifies socialism is the principle that what benefits society and the economy as a whole benefits the individual enterprise and its workers" (*PSE,* 29). This is a classical dialectical argument, the subsumption of the parts into the whole. Needless to say, like classical dialectics, it also has a totalizing tendency inscribed in it which reflects an idealist impulse. The abstraction of the whole, "society," above the working participants, whose labor constructs the institutions that are abstracted into the formal concept "society," is matched by a similar abstraction in the economic sphere: "Conscious control of the economy by no means implies that people can behave in whatever way they like. The economic laws of socialism operate in accordance with their own internal objective logic, independently of people's wishes and desires"

(*PSE,* 33). The claim is idealist because it assumes a separation of subject and object (thus negating the labor theory of value) and ideological because it uses this false separation to enforce subservience to a planning arrangement that abstracts the setting of aims from the will of the productive participants.

The positing of "basic, stable relationships among economic phenomena" is antihistorical, essentialist, and, ultimately, antimarxist. To distinguish between "the essential nature of economic laws and the forms in which they appear" is to assume the existence of an ideal, quasi-Platonic realm of laws whose immaterial purity is "refracted" as they enter concrete existence in the "specific laws of socialism" (*PSE,* 35). The effect of this idealist postulate is to elevate, isolate, and esoterize the domain of economics, knowledge of which then becomes the privilege of an elite of technocratic experts and the ground for their authority in planning for "society" as a whole. Knowledge, as usual, is an instrument of power.

The basis for Soviet planning is "the basic economic law of socialism . . . the greatest possible satisfaction of the ever-increasing needs of all members of society" (*PSE,* 36). Need is a practical, historical, and material concept. It necessitates input as well as impact planning, participation in determining plans as well as the inclusion of social variables. It would need to be distributional, not single factor optimizing, in orientation. Soviet planning does not seem to fill these requirements. It is, as I have suggested, based on rationalist principles that orient it toward rationalism and essentialism in theory and, hence, directional management in practice: "Thus, the essential conditions for making conscious use of economic laws are: the theoretical elucidation of the nature of economic laws, the elaboration of a scientific methodology for taking them into account and using them in planning; and the establishment of some mechanism for economic management and economic stimulation" (*PSE,* 35). If economic laws are independent of the desires of economic agents, how then can a planning based on the "theoretical elucidation of the nature of economic laws" possibly be geared toward the needs of the economic agents? Are such laws themselves directed toward need satisfaction? Such would have to be the case, but it is hardly true, if we are to believe the Soviet authors:

> The achievement of complete balance in economic proportions on the basis of a highly efficient use of labour, material and financial resources is the chief requirement for the proper running of a socialist economy, starting from the law of planned development and the law of saving labour time.
> . . . The achievement of complete balance in developing the economy on an optimal basis is what is required by the laws of planned development and the saving of labour-time. Two basic methods for drawing up plans arise from these two laws—the method of balances (input-output) and the method of optimising planning decisions. [*PSE,* 38-39]

The primary goal of planning cannot be both need satisfaction and the maintenance of a "proper balance" or "proportionality," because broadly (or socialistically) defined needs would include the elimination of some of the prerequisites of "proportionality"—most important, the labor process regulated by a norm of efficiency. The emphasis on efficiency, proportion, and proper balance requires that such fundamental social needs be treated as "exogenous."

The idealist premise of state socialist planning—abstract economic laws—leads to an idealist conclusion, a goal of ideal formal balance. Balance, proportionality, and optimality are idealist concepts in that their principle of operation is the satisfaction of formal equations, not the satisfaction of historical, material, situationally specific needs. From a practical ground level, such satisfaction requires not a ratio, but strategic imbalances that break the logic of formal proportion. It is argued that "planned proportional development" creates the material conditions for the satisfaction of needs. But in the meantime, the very real risk is run that the "essential" economic laws of proportionality and optimality become ends in themselves, as do all abstract ideals.

The rationale for Soviet planning, then, is ideological from a marxist perspective and metaphysical from a deconstructive point of view. As is usually the case, the rationale *for* a social system is indistinguishable from the rationality operative *in* that system. The rationale of abstract formal idealism, such as proportion and optimality, is matched by the very real social process of rationalization in the labor process and in the management of the economy. Formal abstraction operates both as the positing of goals—efficiency—and as the formalizing of life, the channeling of human energy and labor power into a structure of economic production which makes it "one-sided" or "abstract." The attainment of proportion requires the formalization of the labor process. But the practical contingency at work on the level of the labor process cannot be fully reduced to the necessity that operates as the laws of proper proportion. The world, as Marx remarked in *The Poverty of Philosophy,* does not function according to the pattern of logical categories. This noncoincidence of form and substance leads to the necessity of enforcing coincidence, of making practice cohere with theory, of making workers meet the efficiency conditions for optimality. The imposition of rational, formal (in this case, mathematical) theories on the world is idealist. The world is structured according to rationalist conventions (proportionality, efficiency, optimality), and this process is made to appear natural through a recourse to "objective, scientific laws" and "a *proper* basis provided by standards." Such notions are theoretical fictions; they are constructed at the intersection of certain material political and economic interests in Soviet society and of certain principles—proper proportion—of material rationality operative structuring the social system. Such fictions justify the social world, and they are of the same genre as the other theoretical fictions that are imposed on the economic world. Their shared value is organic proportion; it justifies the subsumption of practice under theory, the parts under the whole, and the hierarchical structure that ensues from the privileging of mental over manual labor. This new idealism ironically chooses a metaphor (which, as they use it, is not really metaphoric, something which in itself demonstrates the extent to which the social system is structured by metaphors or fictions like natural hierarchy, proportionality, optimality, and proper standards) used by the German idealists, who also believed the world could be ordered according to the principles of formal logic: "It is advisable in this connection to construct a 'tree' of goals showing their hierarchy and interdependence. . . . Thus it is possible to show how the task of raising living standards is tackled in the form of a definite 'tree' whose crown represents the goal and whose lower branches represent the sub-goals or sets of goals ensuring that these sub-goals are attained" (*PSE*, 62). The "ultimate goal" remains "to satisfy the growing needs of the working people," but such formalism could never address the substantive question of work itself. It must take for granted that the people in the system are "working," and in order for its own goals of efficiency, optimality, and proportionality to be attained, people must have no say in the question of work. It must remain a constant. Because such formal idealism excludes contradiction, it could never take into account the contradiction between its "ultimate goal" and its fundamental premise.[15]

A socialist construction that took a lesson from deconstruction's critique of logocentric rationality would be dehierarchized only provisionally or functionally centralized; it would begin with participatory input, not with a centralizing, efficiency map, which, from the outset, focuses the social system toward the satisfaction of criteria of proportionality and optimality. Work would take on a different character, defined not by efficiency or inefficiency, but by how well it leads to the satisfaction of social needs, and the process of work would be included as a factor in planning. The telos of social activity would be defined not by an ideal formal ratio of exchange equilibria, which underwrites the administration of work toward satisfying that ideal goal, but rather by the material and practical interplay between productive activity (not "work" by piece, wage, discipline, and so on) and social need. Formal models would serve a coordinating, not an administrative, function.

Andreas Papandreou and Uri Zohar propose an "impact approach" to planning[16] as the necessary correlative of participatory planning. Such an approach would deal explicitly with a multiplicity of social (not merely economic) goals. They contrast the approach with the cost-benefit practice, which is exclusively oriented toward efficiency, which reinforces the status quo, and which cannot accommodate goals set by society as an "organic chooser." These criticisms could in part be directed at the Soviet approach. The problem there is whether or not the criterion of proportionality coincides with the criterion of social need satisfaction. Papandreou and Zohar offer the interesting suggestion that in a decentralized economy, there would be no justification for raising the question of the criteria of project selection. Some new criteria or "Socially Relevant Indicators" which they propose (and which are notoriously absent from Soviet planning) are "pollution," "consumption," and "environmental design."[17] The proposal is deconstructive in relation to classic econometric planning (the kind toward which the Soviets are increasingly attracted), which excludes such variables as "exogenous." The systematic inclusion of the exogeneous is bound to upset endogenous balance or ratio. But choosing the criterion of social need over metaphysical proportion already implies a commitment to the possibility of a regulated imbalance or strategic counterrationality.

As in its critique of metaphysical philosophy, deconstruction, when plugged into the problem of socialist construction, comes out on the side of those who emphasize the necessity of "interactive adaptation," the role of uncertainty, the modifications imposed by diverse situations and different contexts, the need for inclusion, rather than exclusion, of variables, the wisdom of choosing policies over monolithic programs, and the impossibility of mapping a whole reality. In other words, planning, as the Soviets have discovered, cannot be a series of "instructions," as Stalin put it, based on a "scientific analysis" of problems. The necessary limits of knowledge place necessary limits on such "scientific" instructional planning. Frances Stewart seems closer to a model of differential planning when she remarks that planning is constitutively shaped by the past and by the world system,[18] one might say, using a deconstructive vocabulary, by a spatialization and temporalizing movement that cannot be reduced by a logocentric planning agency, based on the model of the rational, conscious mind which is supposedly present (in control or possession of) itself in all its thoughts and actions. The logocentric model, once institutionalized in human behavior, becomes the source of the hubris of social administration, instructional planning, and the teleology of efficiency, proportionality, optimality. As in the classical dialectic, materiality is subsumed under ideal formality. A model of the mind as inscribed in a field of practice and in a system of social relations from which it could never sufficiently extract itself to gain a position of transcendent knowledge and mastery (that is, both a marxist and a deconstructionist model) would call forth a planning that would be differential and beyond exchange. By differential, I mean a planning that entails multiple inputs based on needs, diversification of initiative, situational adaptation (a mechanism for accommodating an interplay between plan and environment, both social and natural), an emphasis on diverse, microstructural, "ground level" plans to counter the theoreticist tendency of macro-structural, singular, global planning, and finally, immediate interfacing between sectors, rather than mediated relaying through the "center." Such a micrological planning clearly could only work as the abolition of the law of value.

A logocentric rationality that deals in equilibrium and identities, the basis of the law of value and of exchange, would be incapable of sustaining such planning. It would require equal compensation, whereas differential planning could afford "expenditure without reserve," that is, a social distribution which, because it is not universalist in character, and, therefore, would not be based on an ideal average which equates all under the legislative norm of equal exchange, could take the counterrational, or unbalanced, special cases into account. The divergence of the particular rather than the abstractly mediated normativity of the general would be the constitutive principle (which is to say there would be no "constitutive principle" separable from the plurality of concrete needs). Sectors poorer in certain resources receive more, richer sectors less, regardless of proportion. The principle of differential distribution according to material need differs significantly from the idealist, logocentric models of formal equality, just exchange, and central directiveness.

The deconstructive critique of centrism and its call to "keep the question open" in theoretical terms, not to close it off in an absolute, totalizing solution, can be appropriated for questionable political conclusions, either conservative liberalism or reactionary pessimism, the Yale School or the New Philosophers. Derrida himself argues against the reactionary possibility, but his "open marxism" can easily succumb to liberalism. And the fear he expressed of political co-optation at the first meeting of the Estates General of Philosophy cuts as much against the left as the right, thus placing him in that middle ground of liberal, anti-"dogmatic" openness.[19]

But there is another political alternative which assumes some of the same anticentrist, antiabsolutist principles that one finds emerging out of deconstructive philosophy—the critical marxism of the nonleninist left, a postleninist marxism. In the following chapter, I will discuss two of the most active wings of this movement: British socialist feminism and the Italian Autonomy Movement.

❧ 9 ❧

Postleninist Marxism—
Socialist Feminism
and Autonomy

The revolution is not a party. That is one strong implication of deconstructively keeping open the question of revolution, because the leninist party means closing the question, putting the proletariat back to work, and declaring the revolution over after a transfer of power which retains domination. That attitude arises from a fear and distrust similar to that which motivates the metaphysical desire for a seamless world, one without fissure, rupture, heterogeneity, or crisis. Similarly, leninist metaphysics is founded on an overcoming of crisis (the potential proliferation of movements and the dissemination of workers' power) through the abstract and formal disciplinary party form. Lenin's justification for that form is laid out in *What Is to Be Done?*, where he concludes by discussing the three periods of the Russian revolution. The third period "was the period of dispersion, dissolution and vacillation. In the third period, the voice of Russian Social-Democracy began to break, began to strike a false note."[1] The third period leaders were confused because they could not separate politics from economics, theory from practice, conscious from spontaneous action, and subsume the second of each pair under the first: "The consciousness of the leaders . . . yielded to the breadth and power of the spontaneous rising. . . . It is . . . characteristic of this period . . . the combination of pettifogging practice and utter disregard for theory. . . . The idea of a party did not serve as a call for the creation of a militant organization of revolutionaries" (*LCW*, 519). All of these problems would be straightened out, however, when adolescence is left behind: "We firmly believe that the fourth period will see the consolidation of militant Marxism, that Russian Social-Democracy will emerge from the crisis in the full strength of manhood, that the place of the rear guard of opportunists will be taken by a genuine vanguard of the most revolutionary class. In the sense of calling for such a 'new guard' and summing up, as it were, all that has been expounded above, my reply to the question: 'What is to be done?' can be put briefly: Liquidate the Third Period" (*LCW*, 519-20).

The answer to the title of the book, then, is to perform the idealizing sublation of the third period—annul the period of vacillation or crisis, place theoretical consciousness over practice, elevate economic struggle into political struggle. The attainment of militant firmness amounts to an accession to manhood. Hitting the target. Good marxmanship. Differential dissonance, relationality, contradiction, conflictuality in practice, the undecidability of "economics" and "politics" are all reduced out and sublated into an abstract, formal locus of power, just as problematic practice is honed and abstracted into the theoretical concept or idea in metaphysical idealism. Lenin is right to call it "the idea of a party."

There is a strict analogy between Lenin's metaphysical practice of sewing up reference into a seamless, theological truth, of "summing up" all that has been expounded in a brief slogan—the essence of a text—and the leninist organizational practice of subsuming heterogeneous social, sexual, economic, and political struggles under one political struggle controlled by a single party, which initiates revolution at the "proper" time on command, just as there is a relation between the "personal" male fear of castration and the "public" proof of "manhood" through disciplined political organization at the head of the masses, all "poky" and hard. Iron workplace discipline is yet another symptom of the syndrome. Derrida's "feminist" vocabulary—"hymen," "invagination," and the like—is in many ways problematic from the feminist perspective. But in that it is designed to trouble the metaphysical assumptions that inform a Lenin's phallocratic, univocal style of thinking and writing (itself merely a symptom), it can point the way toward another style, one that is less repressively erect, more attuned to complexity and difference, less given to the closure of absolute truth because more capable of trusting the apparent danger of an open question, one that others, perhaps workers and women, might answer for him, instead of waiting for his oracular declaration, itself merely a symptom of a different political form, of another less formalist socialism, and of an ever-open possibility that any single revolution will not close the set, satisfying all the axioms and making further extension unnecessary. If Derrida's notion of the dissemination of reference beyond any single or absolute determination of truth has a political equivalent, it would be to provide an answer to a question that raises another question. Sheila Rowbotham says that socialist feminists "are involved in making something which might become a means of making something more. They do not assume that we will one day in the future suddenly come to control how we produce, distribute and divide goods and services and that this will rapidly and simply make us new human beings. They see the struggle for survival and control as part of the here and now. They can thus contribute towards the process of continually making ourselves anew in the movement towards making socialism."[2] For Antonio Negri, a theoretician of the Italian Autonomy Movement, it means that the diffuse multiple struggles of the social worker (not only industrial workers but all those marginalized sectors—houseworkers, students, under- and unemployed, service workers—who indirectly produce surplus value) cannot be sublated into capitalism's resolutive dialectic of economic development. The continuous expansion of needs and of productive potential engenders a crisis for capitalism, which must maintain limitations on needs and on production in order to guarantee the realization of surplus value as profit. But the social workers' potential exceeds capital's limits. And all attempts by leninist-type disciplinary parties to curtail that potential and that expansion fail, as do all formal obstacles to material processes.

Rowbotham, in perhaps the most accurate critique of leninism since Luxemburg, points out how and why leninism is a repressive organizational form: "The form in which you choose to organize is not 'neutral,' it implies certain consequences. . . . If you accept a high degree of centralization and define yourselves as professional concentrating above everything upon the central task of seizing power you necessarily diminish the development of the self-activity and self-confidence of most of the people involved" (*BF*, 75). The arguments she uses are often very close to themes Derrida develops in criticizing the repressive operations of metaphysical ·philosophy in general. That coincidence might be explained by Luxemburg, who accused Lenin, accurately, I think, of being less in the marxist philosophic tradition than in that of the nineteenth-century Russian neo-kantian idealists, who privileged consciousness above all else. He was, in other words, a practicing metaphysician. Rowbotham is closest to Derrida in her attack on "naming" and categorizing as instruments of power: "The power of naming is a real force on the left today. . . . I mean the false power which avoids and actually prevents us thinking about the complexities of what is happening by covering it up in a category. . . . Once named, historical situations and groups of people can be shuffled and shifted into neat piles, the unnamed cards are simply left out of the game" (*BF*, 65-66). This suggests the deconstructive preoccupation with the active work of categorization and naming in the construction of a social world. Because there is no absolutely "appropriate" name or category, one that embodies a necessary relation between word and world, the act of naming is always a political act with political presuppositions and effects of the sort Rowbotham finds in leninism. If there is no "pure abstract reason of correct ideas" (and this is the point of deconstruction), then "the argument is really about who has the power to define how the estimation is made." Who, if the matter is not naturally self-evident, decides what is "real," "essential," "central"? "The woman's movement has broken the circle in the concept of the vanguard Party by questioning the criteria used in assessing the meaning of 'advance' and 'backward' and arguing that this assessment is not a neutral and objective process but a matter of subjective control" (*BF*, 107). Who is in control of the determination of "correct" assessments will decide the hierarchy of goals, and all such assessments imply a hierarchy of the kind Rowbotham criticizes in Bolshevik-influenced left organizations. The seizure of political power comes first, sexual politics last, even though political struggle is, inevitably, in male discourse, especially Lenin's, conceived through a phallocratic metaphorics. How one thinks (names, categorizes, classes), therefore, is linked to how one will act, on what basis and for what ends. "The Leninist approach simply blots out immense but fragile processes of transformation. . . . The feminist approach to consciousness perceives its growth as many faceted and contradictory" (*BF*, 110). Deconstruction would be more attuned to the feminist approach.

It should not be surprising that one slogan of the Italian Autonomy Movement is a quotation from Derrida—"the margins are at the center,"[3] meaning that the traditional leninist centrality of "productive workers," at the expense of the marginalized or proletarianized sectors, leads to exclusivist hierarchization within the movement. With the productive industrial work force at the center, the struggles of women, students, unemployed, and nonparty workers are marginalized. Autonomy displaces that hierarchy by undermining the law of value. The law of value forces workers' struggles to submit to an economic logic that demands adherence to ratios of proportional distribution ("incomes policy"). Communist party trade unions try to convince workers to accept the discipline imposed by the ratio of the law of value. The law of just proportion (identity and exchange once again) says that workers can have only so much. The collaborationist unions also accept capitalist development as a goal, and this divides workers who benefit from development from those social strata which are proletarianized by development. The Autonomy Movement strives to break the law of value altogether through a strategy of refusal to work, and it tries to reunite workers' struggles with those of the proletarianized social workers. From this leftist point of view, keeping the question of revolution open implies broadening the movement to include groups and demands that orthodox party communism ignores. It opens the possibility of alternate organizational strategies that diffuse struggle throughout a society and do not limit it to traditional political or economic routes such as the party, elections, and the union. It clears a space for struggles that are not controlled and limited by a party union apparatus that would channel political energy along lines beneficial to its own survival as a formal organization. In a postrevolutionary situation, it means a disposition that would not equate emancipation with workplace discipline and control, or limit it to "industrial workers" at the expense of women, students, and all other exploited groups. It would not function according to a logic of priority which would ignore relations in favor of things, the relations of power in the factory, the home, and the school in favor of "productive forces."[4]

It might not be altogether illegitimate, then, to bring deconstruction, socialist feminism, and the theory of Autonomy together in a single argument for a postleninist marxism. Each in its own very different way represents a force of opening which operates against the tendency toward closure in leninism and in orthodox marxism. Deconstructive philosophy, in its critiques of the classical resolutive dialectic, idealism, formalism, and teleology, undermines the categorical and normative bases of orthodox marxist practice, from critical analysis, to organizing, to socialist construction. By foregrounding social needs, the complex interdependence of production and reproduction, and the problem of power as one whose solution cannot be deferred until "after the revolution," socialist feminism questions the male-defined and dominated centralism of leninist organizing and of the orthodox marxist privileging of a mostly male point of production. And the theory of Autonomy opens areas of struggle around social issues and needs that are ignored by the legitimate marxist political institutions in Italy. It sees an opening arising in the multiple struggles of social workers which fissures the closure imposed by the party school on that recalcitrant heterogeneity for the sake of a linear, "dialectical" move to a socialism conceived as state-managed capitalism (because it preserves wage work, hence the law of value and exploitation). That one cannot translate any one of these approaches or movements into the others, that they are resistant to being identified, is itself a testament to the openness, plurality, and heterogeneity of material processes (which include consciousness, communication, and theorizing) denied by "dialectical materialism" and leninism. Nevertheless, discussing the socialist feminism of Sheila Rowbotham and the Autonomy theory of Antonio Negri as they relate to the same problems will permit us to gauge how each contributes to the project of developing a postleninist marxim. Those problems are categoricality, need, agency, and organization.

Sheila Rowbotham's critique of British leninism is most deconstructive in regard to categoricality, by which I mean the relationship between compartmentalization and hierarchization carried out through the categories of knowledge and the practical ordering of the world according to these categorical imperatives of reason. To be categorical is to divide (say, the personal from the political or the private from the public), and by so doing, to master. The imposition of a purely "political" line of correct ideas from above in the party hierarchy takes for granted that there is a transcendental realm of pure ideas, uncontaminated by cultural practices, personal experiences, and social interchange. The practice of leninist party politics thus implicitly marginalizes and subordinates anyone concerned with the problem of domination in these domains, most notably, socialist feminists. Leninism blots out the complexity and heterogeneity of historical situations in the security and order of a systematic grid made up of well-known words, definitions, and categories that reduce the world to a rote scenario. It is immune to the fact that master words and ideas can be interpreted differently, depending on the situation of the interpreter, and that words and ideas can therefore have multiple meanings. The problem with the leninist model of the monolithic party is that it cannot deal with the multiplicity of the historical and social scene. To function efficiently, it must reduce the heterogeneity of the social world to centers (productive industrial workers, for example) and margins (women, for example). And it must impose a homogeneous line that recapitulates the capitalist structure of administration by denying participation and active construction from below.

The consequences of categoricality in leninism from a socialist-feminist perspective are exclusivism, hierarchy, and teleology. Categorical names define "others" who retroactively define the sect of knowledgeable ones; the interiority of the group cannot be detached from that projection of an exterior, an excluded other:

> The game is rigged to dispose of the "baddies." The slots for those labelled only come in certain shapes. So criticism of particular forms of organization has to be disposed of down one slot marked "anarchism," questioning of a particular idea of leadership goes down into "spontaneism," some baddies are stricken with a terrible hereditary disease and called "middle class." They have only one chance of survival—join the something party. It all sounds absurd when it is put like this. It is an absurd activity. But nonetheless the power of naming is a real force on the left today. It deflects queries about what is going on. It makes people feel small and stupid. It is a part of the invalidation of actual experience which is an inhibiting feature of many aspects of left politics now. Part of its power is in the strange lack of self-consciousness which the left has towards its own values. The power of defining is reduced as soon as it is itself described. But the silences within the leninist language of politics make it impossible to expose these hidden sources of power. [BF, 66]

What attaches immediately to this operation of exclusion is an internal hierarchy of leaders and led, defined according to the idealist premises of categoricality. Idealism is inseparable from a division between mental and manual labor. When leninism defines belonging as holding correct ideas and when it resorts to the idealist operation of defining institutional boundaries by categories that derive from pure reason rather than material interest or need, it necessarily aligns its internal structure as one of an idealist hierarchy of thinkers and doers, idea knowers and those in the "objective" and "material" world who have no access to ideas and must in consequence receive them from "without." In leninism, Rowbotham argues, "thought comes from thought which means there is no room to qualify certainties with the historical experience which might reveal how actual people arrived at leninist ideas or might lead them to seek alternatives. By disguising the process which went into the creation of ideas they are protected by a timeless inviolability" (*BF*, 117). "The Party possesses Thought." Ideas are conceived as detached from cultural context, the mode of social production, and personal experience. By downplaying these concerns, leninism assumes the ideas it holds over them somehow emerge in a realm of pure thought above history and culture. The absolute power of these ideas resides in the fact that they are taken to be transcendental—hardly a marxist conception of consciousness, but also, hardly one that is likely to lead to any other political form than the absolutist imperativism such idealist formalism has always supported.

Finally, categoricality, as exclusivism and hierarchy, determines teleologically conceived goals that prioritize objectives that reflect the idealist premises of leninism. The target is the state, the locus of command, not the reconstitution of the material texture of social, political, and economic life. The goal is normative, and it regulates and overrides the process of attaining it. There is nothing in the premises or the procedure of leninism to guarantee that after the seizure of the state, the form of social organization will be anything but administrative. Administration is the logical consequence of operating toward transcendent goals rather than materially constitutive activity, which is a principle that leads logically to participation and revolutionary democracy. A political approach founded on materialist, rather than idealist, premises, such as need, production, interest, and the constitutive potential of labor, would work to achieve the multilateral and micrological reconstruction of the social process "from below." That complex undertaking would have to be worked out, in time and over space. It could not take the form of an all-encompassing punctual category (industrial production) or a single goal (state seizure), which mediates the differentiated multiplicity of material life and sublates it into a categorical identity. Rowbotham's point is that leninist compartmentalization defines a hierarchy of goals which marginalizes goals that do not fit the initial idealist criteria. And, of course, this pretty much means everything that has to do with material life, everything that socialism is supposedly about, but also everything that has nothing to do with guaranteeing party power: "Left organizations, particularly since the Bolsheviks, have assumed a kind of pyramid of levels of activity. Near the top are struggles for political power and conflict at the workplace. Community struggles follow, traditionally seen mainly as the housing question and tenants' movements. After them education, welfare and cultural issues may be considered with an optional cluster of sexual politics, ecology and what not under a rather dusty heading of 'quality of life'" (*BF*, 110).

Rowbotham's response to the categoricality of leninism is "deconstructive" in that it musters several antimetaphysical concepts in a political critique, for example, what Derrida calls dissemination, the multiplicity of meaning that is not subsumable under a single paternal instance

of authoritative conscious intention: "It is clear from the feminist experience that ideas can have various meanings for different groups even
within the same movement. By focusing on the specific relationship of
women to radical organizations and thus readjusting how we see men's
position as well, socialist feminism can bring out the complexity of these
different meanings" (*BF*, 62). Deconstruction implies that the world cannot
be compartmentalized according to the categories of consciousness. A
spillover from one compartment to another is unavoidable. Rowbotham
rightly sees in a compartmentalistic notion of consciousness a mechanism
of power which must be criticized along what amounts to deconstructive
lines:

> We also need to challenge the notion of consciousness which is behind this
> approach to activity. For consciousness is also being chopped up into cate-
> gories of significance. The women's movement has enabled us to under-
> stand that such divisions do not reach the roots of oppression. Presenting
> consciousness in the compartments of political, economic, cultural, social,
> personal, makes it impossible to begin to see how the different forms feed
> and sustain one another. Feminism has shown how consciousness spills
> over these boundaries. [*BF*, 110-11]

In addition, feminism sees consciousness as multiple and contradictory,
not as a locus of absolute truth or power. It is not the domain of a pure
reason extracted from history; rather, it is determined by circumstances
and social interaction. Derrida's version of this point in his argument in
Glas that Hegel's concept of absolute knowledge is bound up with his
personal life situation, particularly his relation to his sister. Rowbotham
also argues that the development of autonomous movements puts in
question the privileged consciousness of the party. Such movements
develop without guides, and their range of struggle extends beyond the
perimeter of party-sanctioned activities.

Needs are the second problem that allows autonomy and socialist-
feminism to be related. A focus on needs of the sort Rowbotham espouses
displaces the exclusively political center of leninism. Most important, a
general need for liberation moves beyond the limits of productive
struggle toward an examination of how power, domination, and exploitation operate in social relations and everyday life.

> Although the leninist left eschews discussion of its personal values and self-
> image, it nonetheless carries a version of what it means to be a socialist in
> images and assumptions. . . . For example, what about all those comparisons
> to nineteenth-century armies marching in orderly formation and retreating
> smartly at the officer's command? Why is there such a horror of cosiness, as
> if cosiness were almost more dangerous than capitalism itself? Now it may
> well be true that at certain times we will all practice drill and that cosiness
> is inappropriate for some of the circumstances of conflict. But there seems
> to be an imbalance in the contempt it evokes. The fear seems to be that

cosiness means people get cut off from "real" politics. I think this should be put the other way around. If a version of socialism is insisted upon which banishes cosiness, given the attachment of most people, working-class men and women included, to having a fair degree of it around in their lives, this socialism will not attract or keep most people. [*BF*, 67-68]

People seek what they need, enjoy, and are interested in; the disciplinary "visicatory rigor" of leninism is not something many people need or enjoy. Nor does it jive with what socialists and communists (including Marx in the *Grundrisse*) projected as a good society. Compared to Marx's description of a world where people would be liberated from wage work, Lenin's vision of an administered and disciplined productive army is more dystopic than utopic. It may conform to the fantasies of a boy acculturated in an autocratic society to transform the pain of discipline, through masochistic inversion, into pleasure, but the attempt to transform the peculiarities of patriarchal male socialization into the general principle of socialist political and social organization merely repeats the structure of male power and domination which gave rise to that socialization process in the first place. Hence, Rowbotham argues, what leninists claim must be deferred until later, socialist feminists demand now. The principle of deferred satisfaction which sustains the leninist army of disciplined ascetics no longer applies. Its masochism produces an all too predictable parallel sadism. Working for the immediate satisfaction of needs and for the immediate undoing of all forms of domination counters both the "utilitarian narrowness" and the progressivist teleology of leninism. Clearly, this project is inseparable from the problem of organization:

Feminists have been urging the need for a form of politics which enables people to experience different relationships. The implications of this go beyond sex-gender relationships, to all relationships of inequality, including those between socialists. . . . The notion of organization in which a transforming vision of what is possible develops out of the process of organizing questions some of the most deeply held tenets of leninism. The weight of leninist theory (Gramsci apart) and the prevailing historical practice of leninism is towards seeing the "Party" as the means by which the working class can take power and these "means" have a utilitarian narrowness. Other considerations consequently have to be deferred until the goal of socialism is reached. But socialist feminists and men influenced by the women's movement and gay liberation have been saying that these are precisely the considerations which are inseparable from the making of socialism. [*BF*, 146]

For Rowbotham, the organizational form must be prefigurative, that is, it must already embody socialist principles. One cannot play bureaucrat now with the promise that sometime later radical democracy will be put on the agenda. Feminists require that the immediate organizational form be itself a form of socialism. This means rejecting the formalist and centralist model in favor of more diffuse, smaller groups, in which everyone is encouraged to participate. Rowbotham cites the examples of consciousness-raising and self-help groups. In such groups, there are no formal leaders and no formal party institution that transcends the individual needs of the participants and whose generality absorbs their particularity, legislates a line of universal truth which must be adhered to, even when it contradicts one's own experience.

Regarding the problem of agency, then, Rowbotham sees leninism as denying activity, thought, and participation to people; they become adherents rather than active subjects engaged in responsible and creative work to change their lives. Leninism thus contributes to the sense of powerlessness which capitalism fosters. The form of organization is not neutral, and disciplinary centralism does not further the self-activity that socialism requires. Against the transcendent party, socialist feminists assert the importance of their own concrete experience, an experience of domination and exploitation which leninist theory marginalizes.

What is needed, then, is a new form of organization, founded not on guidance, leadership, a knowing elite, and an abstract set of concepts, but instead on participation, self-activity, a diffusion of the leadership function, differences, and radical participatory democracy. This is the problem Rowbotham poses for the movement, how to move "beyond the fragments" toward a strategy of organization which would generalize the diffuse work socialist feminists have been doing while still respecting the decentered and concretely particular nature of their work. That no single statement in her essay mediates the complexity of the task into the unified form of a thesis is itself prefigurative. The tasks must be worked through, produced, and constructed through labor; they cannot be resolved into a declaration or an imperative. This is an indicator of how a socialist-feminist style already beings to undo the hierarchy of mental and manual labor in leninism. Rather than a thesis or an imperative, Rowbotham offers pointers for work: the political movement should treat people as responsible and creative agents; it should further work to reduce domination in all its forms, public and private; it should attend to real material needs rather than abstract theoretical principles that are concretized as discipline and unity; its generality should not be allowed to transcend situational difference; and it should work to make socialism a reality now, not in some deferred postrevolutionary future:

> We need to make the creation of prefigurative forms an explicit part of our movement against capitalism. I do not mean that we try to hold an imaginary future in the present, straining against the boundaries of the possible until we collapse in exhaustion and despair. This would be utopian. Instead such forms would seek both to consolidate existing practice and release the imagination of what could be. The effort to go beyond what we

know now has to be part of our experience of what we might know, rather
than a denial of the validity of our own experience in face of a transcendent
party. This means a conscious legitimation within the theory and practice
of socialism of all those aspects of our experience which are so easily
denied because they go against the grain of how we learn to feel and think
in capitalism. All those feelings of love and creativity, imagination and
wisdom which are negated, jostled and bruised within the relationships
which dominate in capitalism are nonetheless there, our gifts to the new
life. . . . I don't see the way through this as devising an ideal model of a
non-authoritarian organization but as a collective awakening to a constant
awareness about how we see ourselves as socialists, a willingness to trust as
well as criticize what we have done, a recognition of creativity in diversity
and a persistent quest for open types of relationships to one another and to
ideas as part of the process of making socialism. [*BF*, 147, 149]

Rowbotham closes by saying that "there is no clear post-leninist revolutionary tradition yet." This not altogether true. The beginnings of one
are formulating themselves in Poland and Italy. Antonio Negri, a theoretician of the Italian movement, does not dismiss Lenin; he accords him
importance for Russia in 1917, but he also argues that what Lenin offered
his time and his situation no longer applies. A different political class
situation now exists, and new forms of struggle and of organization are
required. These new postleninist forms make up the Autonomy Movement.

Before describing the theory of autonomy as it relates to the four
problems—categoricality, agency, need, and organization—I will com-
ment on the ways in which it can be considered to be "deconstructive."
My primary text will be Negri's *Marx Beyond Marx*.

It would be an oversimplification to say that Negri's fundamental
category is difference and that Derrida's non-"originary" starting point
is also difference, rather than unity or identity. Negri's category names
the irreducible antagonism between the two subjects in the social class
relation that constitutes capitalism—labor and capital. His emphasis on
the subject and on the political nature of seemingly objective economic
structures is designed to counter the party school of capital logic, which
is characterized by an excessive emphasis on objective economic laws,
which supposedly have a logic of their own, independent and transcendent of the action of subjects which are considered to be residual in
relation to this primary process. I have already suggested that the consequence of this objectivism is to reduce the potential of people to be actors
in their own historical situation and to pave the way for control by a
party bureaucracy that is privileged with knowledge of the objective
laws. On the other hand, Derrida's historically determined nemesis is,
among other things, the excessive subjectivism of phenomenology.
Hence, in his work, difference is a category that undermines the humanist

privilege of conscious subjectivity and emphasizes the role of nonconscious forces that constitute all the categories of consciousness (truth, meaning, will, presence, self-identity, and so on) without being available to conscious mastery. This, however, does not constitute an "objectivism" of the sort Negri opposes in orthodox dialectical materialism. Derrida frequently uses the word "force" or "difference of force" to name his principle of constitutive difference, and this would seem to move him closer to Negri, who also emphasizes force as the relation of forces, the fundamental difference that determines modern capitalism.

What ultimately makes the two compatible is the way each uses the force of difference as an analytic weapon against all philosophies and all political strategies founded on the resolutive dialectic, the classical metaphysical model of a process finalistically and linearly oriented toward resolution and identity as the sublation of all particular difference and conflict into a mediated, abstract, general unity. One could say that whereas Derrida criticizes this dialectic as ideology, that is, as the model of an ideal plenitude of truth or meaning which denies the real differences that spatiality and history introduce irreducibly into any such model (its very articulation situates it as part of that which it hopes to transcend), Negri criticizes this dialectic as capitalist political economy, that is, as the model of a unity of cooperating interests, without difference or antagonism, which develops without crisis. I would argue that the compatibility of the two critiques indicates a necessary interrelation between the two objects of critique. What Derrida criticizes, from Plato to Husserl, is simply the illusion specific to a world outlook nurtured within an exchange economy founded on the division between mental and manual labor[5] and within a phallocratic or male-dominated society based on the division between the public and the private domains. Derrida, Rowbotham, and Negri are partners in critique because their objects—metaphysics, phallocentrism, and capitalism—share certain attributes, one of which is power defined as the reduction of a difference to unity either by means of claims to authority (truth) or assumptions of natural superiority (sexism) or forceful domination parading as the neutrality of a proportionally distributional machine (the market). The dialectic is the form of that reduction.

Negri's theory of Autonomy, especially as it is elaborated in *Marx Beyond Marx*, a reading of Marx's *Grundrisse*,[6] can be said to be deconstructive not only because it bases itself on difference, but also because it emphasizes openness, "inconclusivity" (of the method of the *Grundrisse*), the scission implicit in unity, displacement, and plurality. For Negri, Marx's dialectic is not a hegelian one of necessary mediation and of a synthesis imposed on a historical dynamic; rather, it is a dialectic of antagonism, rupture, and opening. The universe of Marx's method is plural; it is characterized by the refusal of all dialectical totalization, logical unity, and linear continuity. Instead, Marx's method is a constitutive process that operates as a plurality of points of view made necessary by the antagonism that is fundamental to the capitalist world the method analyzes. As that world transforms itself according to the vicissitudes of the subjects engaged in struggle, the analysis must also displace itself. Totality occurs only in the form of a multiplicity of sequences, not as a monolith. Rather than a linear continuity, economic (and methodic) development consists of struggle, breakage, and creation. By this, Negri means that the crisis of capitalism is caused by the emergence of a new subject, the subject of proletarian struggles and of working-class autonomy in relation to capital. That subject's productive potential, which is hemmed in by the law of value (equivalence and measure) in capitalism, is creative both of a crisis and of communism. Marx's dialectic does not consist, therefore, of the restoration of an original essence, as in humanism. Rather, it points forward to the negation of all measure (exchange value) and the affirmation of "the most exasperated plurality." In this light, Derrida's concept of plurality loses some of its liberal implications and can be seen to have radical potential. Or, put another way, Negri makes more clear why plurality can be a category of socialism. Once capitalism is seen as a political structure, the forced closure of a (class) difference, then plurality becomes liberatory in relation to that limitation and that domination. The assertion of the plurality of difference is, in the Autonomy Movement, the liberation of the broad, multiple strata of the proletariat from the repressive unity imposed on all society by the factory command and by the law of value.

Two points of deconstructive analysis for which analogies can be found in Negri are the location of division within unity, which reveals unity to be a form of forced closure and repressive domination, and, on the basis of this insight, the positing of an inverse to the world of unity which is contained and suppressed by unity, but which constantly threatens to explode, subverting unity from within and giving rise to a world characterized less by the power of forced closure than by the open potential of a liberated plurality of productive difference. (And, of course, the antiunitarian philosophic equivalents of such a material transformation are indeterminacy and inconclusivity, both of which appear positively in Negri, first as the indeterminacy proletarian autonomy introduces into capital's attempt to plan and determine development, and second, as the inconclusivity or openness of human productive potential liberated in communism.)

The first point centers on value. In capitalism, value is the function of equivalence, the making identical of difference. But in the value equivalent resides the possibility of crisis because its equivalence is constituted by the forced identification of class difference. The equivalence depends on the stability of necessary labor, the amount paid to workers to maintain them as workers. As long as workers expand their needs and up their demands, value cannot be a self-sufficient category; it must be a horizon. It is shot through with oscillation, conflictuality, and the potential for antagonism. The law of value as equivalence is therefore broken open internally as crisis; identity splits into difference because capitalism rests on difference as its constitutive principle. Prior to the initiation of the capitalist process of production there must take place and be assumed a distribution of social agents into the roles of workers and owners. That original difference determines that the system cannot escape the possibility of scission. Politics, a relation of force, is thus placed at the center of economic analysis as wage struggle by Marx, according to Negri. And capital is shown to be the synthesis of a contrast and the overdetermination of separation. As in deconstruction, what appeared unified is shown to be internally split.

This "logic of separation" leads to the second point, the positing of an inverse world of difference emerging out of its suppressed form in the world of unity. The word "autonomy" means that the proletariat refuses to cooperate in capitalist economic development and instead affirms its own needs and its own use value by refusing work. This is an immediate practice of power by the proletariat. It is in the intensity of this separation, Negri argues, when the difference-cum-antagonism resident in capitalism is exacerbated to the fullest, that one finds a maximum of liberation and of difference (of the proletariat from capital), for which there can be no formal equivalence. Proletarian power—communism as the direct appropriation of social wealth—implies the negation of all homogeneity and the triumph of the plural multilateral method (both in the movement and in Marx's "communist" method). What is significant here is Negri's contention that communism is not the teleology of capitalism, but rather its radical inversion. In the categories of capital, one already finds communism prefigured, if not inversely embodied, for example, in the sociality of money. As the fully developed productive potential of the social individual, communism can now be said to be the motor of capitalist economic development. As the curtailment of the "over"-productive potential of labor for the sake of managing its crisis, capital is not so much the beginning of a transition to communism as the immediate suppression of an already existing communism, defined as the full development of the creative and inventive potential of social workers. The more capital must destroy productive potential in crisis (through unemployment, business failures, deflation, and the like) in order to preserve itself, the more the proletariat must assert its autonomy from capital in order to preserve itself. That liberation of productive potential is both the critical subversion of capital and the immediate transition to communism. The assertion of difference breaks the unity of capitalism from within.

It should be clear why one might think of bringing Rowbotham's and Negri's critiques together; neither one is particularly tolerant of the leninist model of disciplined work in factory socialism, with its authoritative division between elite knowers and mass doers. For Negri, the refusal of work is not only a strategy against capital, but also a goal of communism. Subversion and transition are one, and neither prong is particularly leninist. By considering the problems of agency, need, categoricality, and organization, one can see further how the theory of Autonomy in many ways constitutes an outline of the kind of postleninist revolutionary tradition Rowbotham sees as a necessary correlate to socialist feminism.

Like Rowbotham, Negri argues that orthodox marxism (especially leninism) downplays the role of subjectivity or agency. In the scenario of Third International party communism, history works itself out through objective laws toward an inevitable socialism. The principle at work in this scenario is teleological or finalistic rather than constitutive or creative. Indeed, creative constitution is eliminated altogether in favor of a formal, abstract model to which one can adhere but to whose realization one cannot contribute. Negri refutes this model and the party politics that accompany it by pointing to the autonomous proletarian subject whose struggles in the spheres of production and reproduction have been the determining force in recent Italian history. He argues that the proletariat is the unique source of social wealth, and only by focusing on its subjective composition can one determine a politics that leads to the liberation of that wealth creating potential from the capitalist law of value and from wage work. Communism therefore is not a telos or a goal; it is the potentiality of the proletarian subject as it constitutes itself autonomously from capital and thereby liberates itself. The personal is political, Negri argues, because proletarian love, the self-valorization of the proletariat through the refusal of work and the affirmation of its own use value and its own difference from capital, blends with class hatred, because self-valorization and the affirmation of difference imply the negation of capital.

Rowbotham sees the domain of social need as being essential to the construction of socialism, yet it is precisely what leninism ignores or defers. Equally antiformalist, Negri foregrounds substantive needs as a political weapon and as an essential criterion of communism. Not only must they be addressed immediately in the immediate constitution of communism within capitalism, but also their constant expansion is a form of power against capital. The expansion of needs expands the realm of necessary labor and disequilibrates the proportion required for the extraction of surplus value. The affirmation of need, which is itself prefigurative of the multilateral social individual in communism, is therefore a political instrument for bringing about a crisis of capitalism.

Negri speaks of the needs of the social worker in the sphere of reproduction. As the Autonomy Movement developed in the 1970s after an
initial explosion among industrial workers in the late 1960s, it came to be
made up of the struggles of nonwage workers over social spending cuts,
housing, the guaranteed wage, autoreductions (of utility rates), services,
and so on. If there is a critique of categoricality in Negri, it has to do with
this decentering of the traditional focus of leninist political organizing
on "productive labor" (supposedly the only kind of labor that produces
surplus value). Autonomy theory deconstructs the centrality of that
category by emphasizing the indirect production of surplus value through
seemingly "unproductive" labor or through no labor at all (unemployment). By affirming the expansion of needs as a weapon, Autonomy also
necessarily affirms the plurality of sectors of the movement, because
needs is a multilateral category that breaks open the unity of the focus on
productive labor. All of this necessitates undermining the categorical
distinction between the factory or workplace and society, the domain of
production and the domain of reproduction. As capitalism expands,
according to Negri, it extends the form of factory control over society;
capital becomes socialized, and it makes all of society productive of
surplus value. (The key term here is tertiarization, or the development of
the service sector.) The social worker, then, a category that includes not
only production workers but also the broad proletariat, the social strata
that are marginalized by the orthodox marxist categories, becomes the
new sustainer of capitalist development and, consequently, the new
potential source of antagonism and crisis.

The categorical displacement resulting from the new concept of agency
and of needs in Autonomy clearly has implications for the question of
organization. Like Rowbotham and the other socialist feminists who want
to get "beyond the fragments," the discrete small feminist work groups,
toward a broader organizational configuration, Negri and the other
autonomists have throughout the 1970s confronted the problem of how to
attain the continuity and concentrated power of a large organization
while yet maintaining the multiplicity and impetus of the movement at
the level of the autonomously acting groups. Power in such an organization, according to Negri, would have to remain in the hands of the proletariat. Like Rowbotham, Negri is critical of leninist elitism and of the
abstract mediation of concrete struggles by a leninist party that assumes
general command from above over the particularities of the movement.
As soon as the party takes precedence over the movement, the revolution
is over. Vertical power in the party is merely the obverse of the capital-
state form. In Autonomy, power dissolves into a network of powers; the
independence of the proletariat from capital is constructed through the
autonomy of single, individual revolutionary movements. This is necessary, according to Negri, because only a diffuse network of powers can

organize revolutionary democracy and reduce the party to a functional role as the executor of the will of the proletariat. The party allows unity, but it also maintains the production of moments of power which are pluralistic.

Like socialist feminism, Autonomy marks an advance on leninist marxism. Even if the movement in Italy has been momentarily stymied by the firing of radical workers and the arrest of its theoreticians, the value of a movement, which can occur without the discipline, division of labor, guidance, and control of a leninist party, in other situations is evident, in Poland, most notably. And the diversity of the forms of struggle (not just in production but throughout the sphere of reproduction) implies that no single state action against it can annihilate it. After Autonomy, it is no longer possible to return unproblematically to a precritical leninism as the only mode of proletarian organization. Indeed, after the explosion of diverse sectoral struggles in the 1970s, leninism now appears to be only a partial or tactical solution. Both socialist feminism and Autonomy show that it is a form which is not prefigurative of communism or of socialism, if we mean by communism what Marx describes in the *Grundrisse*—a social arrangement whereby the producers directly appropriate the surplus they produce in order to freely expand their needs and their capacity for enjoyment and invention, a world of liberty, difference, and plurality, rather than of authority and disciplined unity. Its model might be a socialist-feminist self-help group or an autonomous worker-community committee, rather than Lenin's taylorized factory.

Autonomy and socialist feminism each in its own way introduces difference into the identity of leninism. Negri argues that political class composition changes, and, therefore, different political strategies are required at different times. Theory is not absolute, nor is it universal. Against the leninist tendency to make the party transcendent, the one overriding solution always and everywhere, Negri suggests the necessity of a more plural, differentiated approach. Rowbotham suggests that leninism is not simply a case of bad theory that can be remedied with a better theory. She focuses on the practice of theory itself, what it as an activity exalts or ignores. She introduces a practical difference into the theory's self-identity as a theory by suggesting that it is itself a form of practice which, if it were to be held responsible for the practical actions it takes as an activity of theorizing, would find that it does not live up to the ideal goal it projects. The demand to be self-conscious, to be more autobiographical and self-historical, immediately works to concretize leninism as a historically specific activity and to undermine its pretensions to transcendental rationality, the expounding of correct ideas apart from concrete personal experience. In each case, the categories of difference and history perform the same corrective function, which may be one reason why, early on, Derrida thought of equating them. History differs, and difference is historical. As an activity in history, leninism cannot practically attain the ahistorical indifference or transcendental universality it claims for itself in theory. But equally, the more it refuses difference, the more it removes itself from history.

It seems that thought, sexuality, and political economy form an interlocking network. Capitalism is patriarchal; the metaphysics which legitimates it is phallocentric, and the cognitive operation of equivalence in metaphysics is necessary to the operation of an exchange economy. Sexual domination occurs as the division of private and public labor which is sanctioned by the highest conceptual apparatuses of philosophy. One element common to the three domains is that in each a form of difference is subsumed by a form of identity — the identity of indivisible male power, the identity of a goal of development defined as efficiency and accumulation, and the identity of the abstract idea or concept. And in each of the domains, the affirmation of difference can, indeed must, have radical implications. Negri argues that proletarian self-valorization, the assertion of its difference in relation to the forced unity capital seeks to impose, has revolutionary potential. Rowbotham describes the way socialist feminists have rejected the male-defined political unity of the leninist party in favor of multiple, differentiated strategies that undermine the scientificity of the monolithic correct line. And Derrida argues that within our conceptual systems, difference and plurality affirm themselves, against the desire of the metaphysicians, from Plato to Ricoeur, to impose identity and order, as ideal transcendence or self-sufficient causality, on the world. Not that disorder prevails. But that rigorous identity and absolute truth — in metaphysical rationalism with its firm categorical divisions and strict objectivism — may merely be an excuse for power. The contestation of this rationalism, despite its claims to universality, scientificity, and normativity, is necessary because, among other things, it works politically to sanction the phallocratic imperativism of leninist males in Britain and to separate marginalized proletarian sectors from the central "productive" labor force in the rationality of orthodox marxism in Italy.

Unless it is put to these uses, crucial among which is the development of a postleninist marxism along (among other things) Autonomous and socialist-feminist lines, deconstructive analysis will remain a victim of the very disciplinary, categorical divisions whose critique it furthers. But deconstruction is only a function of highly diverse, multiple movements. It would be to repeat the mistake of the Frankfurt School to attempt to substitute philosophical or ideological criticism for, among other things, the political-economic and the sexual-political struggles. Only when articulated with these other struggles is the radical political potential of deconstruction realized. I have tried to show how it can be articulated with these other movements, methodologically as well as substantively.

Methodologically, it relates in that Rowbotham's critique of the leninist method of categorically distinguishing the private from the public, the sociocultural from the abstract political, itself resorts to a deconstructive method of reversal and displacement. It is impossible for the leninist to account for the source of the correct ideas of the party leaders, which are supposedly above sociocultural trivialities, other than through some account of sociocultural training; otherwise, it is a case of ideas engendering ideas in some transcendent realm, and the leninist is obliged to confess his idealism. The categorical distinction between public and private, impersonal party line and personal experience, comes undone and is displaced. The seemingly separable domains become interchangeable. Substantively, deconstruction relates in that it advances a principle of material constitution—difference—which Negri considers to be crucial for the emergence of a self-determined, autoconstructed communism. The unity of capitalism is doomed to be merely formal; the concrete separates, divides, and explodes in scission. The proletariat's assertion of its own difference within the forced closure of capitalist development is the material principle of the constitution of communism that, as Negri describes it, would be "deconstructive," that is, it would be characterized by a wealth of difference, plurality, and multilateral liberation from the constraints of forced identity and closure. Deconstruction must be articulated with these diverse movements because the elimination of domination (sexual, political, economic) cannot occur completely without the transformation of the categories and the thought processes that sustain and promote domination. Neither one before or above the others, but all together—different yet articulated.

Conclusion

Deconstructive philosophy emerged at the same time as the New Left, and it is subject to a political problem very similar to one that has dogged the New Left in recent years. But inasmuch as it is an implicit critique of many of the humanist, essentialist, totalist, and subjectivist philosophies (as espoused by Marcuse, Lukacs, and Sartre) that were adhered to by New Leftists, deconstruction cannot be called a New Left philosophy. Nevertheless, it projects certain recognizably new leftish traits: an emphasis on plurality over authoritarian unity, a disposition to criticize rather than to obey, a rejection of the logic of power and domination in all their forms, an advocation of difference against identity, and a questioning of state universalism. It goes one step further and argues for the flawed and structurally incomplete, if not contradictory, nature of all attempts at absolute or total philosophic systems. To understand the common problem shared by deconstruction and the New Left, we must look more closely at this last point.

This argument consistently elicits accusations of "paralysis." How can one do anything if it is inevitably flawed, if indeterminacy precludes absolute truth? This question assumes that the prerequisite of action is some sort of absolute knowledge, which is not necessarily the case. It is not even the case of those who do act on the assumption of possessing such knowledge. Their "absolute knowledge" or truth is incomplete because it is in history; as a historical practice, knowledge is situated and circumscribed by a seriality it cannot transcend. Similarly, their absolute knowledge or truth is self-deconstructive or contradictory because it is possible only through material processes of production whose empiricity contradicts its ideal absoluteness. Truth and knowledge are not aspects of an unchanging Being; they are technological constructs, anchored in a changing historical world that includes the machinery of knowledge in its transformations. The truth of history is that no truth about history is complete and does not, in its historical empiricity, con-

213

tradict that characteristic of truth that supposedly lends it its universality and absoluteness, that is, ideality. The only absoluteness that can be claimed for truth and knowledge is that which characterizes the description of the historical world at a specific moment in the process of material transformation. It is the absoluteness of a relation between two points in two chains which are inseparably interwoven—a linguistic-conceptual chain and the historical world. It is not of the paradigmatic order of an ideal truth, which transcends the seriality of empirical history it describes. Both marxism and deconstruction suggest that this sort of truth is a fiction.

In addition, the world known and the knower are constantly being displaced by their own activities. The accumulation of knowledge changes the act of knowing, just as the expansion and growth of capitalism creates a new object of study. Concepts and words,[1] the material instruments of knowledge, are themselves in history and subject to displacement. They come to one through educational institutions, which are historically defined and are determined by class, sex, race, and geographic considerations (among other things). Knowledge is a matter of technology, construction, and convention. Like all forms of technology, it changes with history; to a certain extent, in order to describe the historical world, the categorical machinery of knowledge *must* be displaced. The most absolute truth would be that which least pretends to absoluteness and instead attends to its own historicity. Fashion would simply be another name for science.

Therefore, those who fear political paralysis from critical philosophies like deconstruction work with too simple a notion of the sort of knowledge (or, if you like, science) required for radical action. Lenin's knowledge was accurate (perhaps even "absolute," within certain highly overdetermined constraints, contexts, and conventions) in regard to his own historical moment and place, but it is not an ideal paradigm which provides absolute knowledge of a completely different historical place and moment. And Lenin's knowledge must be understood in relation to such technological aspects of knowledge as translation, the availability of Marx's texts, his education, and the intellectual environment in Russia. The fact that the dominant intellectual school in late nineteenth-century Russia was lavrovite neokantianism, rather than dialectics, cannot be dismissed as ancillary to the ultimate political formulations Lenin bestowed. I would argue that the conclusions concerning knowledge to which I am led by deconstructive philosophy applied to the question of knowledge and history are more suited to radical action than the opinions held by those who accuse politicized deconstruction of leading to paralysis. Only from the viewpoint of capitalist rationalism or party patriarchalism does the persistent positing of an alternative, of a continuous displacement along a seriality of revolutions which is multisectoral and without conclusion, seem "irrational" or "paralytic." It *is* paralytic of their rationalist power, but it is equally an opening onto a plural diffusion of powers, and this is what is feared, from Hobbes to the party patriarchs. Like political class composition, which changes in relation to the level of struggle, so also the political composition of knowledge practices (which are always conventional constructs, as well as discursive or media practices) must be displaced according to the level of struggle. When I read in a journal of the sectarian left that the leader of the party which publishes the journal defeated "empiricism (1974) and idealism (1977)," I feel this argument may have some relevance.

This discussion has been leading up to a discussion of my suggestion that deconstructive philosophy and the New Left are confronted with a similar political problem. The political problem stems from the sort of argument I have just recounted. Just as, from the point of view I have just criticized, any critique of the assumption that truth can be absolute and rational knowledge universal and transcendental (that is, ideal) is seen as paralysis, so also any critique of the monolithic nature of authority or of the one true party, or patriarchally defined struggle, is seen as leading to anarchy. The New Left has been dogged by charges of excess, of excessive antiauthoritarianism especially, and of an excessive multiplication of inessential, "partial" (i.e., nontotal, nonabsolute) struggles — socialist feminism, ecology, nuclear energy, ideology, housing, health, among others. What has justifiably been called the "Left's Right"[2] would see these excesses curbed for the sake either of returning to older values (the family, patriarchy, authority, party discipline) or of returning to a more organized, authoritative, less diverse movement, if not leninist disciplinarianism, then something close. I will argue here that unity, rather than authority, is needed, and that at this point in history in North America, unity excludes authority. By unity, I mean the articulation of a diverse, differentiated plurality; unity or a whole or identity or a "totality" is never anything but that anyway. Once it is thought to be anything else, an absolute identity or totality, for instance, authority must be wielded to make the material world correspond to the ideal form and to make the technological construct of totality or identity seem natural.

The Left's Right's position is founded on an absolute binary opposition between absolutism and anarchy. The critique of absolutism in the name of something other than paralysis in the domain of knowledge also applies to the political question. The Left's Right sees anarchy as the only other to a firm, masterful, rigorous, and authoritative tightening of the ranks. If you do not want anarchy, then you must accept this. Instead of considering the left's dilemma from the point of view of material considerations like need, interest, the differential relation to the other with which we contend, and historical possibility, the Left's Right tends to sublate that complex texture, which is anchored in a historical seriality of changing political class and social power composition, into an ideal paradigm—*either* authority *or* anarchy. And the solution, of course, is also a paradigm—more authority, rigor, discipline, patriarchal and party values.

A political alternative that addresses the complexity of the historical scene and heeds its own (nonabsolute, nonpatriarchal) anchoring in a shifting material field would not be so anxious to seek refuge in a paradigm of binary opposition. It would see the poles of the supposed opposition—authority or anarchy—as being only two points in a plural field which includes many alternate positions that do not reduce to one side or the other of the metaphysical binary, which escape the logic of division, hierarchy, exclusion, opposition, and so on. I have described Autonomy and socialist feminism as examples, and I have pointed to Solidarity. But even in themselves, authority and anarchy are not self-identical in their opposition. Like Hobbes's sovereignty, the Left's Right's authority is reactive, hence differential. It is meant to be an antidote to excess, to, among other things, excessive antiauthoritarianism. It is the differentiation (the differing from and the deferment of) such excess; hence, it is not a self-sufficient category, but instead a horizon, a relational difference of forces. Where there is authority, there is always the possibility of insubordination. Authority always implies a potential force working against authority, and that difference or limit of resistance precedes and determines the integrity of authority, which means authority can never be self-identical or absolute. No matter how natural or necessary or universal it is made out to be, it is a force of imposition and resistance, the reduction of differences and alterity, of alternatives, to the singularity of one particular group's nongeneral position. A similar argument applies to anarchy. It is a false opposite of authority. From the point of view of the opposition created by those calling for more authority on the left, what they perceive as "anarchy" is dangerous because it creates a power vacuum. Therefore, authority is needed to forestall fascism, the power of the right. Yet, authority fulfills the promise of the "danger of anarchy" by forestalling it. Only from the point of view of power, authority, and identity do difference and diversity seem dangerous. The extraction of one possible strategy (authority) from a complex field of multiple strategies and its transformation into a paradigmatic value permit the multiplicity or seriality that encompasses authority as one determined moment in its material and historical chain to be congealed into a self-identical opposite—"anarchy."

There are alternatives to this simplistic metaphysical binary. It is possible to combine a sense of commonality amid diversity, firmness of resistance, and aggressivity of attack with a plurality of different struggles. It is possible for socialist feminists, workers, nonwhites, and others to pursue their separate, yet articulated, struggles with the unflinching perseverance that is usually associated with authority, without submitting to a point of authority that abstractly and formally mediates their differences into an identity of power. Such a point can be abstract and ideal only in relation to the material and historical differences of the diverse struggles. We are at a point in history when the wealth of struggles has outrun the abstractly mediating form of authority. No one needs authority any more, except left patriarchs. More than authority, the left needs diverse unity, an articulation of different movements and organizations that elicit multiple interests and address plural needs. Materiality is plural and differentiated; it separates and multiplies, rather than forming identities that have a permanence akin to that of ideal forms which bear authority. Only those materially anchored in different struggles can pursue those struggles, because only they have interests and needs at stake. A material principle of articulated unity cannot, therefore, pretend to the ideal identity of interest or need that characterizes traditional disciplinarian organizations. It can be the principle of an organization which relates or articulates without mediating or transcending the diverse struggles. Workers cannot legislate for socialist feminists, nor students or intellectuals for workers. It is not accidental that the various leninist parties in the United States constantly fail to attain the identity of authority (of truth as of command) they assume for themselves, instead generating a multiplicity of leninisms, or that the only organization in recent years to pull off something resembling cooperation is one based on diverse unity — the People's Anti-War Mobilization.

It is easier now to threaten capital without authority than with. Authoritarian state socialism provides liberal capitalism with an easy ideological enemy that allows the real political-economic question to be deflected and allows capital to muster weapons that appear to answer people's material needs for freedom from domination. Antiauthoritarian socialist organizing takes the capitalist weapons of democracy and freedom one step further, radicalizing them as demands against capital. And by so doing, it poses a greater threat to capitalism by putting capital on the defensive, without any ideological recourse, and with only the exercise of force to defend itself, an exercise that constitutes an admission that capitalism is a regime of domination, and nothing else. In addition, there is no evidence to prove that authority-oriented formalist organizations succeed better than antiauthoritarian ones. Indeed, if organizing is to be guided, not by ideal principles, but by the differential material relations that exist between classes, races, and sexes at different historical moments, then capital and race superiority and the patriarchy can no longer be attacked at only one point by only one organization. The political-institutional state whose power is seized would be crushed in a moment by a more powerful multinational network of economic power independent of political institutions. The capitalist state, except for the various third world states of exception, is already merely a subset of capitalist power.

Any organizational strategy that measures itself against its adversaries in methods of answering needs cannot be anything but multiple, diverse, and differential. It must operate on numerous fronts, traditional as well as new: wage demands, consumer action, social power struggles, contestation for state power, liberation struggles, the ideological battle. The more those struggles are articulated the better, but the demand that they must succumb to a formal organization guided by an ideal instance of transcendental authority bears no relevance to their success or failure.

Whatever one may think of the incremental or gradualist nature of these struggles, they attack parts that can prove to be larger than the whole into which they are supposedly subsumed. Squatting, for example, is a "partial" struggle that nonetheless puts the totality of bourgeois property right into question by pointing to the disjunction between the convention of property ownership and the nonsatisfaction of needs. Need, like desire, is a small part of the capitalist whole. Yet capitalism could not exist without needs transformed into desires in the market. Need, like labor, is a material principle around which organizing can coalesce, a part that can prove to be larger than the whole. Whereas authority is a formal and ideal principle that can induce action only on the basis of belief, need, on the other hand, moves action without conventional constraints; it is the locus of the "instinctive" revolt Marx talked about. This is why new leftist organizing around needs is more based in material history than organizing around authority. The crucial moment for this sort of struggle is the point where need and right articulate. It is also the point where a liberal capitalist principle—the doctrine of right—can be used from inside capitalism against capitalism. Increasingly, in capitalism, rights are divorced from needs; it is through the advocacy of needs as rights (housing, economic well-being, political participatory control, exemption from domination, health, and the like) that this point can become a radical way of making the ideological principle of early capitalism—the doctrine of rights—work against capitalism. Unlike the principle of authority, which posits ideal forms of intellectual elitism, discipline, and patriarchal leadership, need-as-right mobilizes multiple struggles against the capitalist patriarchy from inside, stealing both its material basis and its fundamental ideological tool.

Parts that are larger than the whole of which they are a part: what I am advocating is a strategy of enclaves. By an enclave, I do not mean a communal alternative, a withdrawal to utopia. What I mean is pockets within the body of capitalism which work against the principles of the whole. An enclave would be the immediacy of socialism, as much of it as can possibly be made.[3] Without any delusions about the possibility of extracting oneself from the capitalist market, the makers of an enclave nonetheless attempt to create as much as they can the reality of socialist productive and social relations. The point would be to make an enclave work materially in a way that answers needs better than under capitalism. Like a parasite, the enclave would live off capitalism, being outside it yet within it, exploiting capitalist property in order to put capitalist property right in question. An enclave would be the political-economic equivalent of a socialist-feminist self-help group, both a space of resistance and a prefiguration of future social forms. And the place where such a thing is likely to succeed is the north central and northeastern states.

We have learned that socialism cannot be a punctual event, self-contained and immediate, proper and present, or natural. The construction of socialism entails a working out, extended in time and space. The constructive working out of socialism, in all its plural facets, can occur either as the incremental accumulation of struggles, within which, eventually, state power is displaced, or after the seizure of state power. But both are equally extended, plural, and serial. Constructed on the basis of materiality, socialism is necessarily extended temporally and spatially. It is at this point that the principle of authority, with its implicit privilege of mental over manual (of the concept and of the ideal form over the historical, material, and differential) is displaced once and for all. Socialism can no longer be conceptualized or commanded (and the two operations conjoin, at least in Lenin's metaphysical "idea of a party"); it must be worked out, as a texture and not as a punctual instance of power. Authority can aid this process in a highly constrained, functional way. Only from the standpoint of authority does this necessity of working out seem "gradualist," a term that implies a similarly authoritative conclusivity, a goal to be "gradually" reached. It is fitting that such goals are always ideal, like the principle of authority itself, and that the patriarchs who command on their basis, awaiting the perpetually deferred, because ideal, goal, are least liable to work. Once the goal is made immediate, it splits, fissures, differentiates, becomes undecidable. Materialism, conceived as technology and construction, is open-ended, differentiated, spatially articulated, inconclusive. In materiality, no goal, to be reached "gradually," regulates the movement and work of construction. There is only the immediate construction of socialism, the working out of its plural dimensions—social, political, personal, economic—for the satisfaction of needs and the realization of human potential as further material production, the creation of further needs, and so on.

What critical marxists and new leftists need, then, is not authority, be it of the patriarchy or the party, but instead a diverse unity of organizations and programs and "enclaves" that appeal immediately to the material needs and interests of people, a plurality of struggles that address the plural character of capitalist patriarchal domination in the workplace, the home, the media, the school, the knowledge industry. The conclusions to which I am led by this articulation of marxism and deconstruction are that the monolithic concepts of the organization, of the struggle, of values,

and of the "gradual" construction of socialism held by both leninism and
the New Left's Right are untenable, that in consequence one very important struggle is the one against our own drives (in part metaphysical)
to adhere to such forms of power, forms that are not merely not prefigurative of socialism, but also are inimical to the material concept of
socialism. And authority is one of those forms.

The "autobiographic" impulse of deconstruction is a practical implementation of the deconstructive insight into historical, material, and differential nontranscendence. The desire to extract oneself from the world,
either to conceive or to command it ideally, only anchors one more
deeply in it. Not that the personal is political in a pop-psych sense, but
that the public philosophical and the public political are personal through
and through. The personal here is the name for the cultural, the material-
historical, the social, the familial-institutional, and the linguistic-conceptual network which forms a person. The deconstructive displacement
of the centrality of the cogito is the opening of that personal instance
onto a differential, institutional, and historical text that constitutes it
without being subject to its identitarian form. If the personal is seen as
already being public, as a social text, then the apparent reduction of the
political to the personal loses its radicality. The patriarchal desire for
authority in the public political sphere has personal, that is, social, cultural, and historical origins. It is anchored in a seriality it cannot control
at the very moment it proposes a metaserial paradigmatic solution for
the mastery of seriality. The desire for power is merely a project of the
patriarchs' need, a need scripted for them by institutions, such as the
phallocratic family, which, by tautological projection, become themselves
social paradigms within the patriarchal framework. The relation between
the private phallocratic family and the public patriarchal political institution is more than analogical; it is a material circuit. Working out that
circuit entails undermining or deconstructing the rigorous binary opposition between public and private.

To be "autobiographic," then, like Sheila Rowbotham or Toni Negri,
is not to abdicate from the political. It is the gesture that defuses the
patriarchal power of public authority and reduces the actors on the
public stage to their personal, that is, material and historical, dimensions,
to a matrix of need, interest, and desire. It is to see a necessary relation
between American foreign policy and the phallocratic neurosis, between
capitalist power and a monopoly of enjoyment. The concept of the
political, as a domain of thetic proposition and public action that are
somehow transcendent of the materiality and historicality of the everyday
and of the private, and the concept of the economic, as a realm of objectively necessary laws of production and accumulation which only tan-
gentially relate to political power and the multiplicity of needs, are what
are in question here. These oppositions must be deconstructed before we
can work out a socialism without the "need" for authority.

I would like to find ways of showing how public institutions and public power are cultural conventions sustained by acculturated personal belief, and of showing how that hidden dimension of need, interest, and desire, which is the basis, when channeled and manipulated properly, of capital patriarchal accumulation, can be a privately explosive political instrument. The expansion of the domain of needs, both Rowbotham and Negri argue, can be political, that is, it can disturb and displace public power, in social and political institutions and in the economy. I suppose it is fitting that I should end on this note, with a project of work and a not altogether deliberate sense of inconclusivity.

By way of a brief postface, in reading the page proofs for this book, I have occasionally thought that I was being unfair to certain thinkers to whom I am indebted. For example, I suggest that this book marks a radical departure from mainstream deconstruction, and yet it was Derrida's seminars on Marx, Gramsci, and Althusser that in part inspired it. Similarly, I have expressed disagreement with the Yale School, without distinguishing the work of Paul de Man, which has greatly influenced my own. Finally, I give short shrift to Sartre in chapter 3, but a recent rereading of *Search for a Method* has shown me the high degree of similarity between his critique of orthodox marxism and the deconstructive critique I have proposed here.

Notes

PREFACE

1. See Gayatri Chakravorty Spivak, "Il faut en s'en prenant à elles," *Les fins de l'homme,* ed. Jean-Luc Nancy and Philippe Lacoue-Labarthe (Paris, 1981); "Revolutions That As Yet Have No Model: Derrida's 'Limited Inc,'" *Diacritics* 10, no. 4 (Winter 1980); "Finding Feminist Readings: Dante and Yeats," *Social Text* 3 (Fall 1980); "Unmaking and Making in *To the Lighthouse,*" in *Women and Language in Literature and Society,* ed. Sally McConnell-Ginet et al. (New York, 1980); "Three Feminist Readings: McCullers, Drabble, Habermas," *Union Seminary Quarterly Review* 35, nos. 1 and 2 (Fall-Winter 1979-80); "Explanation and Culture: Marginalia," *Humanities in Society* 2, no. 3 (Summer 1979); "Displacement and the Discourse of Woman," forthcoming in a collection from the Center for Twentieth-Century Studies, University of Wisconsin-Milwaukee; "Sex and History in *The Prelude* (1805): Books 9-13," forthcoming in *Texas Studies in Language and Literature*; "Reading the World: Literary Studies in the 80s," forthcoming in *College English*; "French Feminism in an International Frame," forthcoming in *Yale French Studies*; "Marx after Derrida," forthcoming in *Philosophy and Literature,* ed. William Cain (Bucknell University Press).

2. For an account of the "two marxisms," see Alvin Gouldner, *The Two Marxisms* (New York, 1980). I disagree with Gouldner's identification of critical marxism with leninist elitism and voluntarism. Perhaps, one should rightly speak of three, four, or even more "marxisms." Critical marxism is more suited to Lenin's "others"—Luxemburg, Pannekoek, Korsch, and the other "Council Communists."

3. Meeting of GREPH, the Research Group on Philosophic Teaching, at the Sorbonne, Winter 1976.

4. See *Positions* (Paris, 1972), pp. 51-133; *La dissémination* (Paris, 1972), pp. 37-42; *Glas* (Paris, 1974), pp. 225-30; "The White Mythology," *New Literary History* 6, no. 1 (1974): 14-15.

5. "L'age de Hegel," in *Qui a peur de la philosophie?* (Paris, 1977), p. 107: "If the French state today is afraid of philosophy, it's because the extension of philosophic teaching furthers two types of threatening forces: those who want to change the state (let us say that they belong to the age of left hegelianism) and take it out of the hands who now hold power, and those who, alternatively or simultaneously, allied or not with the first type, tend toward the destruction of the state. [Footnote: Which doesn't necessarily or simply mean some kind of tendential movement (through the integral State) toward the "withering away" of the State in a "planned society" (Engels) or "the State without a State" (Gramsci). But I will try to return to these difficult 'limits' elsewhere.] These two forces do not allow themselves to be classified according to the dominant categories. For example, they appear to me to coexist today in the theoretical and practical field of what one calls marxism."

6. James Kearns and Ken Newton, "An Interview with Jacques Derrida," *Literary Review,* no. 14 (18 April-1 May 1980), pp. 21-22.

INTRODUCTION

1. *Issues in Marxist Philosophy: Volume One Dialectics and Method,* ed. John Mepham and David Hillel-Rubin (Atlantic Highlands, 1979), pp. ix, xiv.

2. Thomas Hobbes, *Leviathan,* ed. Michael Oakeshott (London, 1962), p. 19.

3. I have called this a radically egalitarian and democratic socialism, although I would prefer to use the word "communism" here, in Marx's sense of a community of cooperation, liberty, and nonexploitation, not in the Soviet statist sense of the word. It is a better word than socialism, the one usually used in the West because of the connotations that have attached to communism as a result of the Soviet experience, because socialism too often merely means the preservation of surplus value and the exploitation of labor under more humane forms of planning and self-management. I suppose it is a testament to the political power exercised through language that I am obliged to use "socialism." Whenever I use the word, therefore, feel free to displace the meaning.

CHAPTER ONE

1. Jacques Derrida, *Of Grammatology,* trans. Gayatri Chakravorty Spivak (Baltimore, 1976). Readers should consult the translator's preface for a more extensive introduction to deconstruction. Hereafter cited in the text as *Gram.*

2. See Jacques Derrida, *Speech and Phenomena,* trans. David Allison (Evanston, 1973). Hereafter cited in the text as *SP.*

3. Jacques Derrida, "Limited Inc abc," *Glyph 2: Johns Hopkins Textual Studies* (Baltimore, 1977), pp. 236, 247-48. Hereafter cited in the text as LI.

4. See Harold Bloom et al., *Deconstruction and Criticism* (New York, 1979), where Derrida writes: "If we are to approach a text, it must have an edge. . . . What has happened . . . is a sort of overrun that spoils all these boundaries and divisions and forces us to extend the accredited concept, the dominant notion of a 'text,' of what I still call a 'text,' for strategic reasons, in part—a 'text' that is henceforth no longer a finished corpus of writing, some content enclosed in a book or its margins, but a differential network, a fabric of traces referring endlessly to something other than itself, to other differential traces. Thus the text overruns all the limits assigned to it. . . . I sought to work out the theoretical and practical system of these margins, these borders, once more, from the ground up" (83-84).

5. J. van Jeijenoort, ed., *From Frege to Gödel: A Source Book in Mathematical Logic, 1879-1931* (Cambridge, 1967), p. 593.

6. Douglas R. Hofstadter, *Gödel, Escher, Bach: An Eternal Golden Braid* (New York, 1979), p. 222.

7. Jacob Bronowski, *The Identity of Man* (New York, 1971), pp. 121-23.

8. Jacques Derrida, "The Law of Genre," *Glyph 7: Textual Studies* (Baltimore, 1980), pp. 206-12.

9. Jacques Derrida, *La dissémination* (Paris, 1972), p. 234. Hereafter cited in the text as *Diss.*

10. Jacques Derrida, "Freud and the Scene of Writing," *Writing and Difference,* trans. Alan Bass (Chicago, 1978).

11. Jacques Derrida, "Où commence et où finit un corps enseignant," *Politiques de la philosophie,* ed. Dominique Crisoni (Paris, 1976).

12. See Pierre Bourdieu, *Outline of a Theory of Practice* (Cambridge, 1977).

13. See Ian Steedman, *Marx after Sraffa* (London, 1977).

CHAPTER TWO

1. See Jacques Derrida, *La carte postale* (Paris, 1980), and *La verité en peinture* (Paris, 1978).

2. Jacques Derrida, *Positions* (Paris, 1972), p. 99. Hereafter cited in the text as *Pos.*

3. Jacques Derrida, "Ja, ou le faux-bond," *Digraphe*, II (April 1977), p. 107.

4. James Kearns and Ken Newton, "An Interview with Jacques Derrida," *Literary Review*, no. 14 (18 April-1 May 1980), p. 22.

5. Karl Marx, *Grundrisse*, trans. Martin Nicholaus (London, 1973), p. 245; *Grundrisse der Kritik der politischen Ökonomie* (Moscow, 1939), p. 156. Hereafter cited in the text as *Grun.* The reference to the German edition follows the English.

6. Antonio Negri, *Marx Beyond Marx*, trans. Harry Cleaver, Michael Ryan, and Maurizio Viano (New York, 1981), n.p.

7. Karl Marx and Friedrich Engels, *Collected Works*, vol. 6 (Moscow, 1976), p. 197; *Marx-Engels Werke*, vol. 4 (Berlin, 1964), p. 165. Subsequent references in the text, cited as *CW*; *MEW*.

8. Karl Marx, *Theories of Surplus Value*, vol. 3 (Moscow, 1971), p. 295; *MEW*, vol. 26.3 (Berlin, 1968), p. 290. Hereafter cited in the text as *TSV*; *MEW*.

9. Karl Marx, *Collected Works*, vol. 5 (New York, 1976), pp. 88-89; passage not in *MEW* edition.

10. Ibid., p. 449; *MEW*, vol. 3 (Berlin, 1962), p. 435.

11. Ibid., p. 409; ibid., p. 394.

12. Ibid., p. 92; passage not in *MEW* edition.

13. Jacques Derrida, "Où commence et où finit un corps enseignant," *Politiques de la philosophie*, ed. Dominique Crisoni (Paris, 1976), p. 60.

14. Martin Shaw, *Marx's Theory of History* (Stanford, 1978).

15. Karl Marx, *Capital Volume Two*, trans. David Fernbach (London, 1978), p. 194; *MEW*, vol. 24 (Berlin, 1963), p. 118.

CHAPTER THREE

1. Jacques Derrida, *Writing and Difference*, trans. Alan Bass (Chicago, 1978), p. 248.

2. Jacques Derrida, *Glas* (Paris, 1974), p. 168.

3. Jean-Paul Sartre, *Critique of Dialectical Reason* (London, 1976), p. 263. Hereafter cited in the text as *Crit.*

4. Herbert Marcuse, *Counter-Revolution and Revolt* (Boston, 1972), p. 69.

5. In his late work, Marcuse moved more toward Adorno's point of view. He criticized the neoidealist, progressive nature of dialectical materialism in "The Concept of Negation in the Dialectic" (*Telos*, no. 8 [Summer 1971], pp. 130-32). In the transcript of a more recent talk on negative dialectics given at the University of California at San Diego, he followed up on this critique by arguing that negative dialectics rejects the coincidence of logic and history: "But in contrast to the idealist dialectic, negative dialectics rejects the comfortable notion that the negation of the negation is by the inner logic of things necessarily progressive." I am grateful to the Revolutionary People's party for providing me with a copy of the transcript.

6. (Stuttgart, 1956). The book was originally written in the 1930s.

CHAPTER FOUR

1. Antonio Negri, *Marx Beyond Marx*, (New York, 1981). For a sample of the scientific marxist position, see K. Zarodov, *Leninism and Contemporary Problems of the Transition from Capitalism to Socialism* (Moscow, 1972).

2. Friedrich Engels, *Anti-Duhring* (Moscow, 1969), p. 196.

3. A letter to Bloch, 21 September 1890, in *Marx Engels Correspondence* (New York, 1935), p. 396. I am grateful to Harry Cleaver for bringing this letter to my attention.

4. Negri, *Marx beyond Marx*, n.p.

5. Karl Marx, *Capital Volume One*, trans. Ben Fowkes (New York, 1977), p. 103; *Marx-Engels Werke*, vol. 23 (Berlin, 1962), p. 28. Hereafter cited in the text as *Cap 1*; *MEW*.

6. *Basic Works of Marx and Engels* (New York, 1959), p. 440; *MEW*, vol. 19 (Berlin, 1962), p. 111.

7. *MEW*, vol. 33 (Berlin, 1966), p. 209.

8. For Derrida, the principle of undecidability, incompleteness, and the nonsaturability of contexts does not imply an infinite or inexhaustible richness, but rather a structural dilemma at the very heart of any axiomatic system that pretends to be exhaustive.

9. See the works of Louis Althusser and especially also Nikos Poulantzas, *Political Power and Social Classes* (London, 1975).

10. Karl Marx, "The Class Struggles in France: 1848-1850," in *Surveys from Exile*, ed. David Fernbach (London, 1975), pp. 49, 50, 51, 67; *MEW*, vol. 17 (Berlin, 1964), pp. 23, 24, 25, 39. Hereafter cited in the text as CSF; *MEW*.

CHAPTER FIVE

1. For a leftist feminist critique of deconstructive literary criticism, which states the difference frankly, see Gayatri Chakravorty Spivak, "Finding Feminist Readings: Dante-Yeats," *Social Text* (Fall 1980): 73-87.

2. Rainer Nagele, "The Provocation of Lacan," *New German Critique*, no. 16 (Winter 1979), pp. 7-29. Hereafter cited in the text as *NGC*.

3. Rosa Luxemburg, *Leninism or Marxism* (Ann Arbor, 1977), p. 93.

4. Jacques Lacan, *Ecrits*, trans. Alan Sheridan (New York, 1977), p. 175. Subsequent references in the text.

5. Here, Lacan is not using "all that is real" in the same sense as the "real," which is one of his three categories. In the preceding paragraph, he writes: "Reality in the analytic experience does in fact often remain veiled under negative forms, but it is not too difficult to situate it."

6. Jacques Derrida, "The Purveyor of Truth," in *Yale French Studies*, no. 52 (1975): "As soon as truth is determined as adequation (to an original contract: the acquittal of a debt) and as unveiling (of the lack which gives rise to the contracting of the contract in order to reappropriate symbolically what has been detached), the master value is indeed that of propriation, hence of proximity, presence and preserving: the very same provided by the idealizing effect of speech" (89).

7. In this regard, one must bear in mind that the French leftists, who took up Lacan as a political surrogate that provided an explanation for the failure of the French people to join the students in liberating themselves in 1968, were overwhelmingly masculinist or at best nonfeminist. The development of leftist feminism through the 1970s and into the 1980s promises to redefine the terrain of leftist psychoanalysis, perhaps even to the point of curing it of lacanian phallocentrism. It is conceivable that it may also succeed in getting the leftists off the couch and back to the barricades. For an account of Lacan's relationship to the French Left, see Sherry Turkle, "French Psychoanalysis: A Sociological Perspective," in *Psychoanalysis, Creativity, and Literature: A French-American Inquiry* (New York, 1978).

8. Rosalind Coward and John Ellis, *Language and Materialism* (London, 1977), pp. 93, 94, 119, 120.

9. Gilles Deleuze and Felix Guattari (*Anti-Oedipus* [New York, 1977]) raise the question of whether Oedipus is privileged in Lacan: "Despite some fine books by certain disciples of Lacan, we wonder if Lacan's thought really goes in this direction" (p. 53). They cite Lacan claiming, "I spoke of the paternal metaphor, I have never spoken of an Oedipus complex" (p. 53). What Lacan did speak of was the kernel of the oedipal system—the castration complex: "What is not a myth, and which Freud nevertheless formulated soon after the Oedipus complex, is the castration complex . . . the major mainspring of the very subversion that I am trying to articulate here by means of its dialectic" (*Ecrits*, 318). Deleuze and Guattari question the significance of this shift: "If the first disciples were tempted to reclose the Oedipus yoke, didn't they do so to the extent that Lacan seemed to maintain a kind of projection of the signifying chains onto a despotic signifier, lacking unto itself and reintroducing lack into the series of desire on which it imposed an exclusive use? Was it possible to denounce, and nevertheless maintain that the castration complex itself was not a myth but in fact something real?" (83-84).

10. Lacan's formalism could never take into account, of course, an epidemiology of mental illness that would demonstrate a correlation between downturns in the economy and rises in admissions to mental institutions. See M. Harvey Brenner, *Mental Illness and the Economy* (Cambridge, 1973): "Mental hospitalization will increase during economic downturns and decrease during upturns. . . . The major diagnostic categories of functional psychosis taken as a group (including schizophrenia, manic-depressive psychosis, and involutional psychosis) react more sharply to economic downturns than any other diagnostic group" (10, 44). The mental breakdowns that are amply documented in the daily papers in the wake of the massive plant closings in the North as capital shifts to the Sun Belt cannot be accounted for by shifting signifiers, unless those signifiers happen to be monetary.

11. See Jacques Derrida, "Entre crochets," *Digraphe*, no. 8 (1976), pp. 97-114.

CHAPTER SIX

1. Steve Barnet and Martin G. Silverman, *Ideology and Everyday Life* (Ann Arbor, 1979), p. 36.

2. Kathleen Newland, *Women, Men, and the Division of Labor* (Washington, 1980), p. 11.

3. Gerard Chaliand, *Revolution in the Third World* (London, 1978), p. xiv.

4. James Kohl and John Litt, eds., *Urban Guerilla Warfare in Latin America* (Cambridge, 1974), p. 11.

5. Paul Hirst, *On Law and Ideology* (Atlantic Highlands, 1979), pp. 160-62. Hereafter cited in the text as *OLI*.

6. Andreas Faludi, *Planning Theory* (London, 1973), pp. 42, 51. Hereafter cited in the text as *PT*.

7. Janice Perlman, *The Myth of Marginality* (Berkeley, 1976).

8. Henry Kissinger, *American Foreign Policy* (New York, 1977), p. 48. Hereafter cited in the text as *AFP*.

9. Stanley Hoffmann, "A View From Home: The Perils of Incoherence," *Foreign Policy* (Elmsford, 1979), pp. 463-91. Hereafter cited in the text as *VH*.

10. Stanley Hoffmann, *Contemporary Theory in International Relations* (Englewood Cliffs, 1960), p. 12. Hereafter cited in the text as CT.

11. Hoffman, "View from Home," p. 489.

12. "The World according to Brzezinski," *New York Times Magazine*, 31 December 1978, pp. 9-11.

CHAPTER SEVEN

1. The business version is provided by Kenneth Patrick and Richard Eells, *Education and the Business Dollar* (London, 1969); the radical view by David Smith, *Who Rules the University?* (New York, 1974). See also James Ridgway, *The Closed Corporation* (New York, 1968), and Samuel Bowles and Herbert Gintis, *Schooling in Capitalist America* (New York, 1976).

2. "Angry Tigers; Campaigning to Withhold Contributions because of Faculty Political Views," *Newsweek*, 29 March 1976.

3. American Assembly, *Disorders in Higher Education* (Englewood Cliffs, 1979), p. vii. Hereafter cited in the text as *DHE*. I am indebted to Gayatri Chakravorty Spivak for bringing this book to my attention.

4. *Priorities for Action* (New York, 1973), p. 39. Hereafter cited in the text as *PA*.

5. Aristotle, *Politics*, trans. E. Walford (London, 1908), p. 194.

6. *Power and Empowerment in Higher Education* (Louisville, 1978), p. 16.

7. John Thornton, of *Forbes*, recently sent me a "memo," which contained the following lines: "So let me assure you that Forbes is a most *efficient* way to get business information you need. . . . Forbes articles are concise, to the point. With Forbes, you can take in an incredible amount of information in a very short period of time" (private correspondence).

8. In capitalist management, the analog of rational conceptual determination is called "specification" (of tasks, variables, environment problems, and the like); its practical form is organizational division: "Let us assume a rational owner, that is, one who will attempt to

achieve his goals in an efficient manner. Given high visibility of consequences, the owner will be able to specify those procedures which will maximize efficiency and eliminate inappropriate procedures" (Selwyn W. Becker and Duncan Neuhauser, *The Efficient Organization* [New York, 1975], p. 92). These procedures are what I mean by rational exclusion, isolation, division. Efficiency maximization can be described as an essentialist "rational" operation because, like reason, it must eliminate the "inappropriate" in order to achieve "property" or selfsameness—the point where inefficient complexity and marginal elements are entirely purged. For a description of a similar process of structuration along the lines of rational concept formation, see Magali Sarfatti Larson, *The Rise of Professionalism* (Berkeley, 1977), pp. 40, 55: "What makes the codification of knowledge so important from the point of view of the professional project is that it depersonalizes the ideas held about professional practice and its products. It sets up a transcendent cognitive and normative framework within which, ideally, differences in the interpretation of practice and in the definition of the 'commodity' can be reconciled. . . . The more formalized the cognitive basis, the more the profession's language and knowledge appear to be connotation-free and 'objective.' . . . Professional identity is experienced as shared expertise and therefore involves a sense of at least cognitive superiority. . . . The whole process of setting up a monopolistic market of services [is] based . . . on articulating and enforcing principles of inclusion and exclusion."

9. Marshall Ledger, "Big Business' Big Leader," *Pennsylvania Gazette*, June 1979, pp. 18-21.

10. "Vygotsky sees the schools as that agency of socialisation whose special role it is to promote conceptual development. . . . 'School instruction induces the generalizing kind of perception'" (Maurice Levitas, *Marxist Perspectives in the Sociology of Education* [London, 1974], p. 152).

11. Aristotle, *Economics*, trans. E. Walford (London, 1908), p. 243.

12. Mark Blaug, *The Economics of Education* (New York, 1968); George Kneller, *Education and Economic Thought* (New York, 1968); Herbert Parnes, *Forecasting Educational Needs for Economic and Social Development* (Paris, 1962); E. A. G. Robinson and J. E. Vaizey, eds., *The Economics of Education* (New York, 1966).

13. Karl Marx, "Economic and Philosophic Manuscripts," in *Early Works*, trans. Rodney Livingstone and Gregor Benton (London, 1975): "It can be seen how the history of *industry* and the *objective* existence of industry is an *open* book of the essential powers of man [sic], man's psychology present in tangible form" (p. 354).

14. Adam Smith, *An Inquiry into the Nature and the Causes of the Wealth of Nations* (London, 1893), p. 618.

15. See, for example, the essays of Ira Shor and Jean Bethke Elshtain in *Studies in Socialist Pedagogy*, ed. Bertell Ollman and Theodore M. Norton (New York, 1978).

16. Edward Said, *The Question of Palestine* (New York, 1980).

17. See, for example, Alfred Watkins and David Perry, "Giving Cities the Business," *The Nation*, 1 March 1980.

CHAPTER EIGHT

1. V. I. Lenin, *Collected Works*, vol. 25 (London, 1964), p. 386. Hereafter cited in the text as L *CW*.

2. Karl Marx and Friedrich Engels, *Collected Works*, vol. 6 (New York, 1976), p. 87; *Marx-Engels Werke*, vol. 4 (Berlin, 1964), p. 483. Translating Marx has a politics all of its own. A celebrated example is *"aufheben"* (to sublate, or more properly, to annul, to preserve, and to raise to a higher level all at one go), which is rendered as "to abolish," a choice that suggests Marx was interested in abolishing such things as conflict and democracy. In this passage, for example, *"assoziierten Individuen,"* which I render literally as "associated individuals," is translated as "a vast association of a whole nation"—rather convenient for a nationalist central state pretending to operate under Marx's sanction. Here, as before, the phrase *"Produktionsverhältnisse"* or productive relations is rendered by the Soviet translators

as "conditions of production." The hegemony of Soviet scientific marxists' emphasis on productive forces, despite the preservation of capitalist work relations, is assured because in the new edition of the collected works, Marx no longer even has a concept of productive relations which can be mustered as a counter to the Soviets' argument—a convenient device for a regime interested in legitimating capitalist work relations under the title "marxism."

3. Karl Marx, *The First International and After*, ed. David Fernbach (London, 1974), pp. 271, 375 (hereafter cited in the text as *FIA*); *MEW*, vol. 19 (Berlin, 1962), p. 165.

4. Karl Marx, *Early Works*, trans. Rodney Livingstone and Gregor Benton (London, 1975), pp. 193, 196; *MEW*, vol. 1 (Berlin, 1964), pp. 328, 331. Hereafter cited in the text as *EW*.

5. Karl Marx, *The Revolutions of 1848* (London, 1973), p. 87. Hereafter cited in the text as *Rev*.

6. Karl Marx, *Capital Volume Three*, trans. Ernest Untermann (New York, 1977), p. 481; *MEW*, vol. 25 (Berlin, 1964), p. 498. Hereafter cited in the text as *Cap 3*; *MEW*.

7. Marx's discussion of "fictive capital" is of interest in this context. See *Capital Volume Three*, pp. 457-70. Rudolf Hilferding extends the analysis of fictive capital in the banking system and the increased centralization it permitted. The fabrication (*Schaffung*) of fictive capital allowed the necessary mobilization of capital that led to the centralization and the concentration of power in "finance capital." See *Das Finanzkapital* (Vienna, 1910), p. 164.

8. For good discussions of the world monetary system from a radical perspective, see Fred Block, *The Origins of International Economic Disorder* (Berkeley, 1977); Jim Hawley, "The Internationalization of Capital: Bankers, Eurocurrency and the Instability of the World Monetary System," *Review of Radical Political Economics* 25, no. 4 (Winter 1979): 78-80; Christian Marazzi, "Money in the World Crisis," *Zerowork* 2 (1977): 91-112. For descriptions of SDRs, see Wilbur F. Monroe, *International Monetary Reconstruction* (Lexington, 1974); George N. Halm, *A Guide to International Monetary Reform* (Lexington, 1975); Benjamin J. Cohen, *Organizing the World's Money* (New York, 1977). The best book on the subject remains Fritz Machlup, *Remaking the International Monetary System* (Baltimore, 1968).

9. *Class Struggles in the USSR: Second Period, 1923-30* (New York, 1978), p. 11.

10. *The Development of Capitalism in Russia* (Moscow, 1895), p. 387.

11. For some unexceptional discussions of the epistemology of planning, see Colin Lys, "A New Concept of Planning," in *The Crisis in Planning*, ed. Mike Faber and Dudley Seers (Edinburgh, 1972); and Sobanlal Mookerjea, *The Sociology of Planning* (Calcutta, 1968).

12. See especially Cornelium Castoriadis, "Reflexions sur le 'developpement' et la 'rationalité,'" in *Le mythe du developpement* (Paris, 1977).

13. *Models, Planning and Basic Needs*, ed. Sam Cole and Henry Lucas (Oxford, 1979).

14. *Planning a Socialist Economy*, ed. L. Y. Berri (Moscow, 1977). Hereafter cited in the text as *PSE*.

15. For a description of this problem, see Michael Ellman, *Socialist Planning* (Cambridge, 1979).

16. *Project Selection for National Planning* (Toronto, 1974).

17. See also Andreas Papandreou, *Paternalistic Capitalism* (Minnesota, 1972), where he discusses "polycentric planning" (p. 175).

18. *Development Paths of Africa and China*, ed. U. G. Damachi, G. Rouht, A. E. Ali Taha (London, 1976), p. 80.

19. *Etats generaux de la philosophie* (Paris, 1979), pp. 27-46.

CHAPTER NINE

1. V. I. Lenin, *Collected Works*, vol. 5 (Moscow, 1961), p. 518; hereafter cited in the text as *LCW*.

2. "The Woman's Movement and Organizing for Socialism," in Sheila Rowbotham, Lynne Segal, and Hilary Wainwright, *Beyond the Fragments: Feminism and the Making of Socialism* (London, 1979), p. 140. Hereafter cited in the text as *BF*.

3. Eric Alliez, "Hegel and the Wobblies," *Semiotexte* 3, no. 3 (1980): 118.

4. For an account of the Autonomy Movement, see the issue of *Semiotexte* cited above, as well as Conference of Socialist Economists, *Working Class Autonomy and the Crisis: Italian Marxist Texts of the Theory and Practice of a Class Movement: 1964-1979* (London, 1979); and Harry Cleaver, *Reading Capital Politically* (Austin, 1979).

5. Alfred Sohn-Rethel, *Intellectual and Manual Labor: A Critique of Epistemology* (Atlantic Heights, 1978).

6. For a fuller account of Negri's other works, see my "The Theory of Autonomy in the Works of Antonio Negri," a preface to *Marx beyond Marx*. Other works by Negri upon which I have relied for this account of the theory include *Crisi dello stato-piano* (Milan, 1974), "Partito operaia contro il lavoro," in *Crisi e organizzazione operaia* (Milan, 1976), *Proletari e stato* (Milan, 1976), *La fabbrica della strategia* (Milan, 1977), *La forma stato* (Milan, 1977), *Capitalist Domination and Working-Class Sabotage* (London, 1979), and *L'anomalia selvaggio* (Milan, 1980).

CONCLUSION

1. For a good sense of the patriarchal political character of language, see Emile Benveniste, *Indo-European Language and Society* (Coral Gables, Fla., 1973).

2. Paul Breines, "The Left's Right: Remarks on the Relative Autonomy of the Base," *Telos*, no. 46 (Winter 1980-81), pp. 88-91.

3. See Mike Prior and Dave Purdy, *Out of the Ghetto: A Path to Socialist Rewards* (London, 1979), for the outline of a project based on similar assumptions.

Index

DATE DUE

DEMCO, INC. 38-2971